Seven
Medieval
Historians

Seven Medieval Historians

joseph dahmus

Nelson-Hall nh Chicago

Procopius, 7 volumes, translated by H. B. Dewing, Harvard University Press, The Loeb Classical Library. Copyright 1914–1940 by Harvard University Press. Excerpts reprinted by permission.

Bede's Ecclesiastical History of the English People, edited by Bertram Colgrave and R.A.B. Mynors. Copyright Oxford University Press 1969. Excerpts reprinted by permission of Oxford University Press.

The Two Cities and *The Deeds of Frederick Barbarossa* by Otto of Freising, translated by C. C. Mierow, Columbia University Press. Excerpts reprinted by permission.

The Muqaddimah: An Introduction to History by Ibn Khaldun, translated from the Arabic by Franz Rosenthal. Bollingen Series XLIII. Copyright © 1958 and 1967 by Princeton University Press. Reprinted by permission of Princeton University Press.

Ibn Khaldun and Tamerlaine by Ibn Khaldun, translated from the Arabic by Walter J. Fischel. Copyright © 1952 by University of California Press. Excerpts reprinted by permission.

LIBRARY OF CONGRESS CATALOGING IN PUBLICATION DATA

Dahmus, Joseph Henry, 1909-
    Seven medieval historians.

    Bibliography: p.
  Includes index.
    1. Middle Ages – Historiography.   2. Medievalists.
3. Medievalists – Biography.   I. Title.
D116.D29   940.1'072022   81-11332
                           AACR2
ISBN 0-88229-712-0 (cloth)
ISBN 0-88229-795-3 (paper)

Manufactured in the United States of America

10 9 8 7 6 5 4 2 1

The paper in this book is pH neutral (acid-free).

Contents

Introduction

T HE MIDDLE AGES as traditionally defined carried from the decline of Rome to 1500 and encompassed the civilizations of Western Europe, Islam, and the Byzantine empire. The works of the seven scholars considered here are representative of the best historical writing produced in these areas. Their writings also serve to preserve the memory of the events that took place, and the people who lived, during the near-millennium from the sixth to the fifteenth centuries.

Procopius, the leading historian of the Byzantine empire, heads the list in point of time. Of the seven historians, Islam contributes two to this study: al-Tabari, the first important and most representative of Islamic historians, and Ibn Khaldun, who was on all counts the greatest. This leaves the four historians of Western Europe, the Venerable Bede, Otto of Freising, Matthew Paris, and Froissart, who lived through the heart of the medieval period, from Bede in the eighth century to Froissart in the fifteenth.

This study of the writings of these seven historians includes a biographical sketch of each scholar and a discussion of his place in the medieval world of his day. Then follows an analysis of each writer's qualifications as a historian. Extensive excerpts are taken from his works to illustrate the character of his writing and to add the personal flavor that documents can best do.

As centuries pile upon centuries and additional periods of time present themselves to historians for recognition, the pressure grows to compress the cultural achievement of each age into a single mold to simplify its appreciation. There is time left only for trends, for a general appraisal of what that particular age may have contributed in art, thought, science, and the growth of institutions. No time is allotted for the individual, for the exceptional event that may have turned the course of history, for the thinker who was out of step with the times. This is unfortunate. History deals with men and women who thought and acted as individuals, whose thoughts and actions endowed the culture of the age in which they lived with a richness and diversity that belie such attempts at simplification.

This is also true of medieval historians. Although they lived in the same period and are threatened, accordingly, with the danger of receiving a stereotyped identification, they were not faceless scribes. They remain individuals; their writings reflect different personalities and, to a degree, different philosophies of life. Procopius was a different sort of historian than Bede, and Matthew Paris and Froissart appear, at first glance, to have lived in wholly dissimilar worlds, as far apart, presumably, as those that separated Otto of Freising and al-Tabari. On the other hand, the two historians who assumed the most secular, the most modern approach in their recording and analysis of events were Procopius, who lived in the sixth century, and Ibn Khaldun, who died in the fifteenth. Not only did nearly a thousand years separate them but their cultural milieus had little in common.

These two men, Procopius and Ibn Khaldun, remain, nevertheless, exceptional. Much about their writing is not strictly medieval. The same may not be said so readily of the other five. Froissart's chivalry was largely spent by the close of the Middle Ages, even though Sir Walter Scott would find a host of avid readers for the romantic tales he wove about that chivalrous age. There were men with Otto of Freising's otherworldly philosophy of life who lived long after the Middle Ages, but they stayed inside their monasteries or wrote for an esoteric group committed to the "medieval" approach to history. Al-Tabari's annalistic writing was out of vogue long before the close of the Middle Ages, and the same may be said of Bede's deeply religious interpretation of history. And if nothing else keeps Matthew Paris in the Middle Ages it is his concern over protecting the autonomy of the English church and aristocracy against the encroachments of papacy and crown, a contest that was almost as distinctly medieval as such social types as the burgher and serf.

Granted that these writers were individuals, they all bear the mark of the Middle Ages. First among the characteristics that distinguish them as medievalists was their belief in divine providence. All seven believed that above all men and forces there was the one God who with paternal authority watched the course that events took. There were men in ancient times, even historians in recent centuries, who accepted the intervention of the supernatural in human affairs, but never in so universal and positive a fashion as did men in the Middle Ages. All seven of these historians believed in one God and worshiped him. In all probability they permitted that faith to influence their behavior, to color their thinking, and to guide them in their analysis of events.

The impact of this faith in an omniscient and almighty God is most manifest in the Benedictine Bede and the Cistercian Otto of Freising. But even Procopius confessed to the working of divine providence, as did Ibn Khaldun. What kept the incompetent Honorius from suffering the evil consequences of his inept policies, according to Proco-

pius, was God, who "is accustomed to succour those who
are neither clever nor able to devise anything of themselves, and to lend them assistance, if they be not
wicked."[1] Ibn Khaldun, commenting on the fatal decision
of the two sultans Abou Sa'id and Abou Tsabit to attack
the king of Maghrib, declared that "if God had so wished it
they would not have done this! But the knowledge of the
secret designs of Allah toward his creatures will be one
day manifestly revealed!"[2]

Froissart, who permitted little but fighting and acts of
valor to catch his eye, noted several occasions when God
clearly took a hand in the affairs of men. An evident instance of this was the summary manner in which God
punished an English squire who had struck a priest at the
altar, then ridden off with the sacred vessels. No sooner
had the squire reached a hill near the church than his horse
began to rear in a most mysterious fashion, causing both
man and beast to fall down and break their necks, whereupon they "were immediately turned into cinders and
dust."[3] Al-Tabari's introduction to his universal history
reads like an exegete's commentary on the Book of Genesis,[4] while the note of gloom that touches so many pages
in Matthew Paris' writing reflected that chronicler's conviction that time was running out in Age Six and that God
would shortly bring an end to the world.

God and religion were matters of first importance to
these men. Of the seven historians, four were priests or
monks — Bede, Otto of Freising, Matthew Paris, and
Froissart — and al-Tabari was a ranking theologian. Of the
other two, Procopius promised a volume on the subject of
religion, which he never got around to writing; Ibn
Khaldun insisted that only religion could counteract the
disintegrative forces inherent in every nation. And all of
these historians accepted miracles, the most palpable sign
of the working of divine providence.

The belief of these seven writers in God and divine providence explains the teleological view of history to which

they all more or less subscribed. Least direct in this regard was the Byzantine historian Procopius, who took pains to emulate the secularist approach of Thucydides, among ancient writers the one he most admired. Were it not for the frequent references to God and the devil in the *Secret History* and *Buildings,* one might be tempted to classify Procopius as an exception among medieval writers and say that he held to the cyclical position of his pagan predecessors. As a confirmed Christian he had no choice but to accept God's control of the universe. The same is true of Froissart, who also says little that would positively reveal his teleological approach to history. Of the other three Western writers, Bede, Otto of Freising, and Matthew Paris, there is no question that events took the course God intended. So also al-Tabari, whose opening sentence in his universal history clearly indicates where he stood. "God formed the creatures without their creation being necessary to him. He created them to test them."[5] There is Ibn Khaldun's unequivocal statement to the same effect, namely, that the "end of all things is fixed [in advance]. Allah gives us the ability to submit to his decrees. There is no other divinity than He."[6]

That these seven historians who believed in a paternalistic and just God should have assumed the right to moralize on occasion is not surprising. Otto of Freising, Bede, and Matthew Paris do so consistently, Paris going beyond the other two in his willingness to judge even the motives of the men responsible for what had transpired. Because al-Tabari restricted himself to recording what others had written, he has no time for moralizing. Ibn Khaldun rarely assumes the role of judge, although the suicide of an enemy of the sultan Abou Tsabit who had turned traitor, been captured, then in prison slashed his own throat, drew this observation from him: "the devil [had] directed his hand."[7] Procopius does more moralizing in the *Wars* than the impersonal Thucydides would have approved. That ancient historian would scarcely have added his *Amen* to the justification Procopius had the Gothic king Totila give his troops when they questioned the severe manner in which he had punished a member of his bodyguard for ravishing a Roman girl. Totila warned them that in battles God is on the side of the virtuous.[8] Apart from his inclination to mark the deficiencies of the Scots and English, Froissart abstains from moralizing. He wrote to entertain his readers, not to preach, although so dishonorable a deed as John Lambe's stabbing in the back of the Welsh hero Evan[9] merited denunciation by all.

The disposition of medieval historians to moralize raises the question of objectivity. How objective, how detached, how truthful in effect can that historian hold himself who chooses to moralize? These seven men would not have recognized the existence of any problem. To them the only responsibility resting upon the historian was the intent to tell the truth, and here the pronouncements of these historians are reassuring. Procopius declared that "truth alone is appropriate to history,"[10] a statement that Bede confirms.[11] Otto of Freising in his letter to Rainald, Frederick I Barbarossa's chancellor, admitted the temptation for historians to write what pleased men in power but declared it was "better to fall into the hands of men than to abandon the function of a historian by covering up a loathsome sight by colors that conceal the truth."[12] Froissart became almost indignant when someone suggested he might have colored his account to please a patron.[13] Al-Tabari did not assume it to be his responsibility to do other than report faithfully what others had written. For all of Ibn Khaldun's ability to be on the winning side in the many political vicissitudes that came his way, he strikes the reader as scrupulously honest in dealing with the past.[14] And from the historian most given to moralizing, that is, Matthew Paris, we have his exhortation to writers that they must tell the truth, even though it provokes men: "If they commit to writing that which is false, they are not acceptable to the Lord."[15]

As if to lend credence to their declarations about telling the truth, these medieval writers generally make a point of informing the reader about their sources of information. Most detailed in providing this information was Bede.[16] Procopius in his introduction to the *Wars* states he was eyewitness to what he wrote,[17] which statement, he assumed, should have been proof enough of his accuracy. Al-Tabari normally cites his sources. Otto of Freising lists the principal ancient and contemporary writers whom he consulted.[18] Matthew Paris frequently indicates the sources of his information for the matter at hand, a letter from Frederick II to Henry III, for example, or a visitor from Syria. His *Liber Additamentorum* bespeaks his appreciation of the value of documents. Froissart appears on several occasions to wish to dispel any possible skepticism on the part of the reader by assuring him that he had his information of some particular incident from both sides; furthermore, that the five years he had spent in England, together with his personal acquaintance with the kings of France, enabled him to write a truthful account of the wars in which these monarchs were involved.[19] Only Ibn Khaldun makes little note of sources, which is understandable in the *Muqaddimah* because it is largely analytical in character. In the universal history itself, his handling of Western history, with the exception of Spain, would suggest that he either had few reliable sources at hand or that he went to no great pains to find better ones.

Most representative of what is frequently considered a uniquely medieval concern about natural phenomena was Matthew Paris. Part of this fascination over such phenomena was the tendency of medieval writers to attribute the more alarming and destructive of these to an angry God. When strange animals were the subject, it was the rarity with which they were seen and the almost complete absence of information about them that aroused the interest of medieval men. The appearance of such strange animals might also be portentous of some coming evil; it might simply be a matter of interest. The latter was the case with the elephant that Matthew Paris says Louis IX gave to Henry III. All Englishmen who saw the creature marveled at its size,[20] but that was all. Yet anything disturbingly different was apt to set men to thinking, and even Procopius, the most secular of the Christian historians, attached prophetic significance to the birth of a two-headed baby in Edessa. He declared it foretold the struggle that the Persian and Byzantine empires would engage in over both Edessa and the "greater part of the Roman empire to the north."[21]

What the modern reader usually finds more interesting in medieval chronicles than the notice of phenomena are the tales and anecdotes authors liked to introduce. It was a practice ancient writers employed. So Procopius, after the manner of Herodotus, tells of the infant that was raised by a she-goat as an aside in his description of the war in Italy between the Romans and the Goths.[22] Bede likes to weave similar incidents into his history, as in the case of the conversion of Northumbria when he has Coifi and other of King Edwin's counselors stating their individual positions.[23] Al-Tabari, although limited by the sources he records, must have been happy to introduce the episode concerning al-Abassah and Ja'far.[24] Otto of Freising hoped his readers would find the story of Perillus and the brazen bull both interesting and moralizing.[25] Rather than a simple recording of the death of the son of Llewellyn by a fall from the tower, Matthew Paris tells how the young man fashioned a rope out of the sheets, tablecloths, and hangings he found in his quarters, then fell head downward when the contraption broke—he was a heavy man—landing so hard that his head and neck were "almost buried in his breast between the shoulders."[26] Froissart has no end of stories, among these the clever manner Bertrand du Guesclin contrived to gain his freedom: he told the Black Prince that people were saying his captor was afraid to permit his ransom.[27] Even the scholarly Ibn

Khaldun, who had little time for stories, introduced these in the *Muqaddimah* when he wished to illustrate some point. So to caution the historian against rejecting reports of accomplishments for which he found no observable parallels in his own time, he tells of a vizier's son who grew up in prison; for this reason he could not visualize a sheep as being any different from the rats that scurried about his dungeon, the only four-legged animals with which he was familiar.[28]

It was partly a continuation of a practice from ancient writers, partly because they hoped this would help them hold their readers' attention, that medieval historians often had their principals giving speeches or falling into conversation with those about them. Procopius, the sixth-century historian, made extensive use of this convention, as did the late medieval Froissart. Because al-Tabari was primarily a recorder of documents, there are few speeches in his work, although in a number of instances he has his characters carry on the account in the first person. An example of this is the case of Chosroes' scribe who went to what appeared dangerous lengths to impress upon his king the importance of respecting his official's authority.[29]

If the modern reader is surprised to find speeches, conversations, anecdotes, moralizing, and miracles in the writings of medieval historians, he will also be surprised to find almost nothing of a social or economic nature. Historians of the Middle Ages, except for an unusual scholar such as Ibn Khaldun, considered their responsibilities pretty well discharged once they had recorded information of political or religious importance. Even the description of phenomena could be justified on the argument that it might hold some prophetic significance. Only bits of information that the social and economic historian welcomes find their way into the pages of medieval chronicles, such as the masons whom Bede's abbot at Wearmouth brought from Gaul, for example, or the price of bread in Matthew Paris' England, or the weapons that Froissart's warriors used. In this respect medieval historians were least modern. Still their readers were expecting little more from them than news about political and ecclesiastical superiors, about wars, and about strange peoples beyond their frontiers who might become a threat. If medieval chroniclers enlivened their accounts with interesting stories, so much the better. The kind of information upon which modern social and economic historians would base their studies could wait for a later age.

CHAPTER 1

Procopius

"**F**OR THIS MAN was both an evil-doer and easily led into evil, the sort of person whom they call a moral pervert . . . [and] Nature seemed to have removed all baseness from the rest of mankind and to have concentrated it in the soul of this man."[1] So wrote Procopius of the illustrious Justinian, who ruled the Byzantine empire from 527 to 565. The extreme prejudice revealed in the language of Procopius is patent even to readers who have never heard of Justinian. Why then is Procopius considered the ranking historian of the Byzantine empire and the ablest Greek historian after Polybius (d. c. 118 B.C.)?

The question is more difficult to answer today than it was a generation ago. Until recent years scholars were inclined to deny Procopius' authorship of the *Secret History,* in which the above passage appears, because of the extravagance of its language. They argued that the same man could not have written this slanderous book and the eminently solid volumes of the *Wars.* But scholars today agree that Procopius was the author of both the *Wars* and the *Secret History.* He ranks high as a historian because the excellence of the *Wars* ensures him a solid reputation, the dubious character of the *Secret History* notwithstanding.

Procopius was born about the year 500 A.D. in Caesarea, the civil capital of Palestine. Where he received his education is a matter of speculation, although some of it was probably in Constantinople. That he prepared himself for a legal career or for some administrative post appears certain. His writing reveals a wide acquaintance with Greek classical literature. He also learned Latin because a lawyer would have found that language indispensable anywhere within the empire. And one would conclude from the views he occasionally expressed in his writings that he belonged to the provincial senatorial aristocracy, which was the most conservative element in Byzantine society.

Procopius must have been a budding lawyer in his late twenties or early thirties when he attracted the attention of the imperial court. For it was about this time that he was appointed secretary and legal adviser to Belisarius, the promising young general to whom the emperor Justinian had just entrusted the command of the Byzantine army in the east against the Sassanid Persians. What must have recommended Procopius for this appointment, apart from his legal training, was his knowledge of languages, particularly Aramaic. Together with Greek, Aramaic was spoken by many people of western Asia. His linguistic competency may indeed have been remarkable — scholars have credited him with some knowledge of Armenian, Hebrew, and even of Gothic, Slavic, and Persian.

In 527, the year of his appointment as Belisarius' secretary, Procopius accompanied the general on his campaign in Syria and Mesopotamia. Six years later he followed him to Africa for the short, victorious campaign against the Vandals. In 536 he crossed to Italy where he joined Belisarius for what proved to be only the first years in the long, tragic history of fighting in that peninsula. Not only was he in constant attendance upon the general, but he also received assignments of his own from Belisarius, all of which Procopius assures the reader he executed with complete success. On one occasion he even proposed a tactical maneuver to Belisarius that the general adopted.[2]

Procopius returned to Constantinople after the capture of Rome in 540 and was apparently witness to the terrible plague that struck the city in 542. After that point his movements become obscure. One may assume that the imperial order, which isolated Belisarius from his friends in 542 when the general fell from favor, also included Procopius. He may have broken with Belisarius of his own choosing, for a reading of the *Secret History* leaves the impression that his attitude toward the general underwent a fundamental change at about this time.

What appears reasonably certain is that Procopius made Constantinople his home for the remainder of his life. It is also highly probable that he continued to enjoy Justinian's goodwill despite the bitter denunciation he expresses of the emperor in the *Secret History*. In the introduction to the *Buildings*, Procopius speaks of "subjects who have received benefits have proved themselves grateful toward their benefactors,"[3] a passage that has been interpreted as referring to the writer himself. If so, the favor that the emperor might have shown him may have been the bestowal of the title *illustris*, which Procopius received in 560. This honor placed him in the inner circles of the aristocracy and suggested his possession of a high administrative office. Some writers believe he was the Procopius who is mentioned as Prefect of the City in 562, although this must be viewed as conjecture. We know nothing of his last years. His death may have come shortly after 560, perhaps as late as 565.

The writings of Procopius, which include the *Wars, Secret History,* and *Buildings*, make up seven volumes in the Loeb Classical Library. Considerable controversy turns about the matter of dating the historian's works. What accounts for most of this problem is the *Secret History*. Had this slanderous volume never appeared, the matter of dating Procopius' other works, the *Wars* and *Buildings*, would occasion neither difficulty nor interest. But because Procopius did write the *Secret History*, some scholars are tempted to detect veiled criticism of the emperor between the lines of the *Wars*, assuming that the historian was at work on both books at the same time.[4]

The first seven books of the *Wars* appeared about 550, the eighth book some time after 554. It is customary to assign the *Buildings* to 560. Because the world was not aware of the existence of the *Secret History* before its listing in *Suidas*, a tenth-century Byzantine "encyclopedia," scholars have here no publication problem to vex them. But they do wrangle over its date of composition. One clue is the statement of Procopius that Justinian had been administering the empire for thirty-two years. Because the emperor's official reign began in 527, the passage of thirty-two years would indicate the period 558–9 as the time of composition. Scholars generally prefer the date 550, however, since Procopius dismisses Justin, the uncle of Justinian who reigned from 518, as no more than a figurehead. He makes the nephew the actual ruler.

The *Wars* cover the fighting in the Near East against the Sassanid Persians, in Libya against the Vandals, and in Italy against the Ostrogoths. In his description of the campaigns and battles Procopius proved himself an observant, impartial, and accurate reporter. In the *Buildings* and the *Secret History*, on the other hand, he assumes a different pose. His *Buildings* is a panegyric, the *Secret History* one of the most malevolent philippics ever penned.

The modern reader who is apt to bridle even at mild propaganda finds the *Buildings* scarcely worthy of notice, which is unfortunate. Not only did Procopius and his contemporaries accept the panegyric as a respectable literary genre, but the volume also contains solid information. So much certain information appears about the construction that took place during Justinian's reign, for instance, that the student of architecture knows more about that century than any prior to the twelfth. The volume supplies a mass of information about churches and fortifications, also about reservoirs, monasteries, spas, and granaries that Justinian caused to have erected or restored. Here is Procopius' lyrical description of the interior of Hagia Sophia, the great church whose magnificent dome continues to dominate the city of Istanbul.

The whole ceiling is overlaid with pure gold, which adds glory to the beauty, yet the light reflected from the stones prevails, shining out in rivalry with the gold. And there are two stoa-like colonnades, one on each side, not separated in any way from the structure of the church itself, but actually making the effect of its width greater, and reaching along its whole length, to the very end, while in height they are less than the interior of the building. And they too have vaulted ceilings and decorations of gold. One of these two colonnaded stoas has been assigned to men worshippers, while the other is reserved for women engaged in the same exercise. But they have nothing to distinguish them, nor do they differ from one another in any way, but their very equality serves to beautify the church, and their similarity to adorn it. But who could fittingly describe the galleries of the women's side, or enumerate the many colonnades and the colonnaded aisles by means of which the church is surrounded? Or who could recount the beauty of the columns and the stones with which the church is adorned? One might imagine that he had come upon a meadow with its flowers in full bloom. For he would surely marvel at the purple of some, the green tint of others, and at those on which the crimson glows and those from which the white flashes, and again at those which Nature, like some painter, varies with the most contrasting colours. And whenever anyone enters this church to pray, he understands at once that it is not by any human power or skill, but by the influence of God, that this work has been so finely turned. And so his mind is lifted up toward God and exalted, feeling that He cannot be far away, but must especially love to dwell in this place which He has chosen. And this does not happen only to one who sees the church for the first time, but the same experience comes to him on each successive occasion, as though the sight were new each time. Of this spectacle no one has ever had a surfeit, but when present in the church men rejoice in what they see, and when they leave it they take proud delight in conversing about it. Furthermore, concerning the treasures of this church – the vessels of gold and silver and the works in precious stones which the Emperor Justinian has dedicated here – it is impossible to give a precise account of them all. But I shall allow my readers to form a judgment by a single example. That part of the shrine which is especially sacred, where only priests may enter, which they call the Inner Sanctuary, is embellished with forty thousand pounds' weight of silver.[5]

If Procopius intended the *Secret History* as a corrective to the *Wars,* as he declares, he rarely kept that objective in mind. The volume consists of little more than a deliberate attempt to destroy the reputations of Justinian, his wife, Theodora, Belisarius, and his wife, Antonina. Procopius invests Justinian, Theodora, and Antonina with demonic powers, if he does not make them out to be actual demons. For Belisarius he reserves the role of a despicable cuckold. Because the pictures he draws of these four individuals are so different from those he presents in the *Wars,* many scholars in the past doubted Procopius' authorship.

Concerning the sources of the information Procopius wove into the *Wars,* the *Buildings,* and the *Secret History,* the author is as reticent as his ancient predecessors in the art of writing history were about theirs. The one clear statement that he has left us on this point is in the introduction to the *Wars.* After a word concerning his purpose in writing the work, he declares: "Furthermore he had assurance that he was especially competent to write the history of these events, if for no other reason, because it fell to his lot, when appointed adviser to the general Belisarius, to be an eyewitness of practically all the events to be described."[6]

It is almost certain that Procopius had access to the imperial archives in his preparation of the *Buildings.* The description he gives of so very many buildings erected or restored during Justinian's reign makes this conclusion inescapable. If Justinian actually commissioned him to prepare this volume, as some scholars believe, Procopius could surely have counted on the cooperation of the government in furnishing him this information. As for the sources for the disgraceful anecdotes and lurid details concerning Theodora, the wife of Justinian, and Antonina, the wife of Belisarius, with which Procopius titillates the reader of the *Secret History,* one can only suggest gossipmongers who are ever at hand ready to accommodate those who seek their merchandise. In addition, Procopius' own morbid imagination led him to attribute the worst possible motives to the persons whose characters he was seeking to assassinate.

Procopius writes a clear, vigorous style. Strongest proof that he was schooled in the arts of the rhetorician appears in the frequency with which his characters make speeches and in the sententious statements he puts into their mouths. Another mark of the rhetorician at this time was his adoption of phrases and figures of speech that his countrymen of the ancient past, notably Herodotus and Thucydides, liked to employ. Some of these are apt: others had been best left to antiquity. One delights in the imagery of Homer's favorite aphorism that such and such "lies on the knees of the gods." When Procopius has the scoundrel John the Cappadocian declaring that "these things lie on the knees of God,"[7] the reader is likely to squirm.

The scholar curious about the motives that prompted Procopius to write the *Wars,* the *Buildings,* and the *Secret History,* will find the author most accommodating. At the beginning of each work, he states his inspiration. In the case of the *Wars* he is writing "to the end that the long course of time may not overwhelm deeds of singular importance through lack of a record, and thus abandon them to oblivion and utterly obliterate them. The memory of these events he deemed would be a great thing and most helpful to men of the present time, and to future generations as well, in case time should ever again place men under a similar stress."

What Procopius had in mind were circumstances that led men to go to war, and for such he has much in the *Wars* that they will find valuable. "For men who purpose to enter upon a war or are preparing themselves for any kind of struggle may derive some benefit from a narrative of a similar situation in history, inasmuch as this discloses the final result attained by men of an earlier day in a struggle of the same sort, and foreshadows, at least for those who are most prudent in planning, what outcome present events will probably have."[8]

Procopius does not say specifically what particular lesson men who contemplate war may derive from his history, although it becomes clear in the end. He leaves no doubt in the reader's mind that war is an evil. Beyond teaching this lesson, history serves other ends. Procopius appreciates the interest value even wars might possess. For this reason he insists that in no previous conflicts were "more important or mightier deeds . . . to be found in history than those which have been enacted in these wars. . . . For in them more remarkable feats have been performed than in any other wars with which we are acquainted."[9]

In his introduction to the *Buildings* Procopius justifies the writing of history for the examples of virtue and vice it records. Subsequent generations should emulate the first and avoid the second, and he marvels at "how many and how great are the benefits which are wont to accrue to states through History, which transmits to future genera-

tions the memory of those who have gone before, and re-
sists the steady effort of time to bury events in oblivion;
and while it incites to virtue those who from time to time
may read it by the praise it bestows, it constantly assails
vice by repelling its influence. Wherefore our concern
must be solely this — that all the deeds of the past shall be
clearly set forth, and by what man, whosoever he might
be, they were wrought."[10]

Procopius' intent in writing the *Secret History* was to
introduce for the record damaging information about men
and women in high places that he had not dared to incorpo-
rate in the *Wars*. He could not do this, he explains, "as long
as the actors were still alive. . . . For neither was it possible to elude the vigilance of multitudes of spies, nor, if
detected, to escape a most cruel death. . . . It will therefore
be necessary for me in this book to disclose, not only those
things which have hitherto remained undivulged, but also
the causes of those occurrences which have already been
described."[11]

Procopius confesses that what he will be writing in this
volume will "seem neither credible nor probable to men of a
later generation." For a time he had hesitated to reveal the
black deeds of present rulers lest evil-minded men copy
them. Later he decided otherwise, persuaded "by the
thought that it will assuredly be clear to those who hereafter shall hold sovereign power that, in the first place, punishment will in all probability overtake them likewise for
their misdeeds, just as befell those persons; and, in the
second place, that their own actions and characters will
likewise be on record for all future time, so that consequently they will perhaps be more reluctant to trans-
gress."[12]

The diverse character of Procopius' writings makes it
necessary to consider each work individually when weigh-
ing the historian's credibility. One may assume, for instance, that many violations of the canons of strict truth-
fulness will come to light in the *Buildings* because this

volume was intended as a panegyric to Justinian. Surely an illustration of such departure from the truth appears in the course of the historian's description of the construction of Hagia Sophia. He writes that before the center of one of the great arches had been put into place, the piers that supported it began to crack, "unable to carry the mass which bore down upon them. . . . So Anthemius and Isidorus,[13] terrified at what had happened, carried the matter to the Emperor, having come to have no hope in their technical skill. And straightway the Emperor, impelled by I know not what, but I suppose by God (for he is not himself a master-builder), commanded them to carry the course of this arch to its final completion. 'For when it rests upon itself,' he said, 'it will not longer need the props beneath it.' . . . So the artisans carried out his instructions, and the whole arch then hung secure, sealing by experiment the truth of his idea."[14]

Apart from such licenses that the laudatory character of the *Buildings* permitted him and what contemporaries would have accepted without protest, there is no reason to question the essential accuracy of the information Procopius supplies concerning the churches and fortifications the emperor caused to be built or restored. Because Procopius spent some time in many of the places he mentions in the *Buildings*, the reader may also accept with some confidence the descriptions he offers concerning topography and climate.

The reader may assume much the same position concerning the credibility of the *Wars*. As noted above, Procopius made a point of assuring the reader in the introduction that "he was especially competent to write the history of these events" in that he had been "an eyewitness of practically all the events to be described." In nearly the next sentence he sets down the first rule of the historian, namely, that "truth alone is appropriate to history." Although some scholars insist on finding oblique criticisms of Justinian in the *Wars*, the volumes will strike the ordinary reader as the work of an observant writer whose only concern was to present a true account of what happened. Errors do exist in the *Wars,* however, a few of which one would not expect of a writer so well educated as Procopius. He has Attila dying after Aetius,[15] for example, and he declares Totila's capture of Roman standards was "a thing which had never before happened to the Romans."[16]

But as one would expect of so ancient a writer, Procopius also makes mistakes in geography. "Now the earth is surrounded by a circle of ocean," he writes,

> either entirely or for the most part (for our knowledge is not as yet at all clear in this matter); and it is split into two continents by a sort of outflow from the ocean, a flow which enters at the western part and forms this Sea which we know, beginning at Gadira (Cadiz) and extending all the way to the Maeotic Lake (Sea of Azov). Of these two continents the one to the right, as one sails into the Sea, as far as the Lake, has received the name of Asia, beginning at Gadira and at the southern of the two Pillars of Heracles. . . . And the whole continent opposite this was named Europe. And the strait at that point separates the two continents by about eighty-four stades, but from there on they are kept apart by wide expanses of sea as far as the Hellespont.[17]

The question of the credibility of the *Secret History* is a subject all its own and the one that has received most attention in the evaluation of Procopius as a historian. Procopius anticipated the doubts of his reliability this volume would leave in the minds of his readers. What he had to write, he warned, "will seem neither credible nor probable to men of a later generation."[18] As suggested, the intemperate language is not that of a responsible writer; it was for this reason that scholars hesitated so long to recognize it as Procopius' work. If there is a measure of truth in what Procopius writes, the preposterous distortion to which he subjects it leaves the characters scarcely recognizable. As one scholar observes: "The unedifying picture [of Theodora] omits no detail of depravity which can be imagined as possible for the most shameless of women, and the author succeeds only in discrediting his own testimony, which he seems to offer in full confidence, but which falls to the ground through the weight of its own extravagance."[19]

Procopius, who is the only source one can turn to for information about Theodora's youth, has her growing up in the rough atmosphere of the Hippodrome. Her father, who was the keeper of the animals in the circus, had died. Her financially pressed mother then hurried her three daughters on to the stage as soon as their ages would permit.

> Now Comito, the first one, had already scored a brilliant success among the harlots of her age; and Theodora, the next in order, clothed in a little sleeved frock suitable to a slave girl, would follow her about, performing various services and in particular always carrying on her shoulders the stool on which her sister was accustomed to sit in the assemblies. Now for a time Theodora, being immature, was quite unable to sleep with a man or to have a woman's kind of intercourse with one, yet she did engage in intercourse of a masculine type of lewdness with the wretches, slaves though they were, who, following their masters to the theatre, incidentally took advantage of the opportunity afforded them to carry on this monstrous business, and she spent much time in the brothel in this unnatural traffic of the body. But as soon as she came of age and was at last mature, she joined the women of the stage and straightway became a courtesan, of the sort whom men of ancient times used to call "infantry."[20]

As Theodora grew more mature and experienced, Procopius writes, so did her lechery. So absurd becomes his testimony, however, that it collapses of its own ridiculousness. What further weakens Procopius' credibility in the *Secret History* is his effort to portray Antonina, the wife of Belisarius, as the same sort of lewd woman. It seems Pro-

copius believed nothing more heinous could be said of a
woman than to make her out a nymphomaniac, although
in the case of both Theodora and Antonina, the grossness
of their lewdness marked them as possessed.

Justinian, another person whose reputation Procopius
set out to destroy in the *Secret History*, also seemed possessed, perhaps actually sired by the devil. To advance
this last possibility, Procopius introduces the emperor's
own mother to testify against her son. He writes: "And
they say that Justinian's mother stated to some of her
intimates that he was not the son of her husband Sabba-
tius nor of any man. For when she was about to conceive
him, a demon visited her; he was invisible but affected her
with a certain impression that he was there with her as a
man having intercourse with a woman and then disappeared as in a dream."[21]

If the reader was prepared to believe that Justinian was
the son of a devil, then he would be ready to accept what
Procopius went on to say about the emperor.

> For this man was both an evil-doer and easily led into evil,
> the sort of a person whom they call a moral pervert, never
> of his own accord speaking the truth to those with whom
> he conversed, but having a deceitful and crafty intent be-
> hind every word and action. . . . [Justinian] was insincere,
> crafty, hypocritical, dissembling his anger, double-
> dealing, clever, a perfect artist in acting out an opinion
> which he pretended to hold, and even able to produce tears,
> not from joy or sorrow, but contriving them for the occa-
> sion according to the need of the moment, always playing
> false, yet not carelessly but adding both his signature and
> the most terrible oaths to bind his agreements, and that
> too in dealing with his own subjects. But he departed
> straightway from his agreements and his oaths, just like
> the vilest slaves. . . . He was a fickle friend, a truceless
> enemy, an ardent devotee of assassination and of robbery,
> quarrelsome and an inveterate innovator, easily led astray
> into wrong, but influenced by no counsel to adopt the
> right. . . . How could any man be competent to describe

adequately the character of Justinian? These faults and
many others still greater he manifestly possessed to a degree not in accord with human nature. On the contrary,
Nature seemed to have removed all baseness from the rest
of mankind and to have concentrated it in the soul of this
man.[22]

Although admitting the extravagance of its language,
some scholars attempt to salvage the bulk of the *Secret
History* as credible on the argument that nothing appears
there that directly contradicts what Procopius wrote in
the *Wars*.[23] This is certainly an overstatement.

In the *Wars*, for instance, Procopius attributes the death
of Amalasuntha, the Ostrogothic queen of Italy, to relatives
of certain Goths she had ordered slain.[24] In the *Secret History* Theodora is clearly the real culprit, and she contrived
the death of the physically attractive Amalasuntha lest she
seduce her impressionable husband, Justinian![25] In the
Wars Justinian occasionally appears to desire peace.[26] In the
Secret History he stands forth as an inveterate warmonger
who would stop at nothing short of the destruction of the
entire human race.[27] In the *Wars* Procopius speaks of
Theodora's kindly nature, which "always led her to assist
unfortunate women (prostitutes)."[28] When he tells in the *Secret History* how she had these women removed from the
streets of Constantinople and placed in the Convent of Repentance she had constructed on the Asiatic side of the Bos-
phorus, he leaves the reader the impression that only malice
inspired her action.[29] Beyond these clear inconsistencies between the *Wars* and the *Secret History*, the most palpable
contradiction between the two lies in Procopius' depiction of
Justinian, Belisarius, Theodora, and Antonina in *Wars* as
reasonably normal men and women. In the *Secret History*
they are either demons or moral lepers and conduct themselves accordingly.

Ancient Greek historians such as Herodotus and Thucydides clearly influenced Procopius. Surely to Herodotus one may trace his practice of weaving anecdotes and incidents into his narrative, as well as trivia about mores, geography, and mythology so little linked with the theme at hand that the modern historian would never think of introducing them. Neither the "father of history" nor Procopius ever forgot that the reader wanted to be entertained as much as he might wish to be informed. So in the course of describing the movements of the Byzantine army in the vicinity of Picenum, Procopius takes time for an aside about an infant that had been abandoned by its mother.

Now a certain women of this city had, as it happened, just given birth to a child, and had abandoned the infant, leaving it in its swaddling clothes lying upon the ground; and whether she sought safety in flight or was captured by someone or other, she did not succeed in getting back again to that place; for assuredly it fell out that she disappeared from the world or at least from Italy. So the infant, being thus abandoned, began to cry. But a lone she-goat, seeing it, felt pity and came near, and gave the infant her udder (for she too, as it happened, had recently brought forth young) and guarded it carefully, lest a dog or wild beast should injure it. And since the confusion was long continued, it came about that the infant partook of this food for a very long time. But later, when it became known to the people of Picenum that the emperor's army had come there to injure the Goths, but that the Romans would suffer no harm from it, they all returned immediately to their homes. And when such of the women as were Romans by birth came to Urvisalia with the men, and saw the infant still alive in its swaddling clothes, they were utterly unable to comprehend what had happened and considered it very wonderful that the infant was living. And each of them who chanced to be at that time able to do so offered her breast. But neither would the infant now have anything to do with human milk, nor was the goat at all willing to let it go, but as it kept bleating unceasingly about the infant, it seemed to those present to be feeling the greatest resentment that the women came near it and disturbed it as they did, and, to put all in a word, she insisted upon claiming the babe as her own. Consequently the women no longer disturbed the infant, and the goat continued to nourish it free from fear and to guard it with every care. Wherefore the inhabitants of the place appropriately called this infant Aegisthus.[30] And when I happened to be sojourning in that place, by way of making a display of the strange sight they took me near the infant and purposely hurt it so that it might cry out. And the infant, annoyed by those hurting it, began to cry; whereupon the goat, which was standing about a stone's throw away from it, hearing the cry, came running and bleating loudly to its side, and took her stand over it, so that no one might be able to hurt it again. Such then is the story of this Aegisthus.[31]

Procopius could vouch for the truth of this particular story — he says he saw the infant himself. Not all the anecdotes that he introduces carry this assurance. Like Herodotus, he occasionally leaves the matter of judging the credibility of a tale to the reader.[32]

The impersonal manner Procopius adopts in the *Wars* is a posture he probably admired in Thucydides. It will be recalled that Thucydides referred to himself but once in the *Peloponnesian War* and then in the third person, so casually in fact, that the reader is usually not aware the author is speaking of himself. Procopius is not so austerely impersonal, although it is rare for him to employ the first person. Typical of the impersonal manner in which he chose to hide his identity is this description of the assignment with which Belisarius entrusted him at a time when Rome was under siege by the Goths. Belisarius had just addressed the starving Romans, who were demanding action, concerning the danger of staking their fortunes on a single battle with the enemy.

With these words Belisarius encouraged the Roman populace and then dismissed them; and Procopius, who wrote

> this history, he immediately commanded to go to Na-
> ples. . . . And he commissioned him to load as many ships
> as possible with grain, to gather all the soldiers who at the
> moment had arrived from Byzantium, or had been left
> about Naples in charge of horses or for any other purpose
> whatever. . . . And Procopius, accompanied by Mundilas
> the guardsman and a few horsemen, passed out by night
> through the gate which bears the name of the Apostle
> Paul, eluding the enemy's camp which had been estab-
> lished very close to the Appian Way to keep guard over
> it.[33]

To write in an impersonal manner had been the fashion
of the secular historians of the past. They also avoided
references to the supernatural, that is, to the gods as agencies that guided the course of events. Because Procopius
was a Christian, it was not possible for him to go as far as
his professional predecessors in ignoring the hand of the
Almighty. Still, if he wished to remain in good standing
with the circle of sophisticated readers in Constantinople
for whom his writing was intended, he had to try. Although he does speak of God and divine providence, he
prefers to cloak the working of heaven's will through the
mediums of fate and chance. This effort to sound secular
might also explain his customary reference to the pope as
simply the "chief priest of Rome." He is also careful to hold
himself aloof from the theological controversies of the
time, which was, of course, only the proper thing for a
secular historian to do.

Although the title "father of history" is traditionally
reserved for Herodotus, it is Thucydides who is generally
honored as the father of "scientific" history. He was surely
the first to make a study of war. In his *Peloponnesian War*
he attempted to show how futile and dangerous war is and
how destructive in terms of both physical and moral
values. Procopius, who had certainly joined company with
those who opposed war by the time he neared the end of
the *Wars*, may have shared that ancient historian's con-

demnation of war from the very beginning of his writing. In the very opening paragraphs of the *Wars* he voices, at least by implication, the argument against war that Thucydides had proposed back in the fifth century B.C.: frequently, circumstances of which war-planners are unaware interpose themselves and almost regularly prevent victory.[34]

One of the conventions Procopius inherited from earlier historians, mainly from Thucydides, was that of having the principals in his writing interrupt the narrative with speeches of their own. Relatively few such speeches appear in the *Buildings* and the *Secret History,* but a great many appear in the *Wars.* These speeches serve a variety of purposes. Procopius might simply introduce a speech to break the impersonal monotony of the narrative. When he has his speaker express thoughts of a philosophizing nature the reader may suspect Procopius is airing his own views. If the speaker raises issues that might be offensive to the emperor, one may assume that Procopius is employing the speech to voice with impunity his own criticism of some imperial policy or action.

The best explanation for the large number of speeches is probably that this style was conventional for the times. It had actually been so for centuries before and would continue a popular literary genre into modern times. Today's reader may object to these speeches on several counts. They often interrupt the flow of the narrative both stylistically and logically. But contemporaries of Procopius accepted speeches, like panegyrics, with ease. Since the day of Procopius, history has become, for better or worse, a science. Such literary "aberrations" are no longer tolerated.

How forced one or the other of Procopius' speeches may strike the modern reader is illustrated by the following one. Belisarius made it to his stepson when he learned of the infidelity of his wife Antonina. Not only was she squandering her physical charms upon others but also his wealth. So the general appealed to his stepson, Photius, to do something about it.

> O son most beloved, you have no knowledge of what your father was, since while you were still being nourished at the breast, he fulfilled the term of life and left you and you have profited by no portion of his estate; for he was not very fortunate in the matter of possessions. But you were reared under my care, who am only your stepfather, and you are now of such an age that it is your duty to defend me to the utmost when I suffer injustice; and you have risen to the rank of Consul and have acquired such a mass of wealth, my noble boy, that I might justly be called, and indeed might be, both father to you and mother and all your kindred. For it is not only by ties of blood, but in very truth by deeds, that men are wont to gauge their affection for one another. The time has come, then, for you not to stand by and see me, in addition to the ruin of my home, also deprived of property in so vast an amount and your own mother fastening upon herself a disgrace so great in the eyes of all mankind. And bear in mind that the sins of women do not fall upon the husbands alone, but affect their children even more; for it will generally be their lot to carry with them a certain reputation to the effect that they resemble their mothers in character. Thus would I have you take counsel concerning me, that I love my wife exceedingly, and if it be granted me to take vengeance upon the corruption of my home, I shall do her no harm; but while Theodosius lives, I cannot forgive her the accusations against her.[35]

Procopius appears to have employed the speech occasionally as a means of expressing his own point of view on a particular matter. A probable illustration of this kind of speech is the one Procopius has John the Cappadocian addressing to Justinian in an effort to dissuade him from undertaking a campaign aimed at conquering the Vandal kingdom in north Africa. He cautioned him that the outcome of such an ambitious campaign was at best problematical and asked that "taking example from what has hap-

pened in the past" whether "it [was] not better to love a
state of quiet rather than the dangers of mortal strife?"[36]

The reader of the speech that Belisarius addressed to
Stephanus, an emissary the people of Naples had sent to
him, may feel sure that Procopius was speaking here as
much as his general. Belisarius had had Naples under
siege for some time. His failure to take it had heartened
the defenders into believing their city could *not* be taken.
Then through some accident an aqueduct had been discovered that, after a little chipping away of stone, would permit a detachment of troops to slip into the city. It would
then be a simple matter to open the gates and take the
defenders by surprise. Were the troops of Belisarius to
gain entrance in this manner the populace would be subjected to all the horrors of a "sacking." It was to prevent
such a tragedy that Belisarius spoke to Stephanus of the
evils that would ensue, hoping that he might be able to
convince the city to surrender.

> Many times have I witnessed the capture of cities and I am
> well acquainted with what takes place at such a time. For
> they slay all the men of every age, and as for the women,
> though they beg to die, they are not granted the boon of
> death, but are carried off for outrage and are made to suf-
> fer treatment that is abominable and most pitiable. And
> the children, who are thus deprived of their proper mainte-
> nance and education, are forced to be slaves, and that, too,
> of the men who are the most odious of all – those on whose
> hands they see the blood of their fathers. And this is not
> all, my dear Stephanus, for I make no mention of the con-
> flagration which destroys all the property and blots out
> the beauty of the city. When I see, as in a mirror of the
> cities which have been captured in time past, this city of
> Naples falling victim to such a fate, I am moved to pity
> both it and you its inhabitants. For such means have now
> been perfected by me against the city that its capture is
> inevitable. But I pray that an ancient city, which has for
> ages been inhabited by both Christians and Romans, may
> not meet with such a fortune, especially at my hands as

commander of Roman troops, not least because in my army are a multitude of barbarians, who have lost brothers or relatives before the wall of this town; for the fury of these men I should be unable to control, if they should capture the city by act of war. While, therefore, it is still within your power to choose and to put into effect that which will be your advantage, adopt the better course and escape misfortune; for when it falls upon you, as it probably will, you will not justly blame fortune but your own judgment.[37]

The *Wars* is without question the finest of Procopius' works. Among the qualities that contribute to its excellence is the objective manner with which the historian presents his materials. What renders this the more singular is the woeful lack of detachment manifest in the *Secret History* and *Buildings*. Only one person, for instance, feels the bite of Procopius' pen in the *Wars* — John the Cappadocian, Justinian's ruthless treasurer, the "basest of all men."[38] In the *Wars* Procopius also demonstrates his powers of observation, his knowledge of weaponry and military tactics, and his skill in describing aspects of topography and similar circumstances that enable the reader to follow the narrative more intelligently. He writes with such perceptiveness about tactics that the reader may assume the historian enjoyed the confidence of Belisarius when he mapped strategy.

Because Belisarius regularly found himself outnumbered by larger Gothic armies in the fighting in Italy, he always had to be prepared to extricate himself when a dangerous situation developed or to exploit some possible good fortune. The incident described here took place while the Goths had Rome and the army of Belisarius under siege, but then the arrival of sixteen hundred "Roman" horsemen enabled the general to undertake a kind of limited offensive. The nature of Procopius' description strongly suggests that he had been informed, or at least had learned, of Belisarius' plans.

And Belisarius was pleased by their coming and thought that thenceforth his army ought to carry the war against the enemy. On the following day, accordingly, he commanded one of his own bodyguards, Trajan by name, an impetuous and active fighter, to take two hundred horsemen of the guards and go straight towards the enemy and as soon as they came near the camps to go up on a high hill (which he pointed out to him) and remain quietly there. And if the enemy should come against them, he was not to allow the battle to come to close quarters, nor to touch sword or spear in any case, but to use bows only, and as soon as he should find that his quiver had no more arrows in it, he was to flee as hard as he could with no thought of shame and retire to the fortifications on the run. Having given these instructions, he held in readiness both the engines for shooting arrows and the men skilled in their use. Then Trajan with the two hundred men went out from the Salarian Gate against the camp of the enemy. And they, being filled with amazement at the suddenness of the thing, rushed out from the camps, each man equipping himself as well as he could. But the men under Trajan galloped to the top of the hill which Belisarius had shewn them, and from there began to ward off the barbarians with missiles. And since their shafts fell among a dense throng, they were for the most part successful in hitting a man or a horse. But when all their missiles had at last failed them, they rode off to the rear with all speed, and the Goths kept pressing upon them in pursuit. But when they came near the fortifications, the operators of the engines began to shoot arrows from them, and the barbarians became terrified and abandoned the pursuit. And it is said that not less than one thousand Goths perished in this action. A few days later Belisarius sent Mundilas, another of his own bodyguard, and Diogenes, both exceptionally capable warriors, with three hundred guardsmen, commanding them to do the same thing as the others had done before. And they acted according to his instructions. Then, when the enemy confronted them, the result of the encounter was that no fewer than in the former action, perhaps even more, perished in the same way. And sending even a third time the guardsman Oilas with three hundred horsemen, with instructions to handle the enemy in the same way, he accomplished the same result. So in making these three sallies, in the manner told by me, Belisarius destroyed about four thousand of his antagonists.[39]

Whenever he can Procopius likes to give the reader a careful description of the various turns a battle may take. He also shows real talent in describing the weapons employed in these battles. In the following description the reader is introduced to a number of machines used in storming fortifications and, conversely, in defending them against attackers. The setting has the Gothic king Vittigis about to make an assault on the fortifications protecting the city of Rome.

He constructed wooden towers equal in height to the enemy's wall, and he discovered its true measure by making many calculations based upon the courses of stone. And wheels were attached to the floor of these towers under each corner, which were intended, as they turned, to move the towers to any point the attacking army might wish at a given time, and the towers were drawn by oxen yoked together. After this he made ready a great number of ladders, that would reach as far as the parapet, and four engines which are called rams. Now this engine is of the following sort. Four upright wooden beams, equal in length, are set up opposite one another. To these beams they fit eight horizontal timbers, four above and an equal number at the base, thus binding them together. After they have thus made the frame of a four-sided building, they surround it on all sides, not with walls of wood or stone, but with a covering of hides, in order that the engine may be light for those who draw it and that those within may still be in the least possible danger of being shot by their opponents. And on the inside they hang another horizontal beam from the top by means of chains which swing free, and they keep it at about the middle of the interior. They then sharpen the end of this beam and cover it with a large iron head, precisely as they cover the round point of a missile, or they sometimes make the iron head square like an anvil. And the whole structure is raised upon four wheels, one being attached to each upright beam, and men to the number of no fewer than fifty to each ram move it from the inside. Then when they apply it to the wall, they draw back the beam which I have just mentioned by turning a certain mechanism, and then they let it swing forward with great force against the wall. And this beam by frequent blows is able quite easily to batter down and tear open a wall wherever it strikes, and it is for this reason that the engine has the name it bears, because the striking end of the beam, projecting as it does, is accustomed to butt against whatever it may encounter, precisely as do the males among sheep. Such, then, are the rams used by the assailants of a wall. And the Goths were holding in readiness an exceedingly great number of bundles of faggots, which they had made of pieces of wood and reeds, in order that by throwing them into the moat they might make the ground level, and that their engines might not be prevented from crossing it. Now after the Goths had made their preparations in this manner, they were eager to make an assault upon the wall.

In the meantime Belisarius had prepared counter-weapons and machines that he hoped would be capable of repelling the expected attack.

[He] placed upon towers engines which they call "ballistae." Now these engines have the form of a bow, but on the under side of them a grooved wooden shaft projects; this shaft is so fitted to the bow that it is free to move, and rests upon a straight iron bed. So when men wish to shoot at the enemy with this, they make the parts of the bow which form the ends bend toward one another by means of a short rope fastened to them, and they place in the grooved shaft the arrow, which is about one half the length of the ordinary missiles which they shoot from bows, but about four times as wide. However, it does not have feathers of the usual sort attached to it, but by inserting thin pieces of wood in place of feathers, they give it in all respects the form of an arrow, making the point which they put on very large and in keeping with its thickness. And the men who stand on either side wind it up tight by means of certain appliances, and then the grooved shaft shoots forward and stops, but the missile is discharged from the shaft, and with such force that it attains the distance of not less than two bow-shots, and that, when it hits a tree or a rock, it pierces it easily. Such is the engine which bears this name, being so called because it shoots with very great force. And they fixed other engines along the parapet of the wall adapted for throwing stones. Now these resemble slings and are called "wild asses." And outside the gates they placed "wolves," which they make in the following manner. They set up two timbers which reach from the ground to the battlements; then they fit together beams which have been mortised to one another, placing some upright and others crosswise, so that the spaces between the intersections appear as a succession of holes. And from every joint there projects a kind of beak, which resembles very closely a thick goad. Then they fasten the cross-beams to the two upright timbers, beginning at the top and letting them extend half way down, and then lean the timbers back against the gates. And whenever the enemy come up near them, those above lay hold of the ends of the timbers and push, and these, falling suddenly upon the assailants, easily kill with the projecting beaks as many as they may catch. So Belisarius was thus engaged.[40]

As noted above, Procopius never forgot that a writer of history must seek not only to inform his reader but to entertain him as well. To this end he enlivens his account whenever possible by introducing episodes involving individuals who are engaged in activities that he hopes will engage his reader's attention. The setting for the incident that follows was what was shortly to become the battlefield near Daras, a major fortress in northern Mesopotamia. It was here in 530 that Belisarius gained his spurs by defeating a much larger Persian army. The two armies were ready to fight, but neither appeared willing to make the first move. To break the impasse, a young Persian warrior

riding up very close to the Roman army, began to challenge all of them, calling for whoever wished to do battle with him. And no one of the whole army dared face the danger, except a certain Andreas, one of the personal attendants of Bouzes, not a soldier nor one who had ever practised at all the business of war, but a trainer of youths in charge of a certain wrestling school in Byzantium. Through this it came about that he was following the army, for he cared for the person of Bouzes in the bath; his birthplace was Byzantium. This man alone had the courage, without being ordered by Bouzes or anyone else, to go out of his own accord to meet the man in single combat. And he caught the barbarian while still considering how he should deliver his attack, and hit him with his spear on the right breast. And the Persian did not bear the blow delivered by a man of such exceptional strength, and fell from his horse to the earth. Then Andreas with a small knife slew him like a sacrificial animal as he lay on his back, and a mighty shout was raised both from the city wall and from the Roman army. But the Persians were deeply vexed at the outcome and sent forth another horseman for the same purpose, a manly fellow and well favoured as to bodily size, but not a youth, for some of the hair of his head already shewed grey. This horseman came up along the hostile army, and, brandishing vehemently the whip with which he was accustomed to strike his horse, he summoned to battle whoever among the Romans was willing. And when no one went out against him, Andreas, without attracting the notice of anyone, once more came forth, although he had been forbidden to do so by Hermogenes. So both rushed madly upon each other with their spears, and the weapons, driven against their corselets, were turned aside with mighty force, and the horses, striking together their heads, fell themselves and threw off their riders. And both the two men, falling very close to each other, made great haste to rise to their feet, but the Persian was not able to do this easily because his size was against him, while Andreas, anticipating him (for his practice in the wrestling school gave him this advantage), smote him as he was rising on his knee, and as he fell again to the ground dispatched him. Then a roar went up from the wall and from the Roman army as great, if not greater, than before, and the Persians broke their phalanx and withdrew to Ammodios, while the Romans, raising the paean, went inside the fortifications; for already it was growing dark. Thus both armies passed the night.[41]

A question commonly raised in the study of any historian concerns his interpretation of history. What are the writer's views regarding the forces that shape events, whether these forces pertain to an individual ruler, to a people, or to an age? What, in short, is his philosophy of history? In the case of Procopius, did he hold to any particular philosophy? Did he believe that factors and agencies existed that determined or influenced the flow of history? Or did he, as was true of most earlier historians, refrain from expressing any thoughts on the subject? Was history for Procopius simply a sequence of events that it was his duty to record as accurately and objectively as possible? And if he did remain silent about the forces that influenced history, can the reader perhaps detect any theme in the manner in which he presents his narrative or events?

Procopius' ancient predecessors in the art of writing history, above all Herodotus and Thucydides, appear to have accepted a cyclical interpretation of history. They believed that nations have life spans like people. They rise, mature, and decline, and as they wane and pass from the scene, others appear to take their place – and so on until the end of time. It seems Polybius and Livy did not fully endorse this view. They believed that destiny or the gods intended something special for Rome, that the Roman empire might well endure into the indefinite future. Procopius did take pride in being a citizen of the Hellenized Roman empire. But given the condition of that empire in his day, when much of the west had been irretrievably lost and the unceasing war in Italy was turning that peninsula into a shambles, he could scarcely have subscribed to the views of Polybius and Livy.

One may find considerable agreement between the views of Herodotus and Thucydides and those of Procopius concerning the flow of history. For one thing neither they nor Procopius formally expounded their views on the subject. Procopius was in agreement with his ancient predecessors in believing that history would continue in the future as it had in the past, with nations rising and falling, some more powerful than others and enjoying greater longevity, but all inevitably declining and disappearing. Herodotus was willing to permit a factor apart from the doings of human beings to influence or alter this pattern of events. With him the gods might interpose their will. They had done so in the conflict between the Greeks and Persians when they gave the victory to the outnumbered Hellenes to punish the Asiatics for their pride.

Thucydides, the idol of all secular historians, including Procopius, studiously avoided mention of the gods. If they existed, they lived their own lives apart from the world of human beings. For Thucydides history unfolded its seemingly unending twists and turns simply as men and circumstances determined, but with one exception – chance. Chance existed; it might interfere with the best of plans and it frequently did. With those two exceptions, in the interference of Herodotus' gods and Thucydides' chance, history would go on and on and on.

Because Procopius was a devout Christian, he could accept neither Herodotus' gods nor Thucydides' chance in quite the way they were presented. What he managed to do was to combine the views of these two ancient historians, then fit them into a Christian framework. To transform the gods of Herodotus into the one Christian God was a simple matter. What could he do with Thucydides' chance? He retained it, but to reassure his Christian readers and not alienate his secular friends, he designated divine providence as the ultimate authority behind chance. Because Procopius was genuinely convinced of the omnipotence of God and God's wont to interfere in human affairs, one might admit that he retained Thucydides' element of chance to preserve the goodwill of his sophisticated readers. In any event, because he was a secular historian, it was impossible for him to accept, at least formally, the teleological view of history generally adopted by later Western chroniclers.

At times Procopius writes as a thoroughly committed Christian with no apparent concern for the possible reaction of his secular friends. So when telling of the weak Honorius who found his limited talents unequal to the task of dealing with Alaric in southern Italy and pacifying his western provinces, he has God coming to the emperor's rescue. "But while Honorius was thus anxiously awaiting the outcome of these events and tossed amid the billows of uncertain fortune, it so chanced that some wonderful pieces of good fortune befell him. For God is accustomed to succour those who are neither clever nor able to devise anything of themselves, and to lend them assistance, if they be not wicked, when they are in the last extremity of despair; such a thing, indeed, befell this emperor."[42]

Then somewhat later in the *Wars* the reader finds himself confronted with a passage in which Procopius philosophizes over the course of events in a manner typical of a pagan student of history. In this particular instance he is soliloquizing, as it were, over the Roman general Narses' capture of Rome. "At this point in the narrative," he writes,

it occurs to me to comment on the manner in which Fortune makes sport of human affairs, not always visiting men in the same manner nor regarding them with uniform glance, but changing about with the changes of time and place; and she plays a kind of game with them, shifting the value of the poor wretches according to the variations of time, place, or circumstance, seeing that Bessas, the man

who had previously lost Rome, not long afterward recovered Petra in Lazica for the Romans, and that Dagis-
thaeus,[43] on the contrary, who had let Petra go to the enemy, won back Rome for the emperor in a moment of time.
But these things have been happening from the beginning
and will always be as long as the same Fortune rules over
men.[44]

Procopius expresses himself in much the same secular
fashion when commenting on the death of Totila, the valiant king of the Goths. At the height of his success Totila
had succeeded in recovering almost the entire peninsula
from Belisarius, including the city of Rome. Now he was
dead and his army destroyed. "And there his followers
buried him in the earth and departed.

> Such was the conclusion of the reign and the life of Totila,
> who had ruled the Goths eleven years. But the end which
> came to him was not worthy of his past achievements, for
> everything had gone well with the man before that, and his
> end was not commensurate with his deeds. But here again
> Fortune was obviously disporting herself and tearing hu-
> man affairs to shreds by way of making a display of her
> own perverse nature and unaccountable will; for she had
> endowed Totila of her own free will with prosperity for no
> particular reason for a long time, and then after this fash-
> ion smote the man with cowardice and destruction at the
> present time for no fitting cause. But these things, I be-
> lieve, have never been comprehensible to man, nor will
> they ever become so at any future time. And yet there is
> always much talk of this matter and opinions are being for
> ever bandied about according to each man's taste, as he
> seeks comfort for his ignorance in an explanation which
> seems reasonable.[45]

Procopius also confesses his unwillingness to explain
the cause of the plague that struck Constantinople and
"the entire world" in 542 and "blighted the lives of all men,"
regardless of age, sex, or condition. But he can describe
what it did and how. "Now let each one express his own

judgment concerning the matter," he wrote, "both sophist and astrologer, but as for me, I shall proceed to tell where this disease originated and the manner in which it destroyed men."[46]

Not only does man find it impossible to interpret the course of events; he is himself incapable of reversing a sequence of happenings should fate or God have decided otherwise. Man is even obliged to let Fortune make him famous should that be her desire. That was the case with Chosroes, the king of the Persians, the man who had captured and destroyed the great city of Antioch.

> For every time when Fortune wishes to make a man great, she does at the fitting time those things which she has decided upon, with no one standing against the force of her will: and she neither regards the man's station, nor purposes to prevent the occurrence of things which ought not to be, nor does she give heed that many will blaspheme against her because of these things, mocking scornfully at that which has been done by her contrary to the deserts of the man who receives her favour; nor does she take into consideration anything else at all, if only she accomplish the thing which has been decided upon by her. But as for these matters, let them be as God wishes.[47]

In this last line Procopius clearly leaves God the master of Fortune, and this was surely his own position, even though it pleased him to write about chance in a manner reminiscent of Thucydides. And where Thucydides would leave chance and fate free to do as circumstance or whim suggested, Procopius placed God above them and also on the side of justice.[48] He has Belisarius saying as much in a case involving two of his soldiers—they were Massagetae—who had slain a comrade for ridiculing them. Belisarius "straightway impaled these two men on the hill which is near Abydus." When the friends of the two executed soldiers remonstrated with Belisarius that he had acted with unnecessary severity (the two men had been intoxicated), the general called them together and spoke to them of the importance of always being worthy of God's goodwill.

> If my words were addressed to men now for the first time entering into war, it would require a long time for me to convince you by speech how great a help justice is for gaining the victory. For those who do not understand the fortunes of such struggles think that the outcome of war lies in strength of arm alone. But you, who have often conquered an enemy not inferior to you in strength of body and well endowed with valour, you who have often tried your strength against your opponents, you, I think, are not ignorant that, while it is men who always do the fighting in either army, it is God who judges the contest as seems best to Him and bestows the victory in battle. Now since this is so, it is fitting to consider good bodily condition and practice in arms and all the other provision for war of less account than justice and those things which pertain to God.[49]

Procopius showed far greater reserve than the majority of his contemporaries in his willingness to accept omens. When writing of what many people interpreted as omens, he customarily withheld judgment and left the matter to his readers. The comet that appeared in 539 precipitated the usual spate of predictions, but none from Procopius. He writes:

> At that time also the comet appeared, at first about as long as a tall man, but later much larger. And the end of it was toward the west and its beginning toward the east, and it followed behind the sun itself. For the sun was in Capricorn and it was in Sagittarius. And some called it "the swordfish" because it was of goodly length and very sharp at the point, and others called it "the bearded star"; it was seen for more than forty days. Now those who were wise in these matters disagreed utterly with each other, and one announced that one thing, another that another thing was indicated by this star; but I only write what took place and I leave to each one to judge by the outcome as he wishes.[50]

In 547, a series of phenomena took place that had people wondering whether something extraordinary was in the offing. Apart from a number of earthquakes, there was the flooding of the Nile, which had risen to heights never before recorded. Then there was an enormous whale, some forty-five feet long, which for fifty years had been causing havoc to shipping in the vicinity of Constantinople. It had finally run itself aground in the mud and had been killed. After a detailed description of the episode of the whale, Procopius gives this summary.

> Now the Byzantines, observing the earthquakes and learning the circumstances of the Nile's rise and the capture of this whale, began straightway to prophesy that such and such things would take place, according to the taste of each. For men are wont, when present events baffle them, to utter awesome prophecies of the future, and, distracted by occurrences which trouble them, to infer, with no good reason, what the future will bring forth. But as for me, I shall leave to others prophecies and explanations of marvels.[51]

Mention of Procopius' position concerning omens leads to a question regarding his attitude toward mythology. Did he accept the romantic tales told by Homer or the stories upon which Sophocles and other Greek dramatists drew for their plots? The answer is yes and no: yes, he believed, or appeared inclined to believe, that these people had existed; no, he did not accept, at least he does not appear to have accepted, the marvelous tales told about them. Such an analysis finds support in what Procopius wrote of the region about Terracina.[52] He speaks of the luxuriant pasture there that made it an ideal camp for the Roman army. He then mentions nearby Mt. Circaeum and a river flowing by the place

> where they say Odysseus met Circe, though the story seems to me untrustworthy, for Homer declares that the

habitation of Circe was on an island. This, however, I am able to say, that this Mt. Circaeum, extending as it does far into the sea, resembles an island, so that both to those who sail close to it and to those who walk to the shore in the neighbourhood it has every appearance of being an island. And only when a man gets on it does he realize that he was deceived in his former opinion. And for this reason Homer perhaps called the place an island.[53]

Procopius also draws a sharp distinction between history and mythology. He does this in the course of describing the geography and topography of Lazica, a small country touching the eastern end of the Black Sea. He maintains that the Lazi who occupied this region in his day were none other than the ancient Colchians who "have merely changed their name at the present to Lazi, just as nations of men and many other things do." For this reason the ancient accounts concerning the region no longer apply. New conditions now exist and other peoples have moved into the area. All these changes must be examined, "not relating the mythological tales about them nor other antiquated material, nor even telling in what part of the Euxine Sea the poets say Prometheus was bound (for I consider that history is very widely separated from mythology), but stating accurately and in order both the names of each of those places and the facts that apply to them at the present day."[54]

Although Procopius refused to accept the miraculous in ancient mythology, he did believe that the Christian God did work miracles. He describes how Justinian himself became the beneficiary of a miracle. The emperor was suffering an infected knee that was causing him grievous pain. He had brought it on himself, so Procopius writes, by the rigor of the Lenten mortifications he had observed. The emperor would go without food for several days, scarcely took any sleep, and when he did eat he "abstained from wine and bread and other foods and ate only herbs, and those, too, wild ones thoroughly pickled with salt and vinegar." Procopius continues:

> Hence, then, his malady gathered strength and got beyond the help of the physicians, and for a long time the Emperor was racked by these pains. But during this time he heard about the relics which had been brought to light, and abandoning human skill, he gave the case over to them, seeking to recover his health through faith in them, and in a moment of direst necessity he won the reward of the true belief. For as soon as the priests laid the reliquary on the Emperor's knee, the ailment disappeared instantly, driven out by the bodies of men who had been dedicated to the service of God.[55]

That the account of this miracle appears in the *Buildings* may leave the reader wondering whether Procopius actually believed what he wrote. But he does tell of another miracle, this one in the *Wars,* which should remove any question about the matter. This miracle concerned a Syrian ascetic,

> Jacobus by name, who had trained himself with exactitude in matters pertaining to religion. This man had confined himself many years before in a place called Endielon, a day's journey from Amida, in order that he might with more security devote himself to pious contemplation. The men of this place, assisting his purpose, had surrounded him with a kind of fencing, in which the stakes were not continuous, but set at intervals, so that those who approached could see and hold converse with him. And they had constructed for him a small roof over his head, sufficient to keep off the rain and snow. There this man had been sitting for a long time, never yielding either to heat or cold, and sustaining his life with certain seeds, which he was accustomed to eat, not indeed every day, but only at long intervals. Now some of the Ephthalitae who were overrunning the country thereabout saw Jacobus and with

great eagerness drew their bows with intent to shoot at him. But the hands of every one of them became motionless and utterly unable to manage the bow.[56]

This passage should refute the position of those scholars who attempt to make Procopius out to have been something of a free thinker in matters of religion. That Procopius always left the working of fate under God's direction should also refute their argument that his references to fate and fortune were quite after the manner of the pagan Thucydides. That Procopius spoke of the pope simply as the "chief priest of Rome" may not be counted as evidence of his supposed agnosticism. He may have employed that phrase to please his secular readers. That kind of reference, scarcely one of reverence, would surely have gratified the large element in Constantinople that was unsympathetic toward Rome's claim to primacy. Still this element probably included the majority of the people living in that city, both clerical and lay, who, along with Procopius, simply did not subscribe fully to the Petrine Doctrine[57] as this was presented by Western apologists.

Procopius did express some impatience with men who argued incessantly over theological subtleties. The neverending controversy over the nature of Christ left him cold. He wrote:

As for the points in dispute, although I know them well, I shall by no means make mention of them; for I consider it a sort of insane folly to investigate the nature of God, enquiring of what sort it is. For man cannot, I think, apprehend even human affairs with accuracy, much less those things which pertain to the nature of God. As for me, therefore, I shall maintain a discreet silence concerning these matters, with the sole object that old and venerable beliefs may not be discredited. For I, for my part, will say nothing whatever about God save that He is altogether good and has all things in His power.[58]

It is true that Procopius did not approve of the stern

measures Justinian took to suppress heresy, but neither did many others. Had he written the book on the subject of religion that he once planned, most questions concerning his religious views would probably have been answered. For although Procopius was no agnostic, there is little evidence in his writing that he was a man of deep faith. He does not write with any expression of feeling about Christ or the saints or the church. And when he tells of something that sounds mysterious, such as the way the Goths did not attempt to penetrate the city of Rome through the "Broken Wall," which tradition had it the Apostle Peter had agreed to guard, he contents himself with stating that fact and that he was among those who "marveled" about the matter. But then follows a cryptic, "So much then, for this."[58] The reader might expect Procopius to have made some acknowledgment of God's wonderful ways. There is none. Yet such was the mark of the "secular" historian.

CHAPTER 2

The Venerable Bede

BEDE, "THE FIRST HISTORIAN of medieval Europe and its master in chronology,"[1] was probably born in 673 off the bleak coast of northeastern England near where the monastery of Wearmouth would raise its humble walls a year later. This little about Bede and not much more concerning his personal life we learn from the autobiographical note the historian appended to his *Ecclesiastical History of the English People.* Bede tells how, when he was seven, his kinsmen brought him to the monastery at Wearmouth and gave him over into the care of the monks. Two years later, in 682, Abbot Benedict Biscop sent him with a group of some twenty members of the Wearmouth community several miles away to the south bank of the Tyne, where they established the sister community of Jarrow. There at Jarrow Bede remained for the rest of his life except for a visit to Lindisfarne fifty miles to the north and another to York, which lay somewhat farther to the south. If he made other trips, none can be firmly established, surely not the one to Rome about which legend persisted.

For Bede the years from 673 until his death in 735 were those of a student, monk, teacher, and writer. We have this on his own testimony. "From then on," that is, from the time he became a member of the community at Wearmouth-Jarrow, "I have spent all my life in this monastery, applying myself entirely to the study of the Scriptures; and, amid the observance of the Discipline of the Rule² and the daily task of singing in the church, it has always been my delight to learn or to teach or to write."³ At the age of nineteen, six years before the twenty-five canonically required, he was ordained deacon. His ordination to the priesthood came properly at thirty. During a dozen of his learning years he studied under the distinguished scholar Benedict Biscop, the founder of the monastery. Bede's death came just after he had dictated the last line in a vernacular translation of the Gospel of St. John. According to the monk who attended him in his last hours, once Bede had dictated this last sentence, he spoke up: " 'Hold my head in your hands for it is a great delight to me to sit over against my holy place in which I used to pray, that as I sit there I may call upon my Father.' And so upon the floor of his cell, singing 'Glory be to the Father and to the Son and to the Holy Spirit' and the rest, he breathed his last."⁴

While accepting a measure of pious editing on the part of Bede's "biographer" in his description of the saint's last hours, the manner in which Bede died is pertinent to understanding the scholar. From all available evidence it appears he died the saint he lived. As far as can be ascertained from what he wrote and from what others wrote about him, he dedicated his whole life to the service of God. Nothing else counted for him—would, in fact, have constituted an infraction of his monastic vows. And while subsequent centuries, including our own, are grateful to him for the pages of early English history that today would be largely blank had his *History* never taken shape, his interest in history was limited to what he considered relevant to the history of the church and of Christianity in England. No doubt in his charity he would have been pleased to accommodate the secular interests of later generations as far as this was proper. For himself, he never strayed from what he viewed to be his responsibilities as monk and scholar. In terms of historical writing, he was first a church historian, then hagiographer, and, fortunately for us, a true scholar at both tasks.

Bede's thoroughly spiritual posture explains his attitude toward classical literature. He drew upon pagan writers, upon Pliny the Elder in particular in his scientific writings, but he did so with reluctance and without acknowledgment. For apt quotations to point up his writings he appealed to the Bible and the church fathers. Even his treatise on metrics offers illustrations from Christian poets, rarely from pagan. The one exception is Virgil for whom he felt a reverence typical of the Middle Ages.[5] Because of Bede's exclusive concentration on things spiritual, the reader of his *History* will seek in vain for information of economic or social importance, except for such incidental bits as that Benedict Biscop was obliged to import masons and glassmakers from Gaul to build the monasteries at Wearmouth-Jarrow. Still it is strange that Bede evinces so little interest in storms, eclipses, and earthquakes. Phenomena of this kind usually caught the attention of medieval chroniclers who were wont to view such things as presaging evil times, especially the end of the world. This is all the more surprising because Bede believed the world was far advanced in the sixth and final age of its existence. He does refer to comets on one occasion and that significantly in the closing pages of his *History*, as portending disaster for the whole world.

A few other items are known about Bede's career. In 686, shortly after the nine-year-old Bede had moved to Jarrow, a deadly plague struck the community and left all dead save Bede and the abbot Ceolfrith. Scholars, at any rate, so interpret the allusion in the anonymous *History of*

the Abbots, which tells of a little boy and Ceolfrith as all
who remained alive. The account goes on to relate how the
two of them, in the singing of the divine office, at first
attempted to dispense with the chanting of the antiphons
except at vespers and matins, then found this so unsatisfactory that they decided to struggle through the entire
office as best they could until new members could join
them.

One last personal item – the title "venerable" by which
Bede is traditionally known carries no special significance.
It was apparently a title used somewhat synonymously
for "distinguished" or "honorable." Had Bede been canon-
ized within a few years of his death,[6] he might never have
been known by the now familiar title. Bede was buried at
Jarrow, but what are believed to be his relics now rest in
the Galilee chapel of Durham cathedral. A monk is said to
have carried them to Durham about 1020.

In view of the voluminousness of Bede's writings, it is
not surprising that controversy long persisted over the
authenticity of many of the works attributed to him. The
spurious number has indeed been large. In the judgment
of one modern scholar, "No writer has had more different
works unknowingly attributed to him than Bede."[7] Many
of these works were the compositions of unknown *savants*
who hoped to give their views wide acceptance by credit-
ing them to Bede. It also happened on occasion that the
extra leaves remaining unfilled in a codex devoted to a
transcription of Bede's works were filled with anonymous
writings, all of which came in time to be ascribed to Bede.
Many spurious writings made their appearance in the
early sixteenth century when Catholic apologists, in their
zeal to refute the claims of Reformation adherents concerning the views of early and still "uncorrupted" theologians, produced *opera Bedae,* which clearly showed them
to be in error.

What aids mightily in arriving at a fairly accurate body
of Bede's writings is the list the historian appended to his

History. Several of the items he listed have disappeared, however, while others he composed failed of mention, including the translation of St. John's Gospel that is no longer extant. What loom largest in number and volume among his writings, and which he considered his most important, are his theological works, homilies, and commentaries on the Scripture. Many of his homilies made their way into the divine office. For five hundred years his exegetical writings assured him a reputation as a theological commentator second only to that of the major church fathers. Because there is little originality to commend these theological works, they became popular for their clarity, their substance, and their manifest orthodoxy.

The Middle Ages attached considerable importance to Bede's so-called scientific writings. As with his theological works, Bede depended heavily upon what others had written. In cosmography and the field of science in general, he drew heavily upon Pliny the Elder and his Christian transmitter Isidore of Seville. Although some scholars may question the value of such derivative work, the Middle Ages would have been much the poorer intellectually without Bede's diligence in studying these earlier writings and digesting them. Of decisive importance were Bede's treatises on chronology.[8] Bede laid to rest a problem perennially harassing Western scholars from the beginning of recorded history. He began using the birth of Christ as the base year in his own writing, a method proposed by the early sixth-century monk Dionysius Exiguus. For Bede the birth of Christ marked the beginning of the Sixth Age of the universe. This was the division of time he inherited from St. Augustine's *City of God* through Isidore of Seville. What may have been Bede's principal motive in devoting so much of his time to the study of chronology was his eagerness to resolve the controversy over the date of Easter. Until that problem had been settled in favor of the Roman system of dating, Celtic Christians would continue to question the authority of the Roman pontiff.

Other writings of Bede that helped to establish his popularity in the early Middle Ages included treatises on orthography and metrics. Though holding no brief for originality, nor excellence for that matter, they proved of value in the schools of Bede's age and the Carolingian that followed. Bede considered most of his works didactic in character. He intended them for use in the schools. Although the lack of originality in these works severely reduces their intrinsic value, the Middle Ages of the eighth century and for several centuries after had nothing better to offer. These works also establish the thoroughness of Bede's own grounding in the subjects of the trivium, his unusual facility at clear exposition, his ability to judge critically what he read and to extract its important points, and his skill in presenting it all in an orderly, lucid fashion. Bede made no pretensions to originality. He was quite content to do the unpretentious work of presenting in an organized manner the knowledge that such earlier scholars as Isidore of Seville had compiled.

Bede also composed several hymns and poems, the most important poem of which honored the memory of St. Cuthbert. The most valuable of the letters credited to him is the one he addressed to Egbert, bishop of York, who had once been his pupil. In this letter he exhorted that prelate to dedicate himself to a reformation of the church in England for which he declared there was a most urgent need.

Closer to the role of historian that Bede assumed in the *History* was martyrology, which contributed to the popularity of that type of writing. As it happens, his own was hardly an improvement over the anonymous work of the same kind that he used. He also wrote a *Lives of the Abbots* (of Wearmouth-Jarrow) and the lives of several saints as well. The most important of these was his *Life of St. Cuthbert.*

There were finally two chronicles, each appended to a work on chronology. The longer of these, and the more important, enjoyed considerable popularity with medieval chroniclers. It began with the Creation and marched quickly and in starkly chronological fashion to 725 A.D. This chronicle bears witness to Bede's acquaintance with several ancient historians including Eutropius, whence his brief reference to Julius Caesar, who "ob insolentiam morum coniurantibus in eum LX vel amplius senatoribus equitibusque Romanis in curia confossus interiit, post annos IIII et menses VI quem regnare coeperat."[9] But his principal source for the chronicle was Eusebius' *Ecclesiastical History* and its continuators. The only interesting statement in Bede's chronicle is the very last entry, which speaks of the coming of Anti-Christ, of judgment, and of heaven and hell. Bede does refer in the entry for the year 725 to the large number of Englishmen, men and women, nobles and commoners, whose devotion led them to make a pilgrimage to Rome.

Except for a few lines in Northumbrian English and the vernacular translation of St. John's Gospel, all of Bede's writing was in Latin. He wrote in a clear, straightforward style, the language of a scholar and teacher concerned with instructing his readers, not with impressing them. Because of the lucidity with which he wrote and the extensive character of his writing, both in amount and comprehensiveness, Bede stands forth as the most important of the transmitters of classical and patristic learning during the period of the so-called Dark Ages. He also represents the finest product of the mingling of the two intellectual streams to which England of the late eighth century owed its preeminence in Western Europe — the Celtic stream that led back through Lindisfarne, Iona, to Ireland, and the southern stream that carried to Canterbury and Rome. In a more direct way Bede owed much of his education to Benedict Biscop, the founder of Wearmouth-Jarrow, who was perhaps the most learned mentor of his day in England.

In no place in England could Bede have found a more impressive collection of books than at Jarrow, where he spent the greater part of his life. Benedict Biscop had been instrumental in bringing most of these books back from Rome on the five trips he made to the Eternal City. Other books were added during the abbacy of Ceolfrith. There is little question but that the majority of these volumes were of a theological nature. They included some by eastern church fathers, which Bede's knowledge of Greek enabled him to read. A number of pagan classics such as Pliny's *Natural History* must also have graced the shelves of Jarrow's scriptorium. Still many of the hundred authors Bede cites must have been known to him only secondhand.

Whatever the degree of Bede's piety or his intellectual accomplishments, were it not for the *Ecclesiastical History of the English People* he would today be no better known to the Western world than Hrabanus Maurus, a Carolingian scholar of similar productivity and learning. For Bede's history, "its method and style, and above all the personality which shines through the style, have made it one of the classics of human history."[10] Bede completed his history in 731 when the ills of old age were beginning to weigh heavily upon him. (A reference to the Battle of Tours, which was fought in 732, suggests he made some slight revisions later.) The structure of the work is chronological, although Bede is likely to permit certain subjects, such as the career of some saint, to carry him far afield. But when Bede strays, he is careful to bring his reader back whence he came.

Bede opens his *History* with a dedication of the work to King Ceolwulf of Northumbria. Ceolwulf had shown much interest in the undertaking and had even been privileged to examine it before its final drafting. Bede writes: "Your Majesty has asked to see the *History of the English Church and Nation* which I have lately published. It was with pleasure, sire, that I submitted it for your perusal and criticism on a former occasion; and with pleasure I now send it once again, for copying and fuller study, as time may permit."[11]

Next Bede goes on to say what in his judgment justified the writing of history: "Should history tell of good men and their good estate, the thoughtful listener is spurred on to imitate the good; should it record the evil ends of wicked men, no less effectually the devout and earnest listener or reader is kindled to eschew what is harmful and perverse, and himself with greater care pursue those things which he has learned to be good and pleasing in the sight of God."[12]

Bede commends King Ceolwulf for being knowing that history possesses this virtue, and he compliments him for wishing to disseminate the knowledge of this history "for the instruction of yourself and those over whom divine authority has appointed you to rule." Time and again, as the *History* unfolds, Bede reminds the reader of this ethical justification for the writing and reading of history.

Bede now goes to considerable length to assure the king and his other readers that he made great effort "to remove all occasions of doubt about those things I have written, either in your mind or in the minds of any others who listen to or read this history." For the period up to the arrival of Augustine in Britain in 597, he drew his material "from here and there, chiefly from the writings of earlier writers." These have been identified as Pliny, Orosius, Gildas, and Prosper of Aquitaine among others, as well as lives of St. Alban and St. Germanus. For the years after 597 he cites as his principal authority Albinus, abbot of the monastery of St. Peter and St. Paul at Canterbury, later known as St. Augustine's, a close friend of Bede and the one who encouraged him to write the *History*, "a man of universal learning who was educated by . . . Archbishop Theodore [of Tarsus] and Abbot Hadrian of blessed memory, both venerable and learned men." Albinus had exhaustively searched for written records and run down ancient traditions that pertained to Kent and other Anglo-Saxon kingdoms. He passed these materials on to Nothelm, a priest of London, who in turn gave them to

Bede. Nothelm had also gone to Rome, where "he got permission from the present Pope Gregory to search through the archives of the holy Romen church" for letters and documents that he thought Bede would find useful.

Bede continues to discuss the sources of his information.

> Daniel, the esteemed bishop of the West Saxons who still survives, communicated to me in writing something of the history of the church of his own kingdom, as well as of the neighbouring kingdoms of Sussex and the Isle of Wight. Further I learned from the brethren of the monastery known as Lastingham which was founded by Cedd and Chad how, through the ministry of these devoted priests of Christ, the kingdom of Mercia achieved the faith of Christ which it had formerly rejected. I also learned from the monks of Lastingham about the life and death of these two fathers. Further, I learned the history of the church of East Anglia, partly from the writings or the traditions of men of the past, and partly from the account of the esteemed Abbot Esi. As to the kingdom of Lindsey, I learned of the growth of their faith in Christ and of the succession of bishops, either through a letter from the reverend Bishop Cyneberht or from the lips of other trustworthy men. But what happened in the church in the various parts of the kingdom of Northumbria, from the time when they received the faith of Christ up to the present, apart from those matters of which I had personal knowledge, I have learned not from any one source but from the faithful testimony of innumerable witnesses, who either knew or remembered these things.[13]

Bede concludes his detailed discussion of the sources he employed in the preparation of the *History* with a statement that marks him a true historian. "So I humbly beg the reader, if he finds anything other than the truth set down in what I have written, not to impute it to me. For, in accordance with the principles of true history, I have simply sought to commit to writing what I have collected from common report, for the instruction of posterity."[14]

It appears from Bede's discussion of the sources of his information that he was concerned chiefly, if not exclusively, with matters pertaining to Christianity and the church. There is some suggestion, however, that he incorporated into his *History* information of a secular sort that his readers might welcome. So he says he introduced "those events which I believe to be worthy of remembrance and likely to be welcome to the inhabitants."[15]

A prime example of the kind of information Bede owed to tradition rather than to written sources is the story concerning the origin of Pope Gregory the Great's interest in the conversion of Britain. Bede tells the story.

> It is said that one day, soon after some merchants had arrived in Rome, a quantity of merchandise was exposed for sale in the market place. Crowds came to buy and Gregory too amongst them. As well as other merchandise he saw some boys put up for sale, with fair complexions, handsome faces, and lovely hair. On seeing them he asked, so it is said, from what region or land they had been brought. He was told that they came from the island of Britain, whose inhabitants were like that in appearance. He asked again whether those islanders were Christians or still entangled in the errors of heathenism. He was told that they were heathen. Then with a deep-drawn sigh he said, "Alas that the author of darkness should have men so bright of face in his grip, and that minds devoid of inward grace should bear so graceful an outward form." Again he asked for the name of the race. He was told that they were called *Angli.* "Good," he said, "they have the face of angels, and such men should be fellow-heirs of the angels in heaven."[16]

Once beyond the preface Bede moves into Book I of his *History.* This covers the sweep of time from the invasion of the island by Julius Caesar in 55 B.C. to the arrival of Augustine and his band of monks in 597 A.D. Here he depends principally on Pliny the Elder, Orosius, and Gildas for his information. His account opens with a description of the geography and natural wealth of both Britain and Ireland. While he may not have recognized geography as an ancillary science in the study of history, he was surely convinced that this information, although not directly spiritual in character, would assist the reader in following the story of the establishment and growth of Christianity in those lands.

Britain, once called Albion, is an island of the ocean and lies to the northwest, being opposite Germany, Gaul, and Spain, which form the greater part of Europe, though at a considerable distance from them. It extends 800 miles to the north, and is 200 miles broad save only where several promontories stretch out farther and, counting these, the whole circuit of the coast covers 4,875 miles.

The island is rich in crops and in trees, and has good pasturage for cattle and beasts of burden. It also produces vines in certain districts, and has plenty of both land and water fowl of various kinds. It is remarkable too for its rivers, which abound in fish, particularly salmon and eels, and for copious springs. Seals as well as dolphins are frequently captured and even whales; besides these there are various kinds of shellfish, among which are mussels, and enclosed in these are often found excellent pearls of every colour, red and purple, violet and green, but mostly white. There is also a great abundance of whelks, from which a scarlet-coloured dye is made, a most beautiful red which neither fades through the heat of the sun nor exposure to the rain; indeed the colder it is the more beautiful it becomes.

The land possesses salt springs and warm springs and from them flow rivers which supply hot baths, suitable for all ages and both sexes, in separate places and adapted to the needs of each. For water, as St. Basil says, acquires the quality of heat when it passes through certain metals, so that it not only becomes warm but even scalding hot. The land also has rich veins of metal, copper, iron, lead, and silver. It produces a great deal of excellent jet, which is glossy black and burns when put into the fire and, when kindled, it drives away serpents; when it is warmed by rubbing it attracts whatever is applied to it, just as amber does. The country was once famous for its twenty-eight noble cities as well as innumerable fortified places equally well guarded by the strongest of walls and towers, gates and locks. . . .[17]

At the present time, there are five languages in Britain, just as the divine law is written in five books, all devoted to seeking out and setting forth one and the same kind of wisdom, namely the knowledge of sublime truth and of true sublimity. These are English, British, Irish, Pictish, as well as the Latin languages; through the study of the Scriptures, Latin is in general use among them all. To begin with, the inhabitants of the island were all Britons, from whom it receives its name; they sailed to Britain, so it is said, from the land of Armorica,[18] and appropriated to themselves the southern part of it.[19]

Bede continues his account with a description of the arrival of the Picts to Ireland where the Irish refused them a home for the reason that the island was too small for all of them. But they did suggest to the Picts that they go "to another island not far from our own, in an easterly direction, which we often see in the distance on clear days." The Picts accordingly sailed to the east and made their home in the land above Northumbria.

Bede's description of Ireland reveals the combination of fact and hearsay that so frequently characterizes the writings of medieval chroniclers.

Ireland is broader than Britain, is healthier and has a much milder climate, so that snow rarely lasts there for more than three days. Hay is never cut in summer for winter use nor are stables built for their beasts. No reptile is found there nor could a serpent survive; and although serpents have often been brought from Britain, as soon as the ship approaches land they are affected by the scent of the air and quickly perish. In fact almost everything that the island produces is efficacious against poison. For instance we have seen how, in the case of people suffering from snake-bite, the leaves of manuscripts from Ireland were scraped, and the scrapings put in water and given to the sufferer to drink. These scrapings at once absorbed the whole violence of the spreading poison and assuaged the swelling. The island abounds in milk and honey, nor does it lack vines, fish, and birds. It is also noted for the hunting of stags and roedeer.[20]

The second chapter of Book I affords an excellent example of Bede's ability to summarize and collate the different accounts of certain events that were his good fortune to find available. Here he is drawing chiefly on Orosius, Gildas, Eutropius, Prosper, and Marcellinus Comes.

Now Britain had never been visited by the Romans and was unknown to them until the time of Gaius Julius Caesar who, in the year of Rome 693, that is, in the year 60 before our Lord,[21] was consul with Lucius Bibulus. When he was waging war against the Germans and the Gauls, who were divided only by the river Rhine, he came to the Morini, from whose land is the nearest and shortest crossing to Britain. He prepared about eighty transport ships and light vessels and sailed across to Britain, where first of all he was roughly handled in a severe battle and then caught by a contrary gale, so that he lost a great part of his fleet and no small number of his soldiers, including almost all of his cavalry. He returned to Gaul, sent the legions into winter quarters, and then gave orders for the construction of 600 ships of both types. With these he sailed to Britain again in early spring. But while he was marching against the enemy with his army, the ships riding at anchor were caught by a storm and either dashed against each other or cast up on the sands and broken up. Forty of them were lost and the rest were only repaired with great difficulty. At the first encounter Caesar's cavalry were defeated by the Britons and there the tribune Labienus was killed. In the second battle, though his men incurred heavy risks, he conquered the Britons and put them to flight. Thence he marched to the river Thames. An immense multitude of the enemy was established on the further bank under the leadership of Cassobellaunus (Cassivelaunus). The bank of the river and almost all the ford beneath the water had been blocked with sharp stakes. The traces of these stakes are visible even today; each of them, on inspection, is seen to be about the thickness of a man's thigh encased in lead and fixed immovably in the river bed. The Romans saw and avoided these, so the barbarians, being unable to resist the charge of the legions, hid themselves in the woods, from which they made constant sallies and frequently did the Romans great damage. Meanwhile the strongest city of the Trinovantes with its leader Androgeus surrendered to Caesar and gave him forty hostages. Several other towns followed their example and made terms with the Romans. With their guidance Caesar, at length, after heavy fighting, captured the town of Cassivelaunus, which was situated between two marshes and further fortified by a belt of woodland and provided with ample stores of every kind. After this Caesar returned from Britain to Gaul.[22]

As Bede continues with his sketch of the history of Britain, he notes the conquest by Claudius but fails to mention the major revolt under Queen Boudicca that broke out during the reign of Nero. He does say that, beyond other countless disasters, Nero "nearly lost Britain as well." Bede follows Orosius' error in attributing Hadrian's wall to Septimius Severus, who died in 211, then speaks of the persecution of Christians that became empire-wide and reached a new intensity under Diocletian. In England it produced that land's first martyr, St. Alban. The account of Alban's death has Bede combining history and hagiography. Here he reveals his willingness to interrupt the chronological flow of the narrative to elaborate upon an incident he believes will edify the reader. He tells how the heathen Alban had been so impressed by the holiness of a Christian priest who was hiding in his house that he himself became a Christian. When the "evil ruler" learned of the presence of the priest, he ordered him seized, whereupon Alban disguised himself in the cleric's clothes and was brought before the judge.

> Now it happened that, when Alban was brought in to him, the judge was standing before the devils' altars and offering sacrifices to them. Seeing Alban, he immediately flew into a rage because this man of his own accord had dared to give himself up to the soldiers and to run so great a risk on behalf of the guest whom he had harboured. He ordered Alban to be dragged before the images of the devils in front of which he was standing and said, "You have chosen to conceal a profane rebel rather than surrender him to my soldiers, to prevent him from paying a well-deserved penalty for his blasphemy in despising the gods; so you will have to take the punishment he has incurred if you attempt to forsake our worship and religion!"
>
> When Alban refused to submit, the judge said to him: "What is your family and race?" Alban answered, "What concern is it of yours to know my parentage? If you wish to hear the truth about my religion, know that I am now a Christian and am ready to do a Christian's duty." The judge said, "I insist on knowing your name, so tell me at once." Then Alban said, "My parents call me Alban and I shall ever adore and worship the true and living God who created all things." The judge answered very angrily, "If you wish to enjoy the happiness of everlasting life, you must sacrifice at once to the mighty gods." Alban answered, "The sacrifices which you offer to devils cannot help their votaries nor fulfill the desires and petitions of their suppliants. On the contrary, he who has offered sacrifices to these images will receive eternal punishment in hell as his reward." When the judge heard this he was greatly incensed and ordered the holy confessor of God to be beaten by the torturer, thinking that he could weaken by blows that constancy of heart which he could not affect by words. Alban, though he was subjected to the most cruel tortures, bore them patiently and even joyfully for the Lord's sake. So when the judge perceived that he was not to be overcome by tortures nor turned from the Christian faith, he ordered him to be executed.

The place of execution lay beyond a river, the bridge over which was so crowded with curious spectators that the executioner and Alban found it impossible to cross. So "St. Alban, whose ardent desire it was to achieve his martyrdom as soon as possible, came to the torrent and raised his eyes towards heaven. Thereupon the riverbed dried up at that very spot, and he saw the waters give way and provide a path for him to walk in."

According to Bede, nature had adorned the place of execution in a manner truly fitting so glorious a martyr.

This hill lay about five hundred paces from the arena, and, as was fitting, it was fair, shining and beautiful, adorned, indeed clothed on all sides with wild flowers of every kind; nowhere was it steep or precipitous or sheer but Nature had provided it with wide, long-sloping sides stretching smoothly down to the level of the plain. In fact, its natural beauty had long fitted it as a place to be hallowed by the blood of a blessed martyr. When he reached the top of the hill, St. Alban asked God to give him water and at once a perpetual spring bubbled up, confined within its channel and at his very feet, so that all could see that even the stream rendered service to the martyr. For it could not have happened that the martyr who had left no water remaining in the river would have desired it on the top of the hill, if he had not realized that this was fitting. The river, when it had fulfilled its duty and completed its pious service, returned to its natural course, but it left behind a witness to its ministry. And so in this spot the valiant martyr was beheaded and received the crown of life which God has promised to those who love him. But the one who laid his unholy hands on the holy neck was not permitted to rejoice over his death; for the head of the blessed martyr and the executioner's eyes fell to the ground together.[23]

Bede concludes his account of this episode by noting that the judge ordered further persecution of the Christians to cease because he had been "astonished by these strange heavenly miracles." Later when toleration came to the Christians, "a church of wonderful workmanship was built, a worthy memorial of his (St. Alban) martyrdom. To this day sick people are healed in this place and the working of frequent miracles continues to bring it renown."

Scarcely had persecution ended, however, and toleration won than heresy showed its ugly face. First there was what Bede refers to as the "Arian madness which corrupted the whole world and even infected this island, sundered so far from the rest of mankind, with the poison of its error." More serious for England because of its greater acceptance there was the heresy of "the Briton Pelagius [who] spread his treacherous poison far and wide, denying our need for heavenly grace. St. Augustine and the rest of the orthodox fathers answered them by quoting many thousands of catholic authorities against them but failed to correct their folly; and, what was worse, the madness which should have been healed by turning to the truth was rather increased by rebuke and contradiction."[24]

Bede recounts next the history of the last decades of Roman rule in Britain. His narrative flows smoothly and concisely, but its general unreliability reveals how dependent his own accuracy was upon that of the sources he employed. Because these were not accurate, neither is he. So he speaks of the wall thrown up during the reign of Antoninus Pius between 140 A.D. and 142 against the Picts and Scots, but credits its building to anxious Britons who hastily erected it about 415 under prodding of a Roman legion that had hurried back to Britain upon the pleadings of the natives. The one noteworthy feature of these early chapters is the sharpness with which Bede castigates the Britons for their lack of courage and character.

After the Romans had gone back to their own land, the Irish and Picts, who knew they were not to return, immediately came back themselves and, becoming bolder than ever, captured the whole of the northern and farthest portion of the island as far as the wall, driving out the natives. There the Britons deployed their dispirited ranks along the top of the defence and, day and night, they moped with dazed and trembling hearts. On the other hand the enemy with hooked weapons never ceased from their ravages. The cowardly defenders were wretchedly dragged from the walls and dashed to the ground. In short, they deserted their cities, fled from the wall, and were scattered. The enemy pursued and there followed a massacre more blood-thirsty than ever before. The wretched Britons were torn in pieces by their enemies like lambs by wild beasts. They were driven from their dwellings and their poor estates; they tried to save themselves from the starvation which threatened them by robbing and plundering each other. Thus they increased their external calamities by internal strife until the whole land was left without food and desti-tute except for such relief as hunting brought.[25]

These Britons were the only people toward whom Bede displayed what approached a racial prejudice. The proba-ble origin of his hostility was their religious laxity, cer-tainly not the cultural differences that usually breed such prejudice. He later attacks them for having made no effort to convert the German invaders who had subjugated them, then for refusing to accept the Roman calendar. At this point in his *History* he condemns them for their disso-luteness, a perverseness that will bring down God's judg-ment upon them.

Historians are largely dependent upon Bede for the his-tory of Britain during the next century and more. Al-though some of Bede's information is from Gildas, it is not easy to identify the ultimate source of such snippets as the names of the Anglo-Saxon chieftains Hengist and Horsa. The Britons were supposed to have invited them to pro-vide protection against the Picts and Scots. Bede supplies the name of Vortigern, the king of the Britons who called in the Saxons. He also identifies the principal Germanic tribes who invaded Britain's shores during these years, namely, the Saxons, Angles, and Jutes. Some of his information is from the life of St. Germanus, which was written about 475 and no longer exists. In fact, so excellent a job did Bede do in his *History* in covering the history of Britain during these centuries that other and more ancient writings, some of which he undoubtedly consulted, were permitted to disappear.

Any item concerned with Christianity catches Bede's eye. He devotes special attention to the introduction of the Pelagian heresy and the inability of the Britons to cope with it. For this reason Bishops Germanus and Lupus came over from Gaul to see what they could do. The ship that was to bring them across

sped along safely with favouring winds and had reached half-way across the channel between Britain and Gaul, when suddenly they were met on their way by the hostile fury of devils; these were enraged that men of such quality should be sent to restore salvation to the people. They raised storms, they darkened the sky, turning the day into night with clouds; the sails could not resist the fury of the winds; the sailors toiled in vain; the ship was supported by the prayers rather than by their efforts. As it happened, their leader, the bishop, was worn out and fell asleep. Their champion having thus deserted his post (or so it seemed), the storm increased in fury and the ship, overwhelmed by the waves, was about to sink. Then St. Lupus and all the rest in their dismay awakened their leader so that he might oppose the fury of the elements. More resolute than they in the face of frightful danger, Germanus called on Christ and in the name of the Holy Trinity took a little water and sprinkled it on the raging billows. At the same time he admonished his colleagues and encouraged them all, whereupon with one consent and one voice they offered up their prayers. Divine help was forthcoming, the adversaries were put to flight, peace and calm followed, and the contrary winds veered round and helped them on their way; after a quick and peaceful rowing they reached the land they sought. There, great crowds gathered together from all quarters to meet the bishops, whose arrival had been foretold even by their enemies. The evil spirits proclaimed that what they feared had come to pass; and when driven out by the bishops' commands from the bodies of those possessed, they owned up to the nature of the tempest and the dangers which they had brought about, confessing that they had been vanquished by the merits and the power of these men.[26]

The two bishops, brought to Britain under such auspicious circumstances, speedily destroyed the hold that Pelagianism had on the people, and Bede writes, a "countless number of men turned to the Lord."

The reader may accept as accurate the account Bede gives of the coming of Germanus and Lupus to England, even though he might attribute the tempest and its abrupt termination to causes less supernatural than those Bede introduces. Still he should give Bede's interpretation a sympathetic hearing. Bede lived in an age when phenomena that could not be explained in a natural way were customarily accorded a supernatural explanation, under the circumstances a wholly rational thing to do. The following incident will occasion the modern reader less dismay. It might have happened just as Bede describes it.

It appears that the invading Saxons turned on their hosts and made common cause with the Picts against the Britons who had invited them in. The latter, therefore, who in Bede's judgment were a people lacking in courage,

were forced to take up arms. Fearing they were no match for their foes, they besought the help of the holy bishops. These came at once to fulfill their promise and inspired such confidence in the timid people that one would have thought that a large army had come to their support. Indeed, with such apostolic leaders, it was Christ Himself who fought in their camp. Now the holy season of Lent had come round and was made more sacred by the presence of the bishops, so much so that the people, instructed by their daily teaching, flocked eagerly to receive the grace of baptism. Vast numbers of the army were baptized. A church of wattle was built in preparation for Easter Day and set up for the army in the field as though it were in a city. So, still soaked in the waters of baptism, the army expectantly awaited the help of God. The disposition and arrangement of the army was reported to the enemy; they were as sure of victory as though they were attacking an unarmed foe and hastened forward with renewed eagerness; but their approach was observed by the British scouts. So when the Easter solemnities had been celebrated and the greater part of the army, still fresh from the font, were beginning to take up arms and prepare for war, Germanus himself offered to be their leader. He picked out the most active and, having explored the surrounding country, he saw a valley surrounded by hills of moderate height lying in the direction from which the enemy was expected to approach. In this place he stationed his untried army and himself took command. The fierce enemy forces approached, plainly visible as they drew near to the army which was lying in ambush. Germanus who was bearing the standard, thereupon ordered his men to repeat his call in one great shout; as the enemy approached confidently, believing that their coming was unexpected, the bishop shouted "Alleluia" three times. A universal shout of "Alleluia" followed, and the echoes from the surrounding hills multiplied and increased the sound. The enemy forces were smitten with dread, fearing that not only the surrounding rocks but even the very frame of heaven itself would fall upon them. They were so filled with terror that they could not run fast enough. They fled hither and thither casting away their weapons and glad even to escape naked from the danger. Many of them rushed headlong back in panic and were drowned in the river which they had just crossed. The army, without striking a blow, saw themselves avenged and became inactive spectators of the victory freely offered to them. They gathered up the spoils lying ready to hand and the devout soldiery rejoiced in this heaven-sent triumph. The bishops thus overcame the enemy without the shedding of blood; they won a victory by faith and not by might.[27]

Bede writes that during the century and more following the departure of the Roman legions the Britons resembled the Hebrews on their sojourn in Sinai on the way to the Promised Land. When they respected God's laws, they prospered; when they sinned God permitted them to suffer the evil consequences of their misdoings. "To other unspeakable crimes" that the Britons committed, "which Gildas their own historian describes in doleful words was added this crime, that they never preached the faith to the Saxons and Angles who inhabited Britain with them. Nevertheless God in His goodness did not reject the people whom He foreknew, but He had appointed much worthier heralds of the truth to bring this people to the faith."[28]

The worthier heralds to whom Bede referred appeared now in the persons of St. Augustine and the band of monks Gregory the Great sent to Britain in 597. Among the instructions Gregory gave to Augustine – these are recorded by Bede – was a warning not to make a clean sweep of pagan practices in his efforts to convert the natives. Augustine and his monks were not to destroy the idol temples, "but only the idols in them." They were to "take holy water and sprinkle it in these shrines, build altars and place relics in them. . . . When this people see that their shrines are not destroyed they will be able to banish error from their hearts and be more ready to come to the places they are familiar with, but now recognizing and worshipping the true God."[29]

Even more effective than Pope Gregory's instructions in converting the people of Kent, the region where Augustine and his missionaries landed, was the cooperation of King Ethelbert. He was already sympathetic toward the new religion because of the influence of his wife, Bertha, the daughter of the Merovingian king of Paris, who was herself a Christian. Bede says Ethelbert placed no pressure upon his people to accept baptism, however, "though none the less he showed greater affection for believers since they were his fellow citizens in the kingdom of heaven. But he had learned from his teachers and guides in the way of salvation that the service of Christ was voluntary and ought not to be compulsory."[30]

Bede opens the second book of his *History* with notice of the death of Pope Gregory the Great, followed by a eulogy of the man. The fulsome praise Bede showered on Gregory contributed to making him the most popular of all popes in medieval England. Bede's eulogy may have influenced Alfred the Great a century after Bede's death to have several of Gregory's works translated into English. Here is Bede's description of Gregory's writings.

> They urged him [Gregory] to unfold by spiritual interpretation the book of Job, a work which is shrouded in great obscurity. Nor could he refuse the task imposed on him by his living brethren, seeing that it was likely to be of great use to many. So in thirty-five books of exposition he taught in a marvellous manner the literal meaning of the book, its bearing on the mysteries of Christ and the Church, and the sense in which it applies to each of the faithful. . . . He composed another remarkable book called the *Pastoral Care,* in which he set forth in the clearest manner what sort of persons should be chosen to rule the Church and how these rulers ought to live; with how much discrimination they should instruct different types of listeners and how earnestly they ought each day to reflect on their own frailty. He composed forty *Homilies on the Gospel,* which is divided into two volumes of equal size, and made four books of *Dialogues* in which, at the request of Peter his deacon, he collected the virtues of the most famous saints he knew or could learn of in Italy, as an example of life to posterity: as in his expository works he taught what virtues men ought to strive after, so, by describing the miracles of the saints, he showed how glorious those virtues are. He also showed in twenty-two homilies how much inner light is to be found within the most obscure sections of the prophet Ezekiel.[31]

The most important development Bede records in Book

II of his *History* concerns the conversion of Edwin, king of Northumbria, Bede's own country. According to Bede, Edwin had succeeded in extending his authority over the whole of Britain and the islands of Anglesey and Man as well. Then he tells the story of Edwin's conversion. Edwin, though a pagan, married the Christian Ethelburgh, daughter of King Ethelbert of Kent, and promised to examine that faith himself and not to interfere with his wife in the practice of her religion. With Ethelburgh there came to Northumbria "the holy bishop Paulinus" who was "to make sure by daily instruction and the celebration of the heavenly sacraments that she and her companions were not polluted by contact with the heathen."

As it happened, Paulinus made little progress converting the heathen despite his zeal, nor did he have any more luck with the king himself until the miscarriage of an attempt on the king's life. Bede describes the incident.

The following year there came to the kingdom an assassin whose name was Eomer, who had been sent by Cwichelm, king of the West Saxons, hoping to deprive King Edwin of his kingdom and his life. He carried a short sword, double-edged and smeared with poison, to ensure that if the sword wound was not enough to kill the king, the deadly poison would do its work. He came on Easter Day to the king's hall which then stood by the river Derwent. He entered the hall on the pretence of delivering a message from his lord, and while the cunning rascal was expounding his pretended mission, he suddenly leapt up, drew the sword from beneath his cloak, and made a rush at the king. Lilla, a most devoted thegn, saw this, but not having a shield in his hand to protect the king from death, he quickly interposed his own body to receive the blow. His foe thrust the weapon with such force that he killed the thegn and wounded the king as well through his dead body. Swords were drawn and the assassin was at once attacked from every quarter, but in the tumult he slew with his hideous weapon yet another of the king's retainers named Forthhere.[32]

The very day this attempt was made on the king's life, his wife gave birth to a daughter. When Paulinus convinced Edwin that it was in answer to his prayers that his wife had been safely delivered of the child, the king promised to renounce his idols and become a Christian. But God must first help him defeat the West Saxons who had sent the assassin to kill him. After he had gained the complete victory he had asked for, he continued to hesitate. He must now first advise with his councillors, so he called a meeting of his chief men and asked each in turn what he thought of the new doctrine.

> Coifi, the chief of the priests, answered at once, "Notice carefully, King, this doctrine which is now being expounded to us. I frankly admit that, for my part, I have found that the religion which we have hitherto held has no virtue nor profit in it. None of your followers has devoted himself more earnestly than I have to the worship of our gods, but nevertheless there are many who receive greater benefits and greater honour from you than I do and are more successful in all their undertakings. If the gods had any power they would have helped me more readily, seeing that I have always served them with greater zeal. So it follows that if, on examination, these new doctrines which have now been explained to us are found to be better and more effectual, let us accept them at once without any delay."[33]

The next of the royal councillors to speak his piece endorsed Coifi's position, then added his own sage observations:

> "This is how the present life of man on earth, King, appears to me in comparison with that time which is unknown to us. You are sitting feasting with your ealdormen and thegns in winter time; the fire is burning on the hearth in the middle of the hall and all inside is warm, while outside the wintry storms of rain and snow are raging; and a sparrow flies swiftly through the hall. It enters in at one door

and quickly flies out through the other. For the few moments it is inside, the storm and wintry tempest cannot touch it, but after the briefest moment of calm, it flits from your sight, out of the wintry storm and into it again. So this life of man appears but for a moment; what follows or indeed what went before, we know not at all. If this new doctrine brings us more certain information it seems right that we should accept it!"[34]

Several of the other councillors who spoke up agreed with what Coifi and the second man had said, whereupon Coifi took the floor for a second time. "For a long time now," he declared,

I have realized that our religion is worthless; for the more diligently I sought the truth in our cult, the less I found it. Now I confess openly that the truth shines out clearly in this teaching which can bestow on us the gift of life, salvation, and eternal happiness. Therefore I advise your Majesty that we should promptly abandon and commit to the flames the temples and the altars which we have held sacred without reaping any benefit."[35]

This last speech of Coifi must have convinced the king, for he now gave his decision in favor of Christianity. When he asked who should be the first to profane the shrine of their pagan idols, Coifi volunteered. "I will," he said,

for through the wisdom the true God has given me no one can more suitably destroy these things which I once foolishly worshipped, and so set an example to all." And at once, casting aside his vain superstition he asked the king to provide him with arms and a stallion; and mounting it he set out to destroy the idols. Now a high priest of their religion was not allowed to carry arms or to ride except on a mare. So, girded with a sword, he took a spear in his hand and mounting the king's stallion he set off to where the idols were. The common people who saw him thought he was mad. But as soon as he approached the shrine, without any hesitation he profaned it by casting the spear which he held into it; and greatly rejoicing in the knowledge of the worship of the true God, he ordered his companions to destroy and set fire to the shrine and all the enclosures. The place where the idols once stood is still shown, not far from York, to the east, over the river Derwent. Today it is called Goodmanham, the place where the high priest, through the inspiration of the true God, profaned and destroyed the altars which he himself had consecrated.[36]

Bede now writes of the baptism of Edwin, of his nobles, and a vast number of his subjects. Edwin's enthusiasm for his new faith led him to convert the king of the East Angles and that people. So much did God bless Edwin and his realm, Bede says, "That, as the proverb still runs, a woman with a new-born child could walk throughout the island from sea to sea and take no harm."

Again at the conclusion of Book II, as was the case with Book I, Bede fills the reader in on the political developments that took place during the years embraced in the section. He notes that in the year 633, after a reign of seventeen years, Edwin became a victim of a revolt to which Penda, the heathen king of Mercia, was a partner. But Bede is happy in being able to open Book III with the information that the pagan resurgence under Penda and Caedwalla, following the death of King Edwin, did not long endure. The army of King Oswald, "small in numbers but strengthened by their faith in Christ . . . destroyed the abominable leader of the Britons together with the immense force which he boasted was irresistible."[37]

Because Book III of the *History* introduces more miracles than any other of the work's volumes, it might be well to comment here on this feature of Bede's writing, a feature that has evoked considerable criticism. The position of perhaps the leading Bede scholar in the English-speaking world, for example, is that the less said about Bede's miracles the better.[38] This is scarcely fair to Bede; it furthermore represents a faulty interpretation of his *History*. Bede accepted miracles, as did all his contemporaries, learned or otherwise. To the people of his day, anything mysterious that lacked a natural explanation demanded a supernatural interpretation. The reader of the *History* should also keep in mind that Bede is writing church, not secular, history. He felt under some obligation to introduce material that he believed his reader would find edifying. Still, as a historian, he informs the reader of the sources of the miraculous tales he introduces. He leaves it up to the reader, as it were, to accept or reject the authenticity of the miracle.

The reader of the *History* will find that miracles often occurred where a saint had died or was buried. The place where the sainted King Oswald was slain was believed to possess such miraculous powers that

> people have often taken soil from the place where his body fell to the ground, have put it in water and by its use have brought great relief to their sick. This custom became very popular and gradually so much earth was removed that a hole was made, as deep as a man's height. Nor is it to be wondered at that the sick are cured in the place where he died, for while he was alive he never ceased to care for the sick and poor, to give them alms, and to offer them help. Many miracles are related which took place either at that site or through the soil taken from it. But we think it is enough to relate two only which we have heard our elders tell.

The two miracles that Bede then describes offer a "natural" explanation to the skeptical reader.

> It happened that not long after his [King Oswald] death a man was travelling on horseback past this place. The horse suddenly began to tire; next it stopped, bending its head to the ground and foaming at the mouth and then, as the pain became unbearable, it fell to the earth. The rider alighted, took off its saddlecloth, and waited to see whether it would recover or whether he would have to leave it for dead. The beast was long tortured by the agonizing pain and twisted about from place to place, until as it turned over, it came

upon the very spot where the famous king had fallen. Forthwith the pain ceased, and the horse stopped its frantic struggles; then, as horses do, after they have been resting, it rolled from side to side, stood up completely cured and began to crop the grass greedily.

When the rider, who was an intelligent man, saw this, he realized that there must be some special sanctity associated with the place in which the horse was cured. He put up a sign to mark the site, shortly afterwards mounted his horse, and reached the inn where he intended to lodge. On his arrival, he found a girl there, niece of the patron, who had long suffered from paralysis. When he heard the members of the household lamenting the girl's grievous infirmity, he told them of the place where his horse had been cured. Why need I say more? They put her in a cart, brought her to the place and laid her down there. In a short time she fell asleep and when she woke up she found that she was healed of her infirmity.[39]

The reader who is distressed over the number of Bede's miracles will find more to his liking what that historian relates of Oswine who shared the rule of Northumbria with the more aggressive and unscrupulous Oswiu. Oswine was "a man of great piety and religion and ruled the kingdom of Deira for seven years in the greatest prosperity, beloved by all." Oswiu coveted Oswine's part of Northumbria. First he sought to accomplish his destruction on the battlefield. When Oswine refused to fight and disbanded his army, Oswiu had him hunted down and murdered. The episode that follows reveals Bede's talents as a storyteller.

King Oswine was tall and handsome, pleasant of speech, courteous in manner, and bountiful to nobles and commons alike; so it came about that he was beloved by all because of the royal dignity which showed itself in his character, his appearance, and his actions; and noblemen from almost every kingdom flocked to serve him as retainers. Among all the other graces of virtue and modesty with which, if I may say so, he was blessed in a special manner, his humility is said to have been the greatest, as a single example is enough to prove.

He had given Bishop Aidan[40] an excellent horse so that, though he was normally accustomed to walk, he could ride if he had to cross a river or if any other urgent necessity compelled him. A short time afterwards Aidan was met by a beggar who asked for an alms. He at once alighted and offered the horse with all its royal trappings to the beggar; for he was extremely compassionate, a friend of the poor and a real father to the wretched. The king was told of this and, happening to meet the bishop as they were going to dinner, he said, "My lord bishop, why did you want to give a beggar the royal horse intended for you? Have we not many less valuable horses or other things which would have been good enough to give to the poor, without letting the beggar have the horse which I had specially chosen for your own use?" The bishop at once replied, "O King, what are you saying? Surely this son of a mare is not dearer to you than that son of God?"

After these words they went in to dine. The bishop sat down in his own place and the king, who had just come in from hunting, stood warming himself by the fire with his thegns. Suddenly he remembered the bishop's words; at once he took off his sword, gave it to a thegn, and then hastening to where the bishop sat, threw himself at his feet and asked his pardon. "Never from henceforth," he said, "will I speak of this again nor will I form any opinion as to what money of mine or how much of it you should give to the sons of God." When the bishop saw this he was greatly alarmed; he got up immediately and raised the king to his feet, declaring that he would be perfectly satisfied if only the king would banish his sorrow and sit down to the feast. The king, in accordance with the bishop's entreaties and commands, recovered his spirits, but the bishop, on the other hand, grew sadder and sadder and at last began to shed tears. Thereupon a priest asked him in his native tongue, which the king and his thegns did not understand, why he was weeping, and Aidan answered, "I know that the king will not live long; for I never before saw a humble

king. Therefore I think that he will very soon be snatched
from this life; for this nation does not deserve to have such
a ruler." Not long after, the bishop's gloomy forebodings
were fulfilled in the sad death of the king.[41]

Aidan's own death followed twelve days after the murder of Oswine, an event that furnished Bede the opportunity to elaborate upon the virtues of this bishop and of the
miracles worked in his name. He concluded his eulogy of
the bishop with these words:

> I have written these things about the character and work
> of Aidan, not by any means commending or praising his
> lack of knowledge in the matter of the observance of Eas-
> ter; indeed I heartily detest it, as I have clearly shown in
> the book which I wrote called *De Temporibus*, but, as a
> truthful historian, I have described in a straightforward
> manner those things which were done by him or through
> him, praising such of his qualities as are worthy of praise
> and preserving their memory for the benefit of my
> readers.[42]

Given the extraordinary importance that Bede attached
to the acceptance of the Roman date for Easter, he would
have considered few events the equal of importance to the
synod held at Whitby in 664 when the Paschal controversy was finally resolved. The historical background for
the discrepancy between the date observed by the Celtic
clergy of northern England and that accepted by those to
the south reached back to the period of the Anglo-Saxon
invasions. When these severed the ties between Ireland
and the rest of Christendom, the date of Easter had not
been universally established. Ireland had come to accept
what was traditional in much of the eastern Mediterranean because Irish monasticism had been molded by eastern rather than by western influences. For more than 150
years, therefore, from about 400 A.D. on, the Celtic church
had been left pretty much to itself in its acceptance of the
eastern date for Easter. Besides this difference in the litur-

gical calendar there were other usages that the Latin church did not observe and the Irish did, such as the use of leavened bread. It was inevitable, therefore, that once Christianity had spread northward from Canterbury where Augustine and clergy from Rome had established it, it would eventually collide with the Christianity practiced by Celtic missionaries from Iona and Lindisfarne, and that is what happened.

What precipitated the summoning of the synod at Whitby over the Paschal question was a minor matter, the inconvenience that the confusion over the date occasioned in the household of King Oswiu of Northumbria each spring of the year. What had happened was this: because the king followed the Celtic calendar while his wife observed the Roman, "the king had finished the fast and was keeping Easter Sunday, while the queen and her people were still in Lent and observing Palm Sunday."

So a meeting was arranged at Whitby with King Oswiu the host. Among the principal theologians present was Colman, a formidable prelate from Ireland, who defended the Celtic calendar. Upon King Oswiu's request, he rose and stated his position.

> "The method of keeping Easter which I observe, I received from my superiors who sent me here as bishop; it was in this way that all our fathers, men beloved of God, are known to have celebrated it. Now should this method seem contemptible and blameworthy seeing that the blessed evangelist John, the disciple whom the Lord specially loved, is said to have celebrated it thus, together with all the churches over which he presided."[43]

When Colman sat down, the priest Wilfrid rose to present the case for the Roman calendar. He was spokesman for Bishop Agilbert of the West Saxons, who excused himself because of his lack of fluency in the "English tongue." Wilfrid emphasized the point that all the world — Italy, Africa, Egypt, Asia, and Rome — "where the apostles St. Peter and St. Paul lived, taught, suffered, and were buried," accepted the Roman calendar. The only people who stubbornly refused to do so were the Picts and the Britons, "who in these, the two remotest islands of the Ocean, and only in some parts of them, foolishly attempt to fight against the whole world."[44]

Wilfrid's use of the word "foolish" fired the combustible Colman who promptly demanded to know how any person could dare call John, the Apostle, foolish. Wilfrid answered that, no, John had surely not been foolish, but it had been his anxiety to win over the Jews to Christianity that led him to accept their calendar. It was for that same reason that Paul had circumcised Timothy. And so the debate between the two men continued with Bede providing the reader what purports to be a verbatim report of their arguments. The matter came to a head when Wilfrid, in his final summation, referred again to that "handful of people in the one corner of the remotest of islands" obstinately holding out against the practice of the universal church, whose direction Christ had entrusted to Peter, the bishop of Rome, when He said, "Thou art Peter and upon this rock I will build my church and the gates of hell shall not prevail against it, and I will give unto thee the keys of the kingdom of heaven."

Wilfrid's reference to the keys of heaven brought an immediate reaction from King Oswiu. He asked Colman whether Christ had actually said those words to Peter. When Colman admitted that such was the case, the king asked, "Do you both agree, without any dispute, that these words were addressed primarily to Peter and that the Lord gave him the keys of the kingdom of Heaven?" They both answered, "Yes."

Thereupon the king concluded, "Then, I tell you, since he is the doorkeeper I will not contradict him; but I intend to obey his commands in everything to the best of my knowledge and ability, otherwise when I come to the gates of the kingdom of heaven, there may be no one to open them because the one who on your own showing holds the keys has turned his back on me." When the king had spoken, all who were seated there or standing by, both high and low, signified their assent, gave up their imperfect rules, and readily accepted in their place those which they recognized to be better.[45]

As Bede continues his account, however, it becomes evident that the conference at Whitby did not end in complete agreement. Colman remained adamant in his position and "took those who wished to follow him, that is, those who would not accept the Catholic Easter and the tonsure in a shape of a crown for there was no small argument about this too, and returned to Ireland in order to discuss with his own party what he ought to do in the matter."[46]

Before dropping this episode, a word of commendation is due Bede for the thoroughly objective manner he reported what transpired at the conference. Though his sympathies, and they were strong, were on the side of the Roman party, he may not be charged with according Colman and his party in the controversy anything less than complete justice. Here again as elsewhere in his *History* he takes the opportunity to extol the signal virtues of the Celtic clergy and the devotion of their people.

The material covered by Bede in Book IV of his *History* involved developments with which the more knowledgeable people of his time must have been familiar. Papal appointment of Theodore of Tarsus as archbishop of Canterbury and his arrival in England with the learned monk Hadrian, prepared the way for a complete reorganization of the church in Britain and the establishment of a diocesan structure based upon episcopal jurisdiction. The coming of these two men also introduced a new current of intellectual activity that carried through Aldhelm and Benedict Biscop to Bede. Both Theodore and Hadrian receive Bede's highest commendation. Theodore "was a native of Tarsus in Cilicia, a man well trained in secular and divine literature, both Greek and Latin." Hadrian was "a man of African race and well versed in the holy Scriptures, trained both in monastic and ecclesiastical ways and equally skilled in the Greek and Latin tongues." Theodore

> was accompanied everywhere and assisted by Hadrian, as he gave instruction on the ordering of a holy life and the canonical custom of celebrating Easter. He was the first of the archbishops whom the whole English Church consented to obey. And because both of them were extremely learned in sacred and secular literature, they attracted a crowd of students into whose minds they daily poured the streams of wholesome learning. They gave their hearers instruction not only in the books of holy Scripture but also in the art of metre, astronomy, and ecclesiastical computation. As evidence of this, some of their students still survive who know Latin and Greek just as well as their native tongue. . . . From that time also the knowledge of sacred music, which had hitherto been known only in Kent, began to be taught in all the English churches.[47]

Chapter V of Book IV presents a fine illustration of the manner Bede wrote "church" history. He first announces the death of King Oswiu of Northumbria. This monarch had so advanced in virtue during his final years that he hoped to end his days "among the holy places" in Rome, but death had intervened. Then in 672, the third year of the reign of Oswiu's son Ecgrith, Theodore summoned the bishops, "together with many teachers of the church who knew and loved the canonical institutions of the fathers," to the first important synod of its kind in the history of the English church. Bede reports the work of the synod and gives the text of the matters discussed and agreed upon by the assembly. He concludes Chapter V of this last book with notice of the death of Egbert, king of Kent, and the accession of his brother Holthhere.

Now and then the reader of the *History* catches a

glimpse of the simple, slow, yet reasonably effective manner that learning came gradually to spread itself through Britain. Bede notes that Benedict Biscop, the founder of Wearmouth monastery, had brought John, the archchanter at St. Peter's in Rome, back with him on lease for a year, so that

> he might teach the monks of his monastery the mode of chanting throughout the year as it was practised at St. Peter's in Rome. Abbot John carried out the pope's instructions (Pope Agatho had released John for this purpose) and taught the cantors of the monastery the order and manner of singing and reading aloud and also committed to writing all things necessary for the celebration of festal days throughout the whole year; these writings have been preserved to this day in the monastery and copies have now been made by many others elsewhere. Not only did John instruct the brothers in this monastery, but all who had any skill in singing flocked in from almost all the monasteries in the kingdom to hear him, and he had many invitations to teach elsewhere.[48]

An item of singular interest to students of early English literature appears here in Book IV where Bede introduces Caedmon, the first English poet known by name. This is Bede's story.

> In the monastery of this abbess (Abbess Hild of Whitby) there was a certain brother who was specially marked out by the grace of God, so that he used to compose godly and religious songs; thus, whatever he learned from the holy Scriptures by means of interpreters, he quickly turned into extremely delightful and moving poetry, in English, which was his own tongue. By his songs the minds of many were often inspired to despise the world and to long for the heavenly life. It is true that after him other Englishmen attempted to compose religious poems, but none could compare with him. For he did not learn the art of poetry from men nor through a man but he received the gift of

song freely by the grace of God. Hence he could never compose any foolish or trivial poem but only those which were concerned with devotion and so were fitting for his devout tongue to utter.[49]

As Bede tells his story, Caedmon was already along in years when he became a monk and learned to compose verse. Until something marvelous happened to him, it had been his wont to leave the room on social occasions when it came time for each to take a turn at singing, so ashamed was he of his inability to versify. On one such occasion

> he left the place of feasting and went to the cattle byre, as it was his turn to take charge of them that night. In due time he stretched himself out and went to sleep, whereupon he dreamt that someone stood by him, saluted him, and called his name: "Caedmon," he said, "sing me something." Caedmon answered, "I cannot sing; that is why I left the feast and came here because I could not sing." Once again the speaker said, "Nevertheless you must sing to me." "What must I sing?" said Caedmon. "Sing," he said, "about the beginning of created things." Thereupon Caedmon began to sing verses which he had never heard before in praise of God the Creator, of which this is the general sense: "Now we must praise the Maker of the heavenly kingdom, the power of the Creator and his counsel, the deeds of the Father of glory and how He, since He is the eternal God, was the Author of all marvels and first created the heavens as a roof for the children of men and then, the almighty Guardian of the human race, created the earth."[50]

At this point in his narrative Bede interjects one of the earliest recorded observations concerning the difficulty of translating verse from one language to another. "This is the sense," he wrote, "but not the order of the words which he (Caedmon) sang as he slept. For it is not possible to translate verse, however well composed, literally from one language to another without some loss of beauty and dignity."

The morning after this strange dream Caedmon reported his experience to the reeve who in turn reported it to the abbess. Caedmon then took monastic vows and joined the community at Whitby. In the course of acquiring knowledge of sacred history during the months which followed, he learned

> all he could by listening to them and then, memorizing it and ruminating over it, like some clean animal chewing the cud, he turned it into the most melodious verse: and it sounded so sweet as he recited it that his teachers became in turn his audience. He sang about the creation of the world, and origin of the human race, and the whole history of Genesis, of the departure of Israel from Egypt and entry into the promised land and of many other of the stories taken from the sacred Scriptures; of the incarnation, passion, and resurrection of the Lord, of His ascension into heaven, of the coming of the Holy Spirit and the teaching of the apostles. He also made songs about the terrors of future judgment, the horrors of the pains of hell, and the joys of the heavenly kingdom. In addition he composed many other songs about the divine mercies and judgments, in all of which he sought to turn his hearers away from delight in sin and arouse in them the love and practice of good works.[51]

The pattern of Bede's writing alters somewhat as he moves into the fifth and final book of his *History*. There are the usual number of miracles, although no battles because the time span is shorter than that of the previous books. And he has few episcopal appointments to record. A new kind of information appears with Bede's mention of the activity of Anglo-Saxon missionaries on the continent. The general impression that all was reasonably well with the church and with Christianity is heightened by the information that Caedwalla, king of the West Saxons, and his successor Ine, both visited Rome, while Cenred, king of the Mercians, and Offa, king of the East Saxons, not only visited Rome but remained there to join monastic communities.

The letter Bede sent to Archbishop Egbert about two years after he had completed the *History* paints a less favorable picture of the church. In this letter he deplores the unworthiness of several bishops, the establishment of monasteries filled with pseudo-monks, their only motive in joining that of escaping the civil responsibilities of secular life, and a general deterioration of discipline on the part of both the regular and secular clergy. A possible explanation for these contrasting pictures is that Bede in his letter to the archbishop knew he could express himself with complete frankness and felt it was his duty to do so. Many people, on the other hand, would be reading (or hearing) the *History*. There he must be more prudent. He could best achieve his end, that of inspiring men to a greater love of God, by pointing to the example of the pious kings. To report the abuses he saw creeping into religious life would only cause scandal.

Somewhat unusual for Bede, yet illustrating the essentially religious character of his *History,* is his inclusion in Book V of excerpts he had taken from the description Abbot Adamnan of Iona, (d. 704) had recently made of places he had visited during his travels in Palestine. Bede explains: "I think that it will be useful to readers to make some extracts and put them into this *History*." The passage describing Hebron and the tombs of the patriarchs reads as follows:

> Hebron, once a city and the capital of David's kingdom, now only shows by its ruins what it once was. A furlong away to the east, in the valley, in a double cave are the tombs of the patriarchs, their heads facing north, surrounded on four sides by a wall. Each one of these tombs is covered by a single stone, hewn after the shape of a church, those of the three patriarchs being white, while that of Adam is darker and of poorer workmanship; he lies not far from them at the farthest end of the northern wall. There

are also some smaller and poorer monuments to their three wives. The hill of Mamre is a mile to the north of these tombs, covered with grass and flowers, with a level plateau on the top. On the north side is Abraham's oak consisting of a trunk only, and twice the height of a man, being enclosed in a church.[52]

More genuinely historical and of greater value to students of history is the information Bede supplies about English monks who crossed to Germany to spread the gospel. Whitberht, one of the first to go, went to Frisia, but two fruitless years of preaching had him returning to Ireland where he had been living in exile (from England). More successful was Willibrord who in 690 crossed the channel with eleven other missionaries. He received the active encouragement of Pepin of Heristal, mayor of the palace in Austrasia, and eventually became archbishop of all Frisia. Bede mentions two other English missionaries, the one called Hewald the White because of the color of his hair, the other Hewald the Black. Both suffered martyrdom in Frisia. After their bodies, by miraculous intervention, had floated forty miles upstream, they were recovered and on Pepin's orders buried in the church in Cologne.

In Book V Bede also introduces the familiar face of Aldhelm. Aldhelm received the first of his schooling from an Irish monk, then had gone to Canterbury where Hadrian instructed him in all the classical learning he had brought from Rome. Later, in 675, when Aldhelm was serving as abbot of Malmesbury, scholars from all over England came to his monastery to benefit from his learning. Here is Bede's description of the scholar.

Aldhelm, when he was still priest and abbot of the monastery (he had since been consecrated bishop of Sherborne) known as Malmesbury, by order of a synod of his own people wrote a remarkable book against the British error of celebrating Easter at the wrong time, and of doing many other things to the detriment to the pure practices and the peace of the Church; by means of this book he led many of those Britons who were subject to the West Saxons to adopt the catholic celebration of the Easter of the Lord. He also wrote a most excellent book on virginity both in hexameter verse and in prose, producing a twofold work after the example of Sedulius. He also wrote several other books, for he was a man of wide learning. He had a polished style and, as we have said, was remarkable for his erudition in both ecclesiastical and in general studies.[53]

In the twenty-third chapter of his *History* Bede furnishes the reader a quick overview of the church and of Britain. He notes the names of all the bishops who were occupying sees, but he mentions no kings save Aethelbald, king of Mercia, to whom he says all kings south of the Humber owed obedience. He does draw attention to two comets that appeared in 729 and "struck great terror into all beholders."

One of them preceded the sun as it rose in the morning and the other followed it as it set at night, seeming to portend dire disaster to east and west alike. One comet was the forerunner of the day and the other of the night, to indicate that mankind was threatened by calamities both by day and by night. They had fiery torch-like trains which faced northwards as if posed to start a fire. They appeared in the month of January and remained for almost a fortnight.[54]

Bede makes note of the manner the Saracens had ravaged Gaul but "not long afterwards they received the due reward of their treachery in the same kingdom."[55] Britain was itself at peace, the Picts and English content to remain within their borders, the Irish in Britain satisfied "with their own territories and devising no plots or treachery against the English." Only the Britons continued a source of concern. They stubbornly held themselves aloof from the English "through their inbred hatred, and the whole state of the Catholic Church by their incorrect Easter and their evil customs but being opposed by the power of God and man alike, they cannot obtain what they want in either respect."

Although it appears to have been Bede's intention to leave his reader satisfied with the state of things as he brought the *History* to a close, he inserted a note of uneasiness with his observation about the reign of Ceolwulf, the king to whom he had dedicated the volume. So numerous were the troubles of this king's reign, Bede wrote "that it is as yet impossible to know what to say about them or to guess what the outcome will be." Shortly after he noted that the enemies of Ceolwulf had seized him, and to show their contempt for the king, had tonsured him. A curious paragraph then tells how so many Northumbrians were laying "aside their weapons" and entering monasteries, "preferring that they and their children should take monastic vows rather than train themselves in the art of war." That this development was not wholly to Bede's liking is clear from his cryptic observation: "What the result will be, a later generation will discover." On the basis of the letter he wrote to Archbishop Egbert a short time later, it becomes clear that he questioned the motives that inspired these young men to take tonsure. In his judgment they did so, not because of their attraction to the monastic life for which he held them to be unsuited, but in order to escape the obligations of the ordinary citizens, one of which was to bear arms.

The final chapter of the *History* consists of a recapitulation of the events covered in the preceding pages, which Bede inserts "in order to assist the memory." In this recapitulation, he begins with Julius Caesar's invasion of Britain, "in the sixtieth year before the incarnation of the Lord," and concludes in 731 with notice of the consecration of Tatwine as archbishop of Canterbury. Next follows a short autobiography, a list of his writings, a prayer to Christ for the grace of final salvation, and, finally, the notice, "Here, with God's help, ends the fifth book of the History of the English Church."[56]

CHAPTER 3

Al-Tabari

AL-TABARI (Muhammad b. Jarir al-Tabari), "the most respected and most frequently imitated Muslim historian,"[1] was born in 839, in Amul, in the province of Tabaristan, which gave him his surname. He must have been an unusually precocious child; by the time he was seven he had already memorized the Koran. His formal studies, which he commenced in Amul, took him to many cities: Rayy, Baghdad, Basra, Kufa, to different Syrian centers of learning, then to Fustat in Egypt, and finally in 872 back to Baghdad. There in Baghdad, except for two short trips to Tabaristan, he spent the most active years of his career. He died there in 923 at the advanced age of eighty-four.

Al-Tabari's father was a landed proprietor, which explains his son's ability to pursue studies in such distant places. The revenue that al-Tabari later realized from these estates also enabled him to pass up lucrative posts in the government he might have had. And had he not been a person of independent means, he could not have devoted so much of his time to scholarly pursuits. He

might, indeed, have found himself dubbed a court historian, in which event he would not now occupy so eminent a
place in the history of Muslim historiography.

By the time al-Tabari returned to Baghdad and assumed the role of teacher, he had acquired both an as-
tounding mass of erudition and universal renown as an
authority on the Koran and *hadith*.[2] His biographers
credit him with a scholar's knowledge of perhaps all the
disciplines with which a Muslim student could acquaint
himself at that time. These included logic, mathematics,
theology, law, history, poetry, lexicography, grammar,
ethics, medicine, and exegesis.

In the world before printing, a savant's influence was
principally exercised through his teaching, and such was
the case with al-Tabari. We are told that he was a most
popular teacher. A contemporary of al-Tabari, and a distinguished theologian in his own right, is quoted as declaring: "Should you undertake the long journey to China, only
to hear Tabari explain the Koran, it would be worth the
trouble."[3] According to the testimony of one of his pupils,
al-Tabari began what proved a full day at noon when he
occupied himself with writing until the afternoon prayer.
Afterward he gave lessons on the Koran in the mosque
until the first evening prayer. He then lectured on jurisprudence before returning to his house.

While al-Tabari was in Fustat he gained a number of
disciples to his own interpretation of the *fikh*,[4] although
his position is considered to have been substantially that
of the Shafi'ite school. Later in Baghdad there is the story
that he incurred the wrath of the Hanbalists for the slight-
ing observations he had made at the expense of their
founder Ahmad ibn Hanbal. The story is also told that he
was buried after dark the day he died for fear of the populace whom his sympathy for the Shi-ah sect had antago-
nized. This account may not be true, and for those who
regret that obsequies more in keeping with the respect due
so illustrious a scholar were not conducted, another ac-

count describes veritable throngs attending his funeral.

Of these and other items concerning the life of al-Tabari there persists some doubt. General agreement prevails, however, concerning the prodigious amount of writing this scholar was able to turn out during his life time. The figure of forty pages (leaves) a day for forty years running is the one that tradition preserves. The geographer Yaqut, who died in 1229, tells that al-Tabari had planned a commentary on the Koran ten times more voluminous than the one he completed—that is, 30,000 pages rather than 3,000. It was only the anguished protests of his pupils that led him to choose the smaller number. Al-Tabari is also said to have projected the precise number of pages for his universal history—30,000—only to reduce that to the same 3,000 because of the same youthful protests. The modern reader may thus be excused for having some reservations concerning the credibility of the tradition. The story may be a pious fabrication, although the fact that al-Tabari was primarily a recorder of what earlier "historians" had written, not an interpreter, puts the voluminousness of his writing in a different light.[5]

Al-Tabari is said to have been particularly proud of his legal works, which were as extensive as his historical. Beyond these he prepared a description of what he believed to be the authentic traditions concerning Muhammad, the founder of Islam, also a juristic treatise entitled al-Basit. Except for fragments, the only works of al-Tabari that have survived are his universal history and his commentary on the Koran. Both enjoyed wide acceptance in his day, and scholars for centuries considered them the most authoritative sources for the study of both the Koran and early Islamic history. Even today scholars find them indispensable for these subjects.

Al-Tabari is among the first writers to be classified as an Arab historian. Before taking up a consideration of his historical writing it is therefore important to examine, if only briefly, the beginnings of Muslim historiography.

That these beginnings lacked non-Arabic influences further recommends such an examination. It seems the Arabs did not even have a word for history during the pre-Islamic period and actually lacked a consciousness of history. That they had remained unaffected by, and unacquainted with, more ancient historical writing, such as that of the Greeks, is explained by their cultural level, which was too low to permit sustained literary effort. This has ordinarily been the case with nomadic peoples, and the Arabs were no exception. An additional circumstance that may explain the absence of historical writing during the pre-Islamic period was the maxim that "Islam cancels all that was before it," that is, that the coming of the Prophet rendered anything before his appearance futile and worthless.[6] Then during the age of the Prophet which followed, the reverence shown the Koran discouraged further historical writing lest this be viewed as questioning the complete adequacy of what was considered the word of God. Some explanation for the tardiness of the Arabs in taking up writing of any kind may also be found in the absence of such need, given the remarkable retentiveness of their memories. It is entirely possible that a major development that helped usher in the age of writing, including historical writing, was the introduction of paper in the seventh century.[7]

There did exist practices in the pre-Islamic period deserving of mention in a discussion of the beginnings of Muslim historiography, even though the extent of their influence upon later historical writing is debatable. The Arabs, like other Semitic peoples, took great pride in genealogies. While these pedigrees rarely preserved more than the barest listing of succeeding generations, with only an occasional aside for noteworthy deeds that might embellish the memory of some progenitor, they did indicate the existence of a historical sense and an embryonic interest in the past. Possibly more important than these genealogies in its influence upon Muslim historiography was the battle-day literature of the pre-Islamic period. The "Battle-Days of the Arabs," as this kind of literature is usually identified, described battles fought among Arabic tribes and the heroic deeds of their warriors. Stories of this kind appear in the Old Testament (for example, those describing clashes between the Israelites and the Philistines) and suggest that this literature was common to Semitic peoples in general. Still, "Battle-Days" as a kind of writing belonged to literature, rather than to history, and it is unlikely that these stories would have survived at all had they not been presented in verse form. Their aim, in any event, was to entertain, not to instruct, and they lacked the continuity historical narrative demands.

The origins of Muslim historiography find more solid footing in the historical allusions contained in the Koran and the general impression that sacred book leaves of a divine pattern for the universe from Adam to the Prophet to the end of time. To early Muslims history would serve the function of telling the story of Allah's plan for mankind, as this had taken place in the past, and how, through the instrumentality of the Islamic community (*ummah*), it would unfold in the future. The Koran also referred to peoples whose misdeeds had brought the wrath of Allah down upon them. Such references pricked the curiosity of pious Muslims, as did gaps in the life of the Prophet that a study of history might fill in.

Of still greater importance in the encouragement it afforded the writing of history was the necessity of collecting, and evaluating, the thousands of sayings and practices attributed to the Prophet (*hadith*). To the majority of Muslims these traditions were quite as much the inspired word of God as the Koran itself. Their theologians discovered overnight, accordingly, the necessity of establishing chains of authorities (*isnad*). These authorities developed as narrators who had passed, from one to another, testimonies concerning sayings and practices of Muhammad, leading finally to the contemporaries of the Prophet who had initially witnessed the items. It was in this need to establish such chains of authorities concerning the traditions associated with Muhammad that Muslim historiography found its principal inspiration. Finally, a further incentive to writing history was the desire to have a record of the victories that the Prophet and Islamic generals had gained in the cause of Allah.[8]

Originally, Muslim historiography constituted a necessary complement to the study of the Koran and *hadith*, and the function of the historian was initially a religious one. He might, in fact he often did, consider himself a theologian.[9] It is no accident, therefore, that the two major works of al-Tabari, his commentary on the Koran and his universal history, served to complement each other in their author's mind. Scholars who used chains of authority to establish the genuineness of the traditions associated with the Prophet early found that same method a logical one to employ in ascertaining the historical past. The practice of historians thus to depend so heavily upon these authorities explains why they eschewed for some centuries the role of interpreters of past events. They contented themselves rather, as did al-Tabari, with simply recording those accounts of past events they considered pertinent to their subjects.

Al-Tabari furnishes below an excellent example of the manner in which Muslim writers, and that included early historians like himself, customarily presented their chains of narrators, whether the matter was doctrinal[10] or historical. The subject here is the conquest of Egypt, which the Muslims under Omar accomplished during the years 640–641. Al-Tabari's account reads as follows:

> Ibn Ishak says, as said Ibn Humaid, that Salamah said on his authority, that: Omar after subjugating the whole of Syria wrote to 'Amr ibn al 'Asi to march to Egypt with his army. So he set out and captured Bab al Yun (Babylon) in the year A.H. 20. . . . Ibn Humaid says that Salamah says thus, on the authority of Ibn Ishak, who says that Al Ka-

sim (an Egyptian) ibn Kuzman told him – on the authority of Ziyad ibn Jazu, who said he was in 'Amr's army when he took Misr and Alexandria – the following story: We took Alexandria in the Caliphate of Othman in the year A.H. 21 or 22. . . .

Tabari writes that Saif says in the letter which As Sari wrote to me (Tabari) that Shu'aib informed him on [Ibn Ishak's] authority and that of Ar Rabia and that of Abu 'Uthman and that of Abu Harithah, as follows: Omar remained at Jerusalem after making the treaty of peace there, and sent 'Amr to Egypt. He also sent Zubair in support.

As Sari has written to me on the authority of Shu'aib on the authority of Saif, who says Abu 'Utham has told us on the authority of Khalid ibn Mi'dan and 'Ubadah, as follows: 'Amr set out to Egypt after Omar returned to Medina, and marched till he came to Bab al Yun.[11]

It was reliance upon such chains of authorities that led early Muslim "historians" to adopt the annalistic form in their writing. The use of annals, which involved the presentation in chronological order of events related to a particular year or reign, recommended itself to them for its simplicity. It was also an easy matter to introduce in sequence the reports different narrators had given of particular events or reigns, and from this a natural step to permitting chronology, rather than the event itself, to be the determining factor in the order in which this historical information was recorded. Little of this annalistic type of historical writing remains extant from the period prior to al-Tabari, who is considered the master of Muslim annalists. That he revealed himself so accomplished at this task, however, leads scholars to accept the existence of earlier efforts from which he drew his inspiration.

To say that the simplicity of annalistic recording recommended it to tyros in the historical profession is to note about its only virtue. True, as a second virtue, it might point to the general impartiality of its tone. The annalist ordinarily believed his task completed with the recording of an account. No obligation rested upon him to interpret or judge its accuracy, neither was he under pressure to alter its contents. The testimony of the earlier writers whose reports the annalist set down could, of course, make no claim to any inherent objectivity. In presenting their accounts of contests between Muslims and the Byzantine empire, for example, the Muslims are customarily in the right.

Still, serious deficiencies were apt to mar annalistic writing. It placed a high premium upon the accuracy of chronology to which the events were related when such accuracy was often beyond confirmation. There was further the difficulty of incorporating information that was authentic enough but that had come down from out of the past without precise dating. In such cases, the temptation was great for the annalist to place the information arbitrarily where he thought it might belong or where he found space. Neither does annalistic writing lend itself readily to the introduction of material from which the reader could derive knowledge of the social and cultural developments of a period. Under no circumstances could annalistic writing lay claim to literary or aesthetic excellence apart from that which the testimony of a particular narrator might happen to possess. It is history presented in its most functional garb, unadorned and starkly informational. Fortunately for the reader of al-Tabari's history, the reports of earlier writers he introduces frequently contain episodes of unusual interest.

Al-Tabari begins his history (*Ta'rikh al-Rusul w-al-Muluk*), the first universal history in the Arabic language, with the Creation, then moves through the patriarchs, kings, and prophets as these appear in the Islamized version of Biblical history. From here he passes quickly to the kingdom of the Sassanid Persians, next to Muhammad, to the caliphs who succeeded the Prophet, and finally to the Ummayads and early Abbasids to 915. Although his work presumes to be a universal history, he restricts himself to Islamic Asia for the most part. He has little time for either north Africa or Europe. That Abbasid authority scarcely extended farther west than Egypt may account for his lack of attention to those areas. Still his preoccupation with Baghdad and the neighboring regions may simply reflect the powerful impact the Islamic capital on the Tigris had upon Muslim thought and culture.

Al-Tabari adopted the annalistic method of presenting his information when he reached the Islamic period, where the Hijrah furnished him his first solid base from which to reckon the passage of time. Almost ritualistic is the sentence with which he opens the annal for each succeeding year: "Then came the year. . . ." Almost as methodical was his practice of concluding the year's annal with some information concerning the leader of the pilgrimage made to Mecca that year; he is also inclined to introduce important events in the beginning of the annal. Obituary notices that appear prominently in Western chronicles are not mentioned and neither are the names of high officials unless they figured in events of some importance. A major departure from pure annalistic recording is al-Tabari's practice of inserting an extensive biography of each caliph at the close of his reign.

The deficiencies that saddled the annalistic method of recording history also burdened al-Tabari's writing. He contents himself with recording the information he has accumulated. This may be by way of chains of authorities or from eyewitnesses, and he presents the details either in the form of annals or simply en bloc – that is, introducing what information the one writer has concerning a particular caliph, for instance, followed by the information another writer has to offer. Unfortunately, he often omits the names of his authorities and the author or eyewitness of some particular excerpt. He makes no effort to fashion a single account from those he had at hand. He does little sorting of facts, even when they are contradictory. For him history was not a rational discipline in the sense that it demanded interpretation and analysis. His responsibility consisted solely of passing on accurately the information he had gathered about the past, whatever this might be.[12] He states his position in the introduction to his universal history.

> The knowledge of the events of past nations, and of the information about what is currently taking place, does not reach one who is not contemporary to, or does not observe, such events except through the reports of historians and the transmission of transmitters. These [historians, transmitters] should not use rational deductions and mental elucidations. Now if there happens to be in this book a report that I have transmitted from some past authority to which the reader objects or which the hearer detests because he does not see how it could possibly be true or correct, let him know that this report did not originate with me, but came from some of those who transmitted it to me and all I did was to deliver it as it was delivered to me.[13]

Because al-Tabari introduces parallel accounts by different authorities of the same event without any attempt to reconcile these, his history suffers from repetitiousness, unevenness of style, a measure of disconnectedness, and some lack of balance. If his authorities have little or nothing to report about Morocco, for example, he has little or nothing to pass on to his reader. Thus, he devotes but six lines to the conquest of Spain. When he reaches his own age and is dealing with recent events, some of this repetitiousness naturally disappears, but then comes to view an apparent inability to distinguish properly the relative importance of these events. He omits such important items as the attack of the Byzantine fleet in 839.[14] And he reveals no greater interest in things cultural and social when dealing with times nearer his own than he did for earlier centuries when he was wholly dependent upon his authorities.

But whatever his shortcomings, al-Tabari was the first historian to furnish the world a reasonably clear and trustworthy view of Islamic history. The most eloquent tribute to the solid character of his work is that later historians did not bother to go over the same early ground themselves. For the summaries they introduced, they depended almost entirely upon al-Tabari, or they simply began their accounts where he left off. To Ibn Khaldun, the most distinguished of all Arab historians, al-Tabari was "the historian and traditioner of the people and no other opinion outweighs his."[15]

In a historian such as al-Tabari who holds himself to be preserving the traditions of the past, the virtues to which the reader gives first priority are accuracy in recording and objectivity, and here al-Tabari's performance deserves highest commendation.[16] He approaches his task with the detachment of a craftsman at his workbench. If one wonders why he abstains from favoring one account at the expense of another, a privilege he claimed in his commentaries on the Koran, the explanation may be that the writing of history had not yet attained so mature a level as to permit or demand analysis and interpretation. The historian's responsibility in his day remained simply that of gathering and recording information. Only after all pertinent material had been assembled could the task of resolving inconsistencies and establishing a single, accurate account become feasible and desirable.

That al-Tabari took considerable pains to arrive at the "orthodox" position in his consideration of the Koran and *hadith* is understandable. Because orthodoxy here was of paramount importance, he could not properly stop with simply reporting what different authorities had to say. The situation regarding history was quite different since historical accuracy was not essential to the preservation of religious orthodoxy. Accordingly, al-Tabari gave little thought to the accuracy of his historical writing beyond a truthful rendering of the various narratives supplied him.

The irony of it is that whereas later scholars subjected to careful scrutiny his commentaries on the Koran to which he had devoted the most fastidious consideration, they accepted almost without question the accuracy of his historical writing to which he had given little thought. What accounts for the qualified acceptance of the commentaries on the Koran is, of course, the presence of similar studies by scholars who may have been as qualified as al-Tabari to do that work. His history, on the other hand, stands alone. It has no competitors.

Here follow several excerpts from al-Tabari's universal history. Good Muslim that al-Tabari was, he believed history began with the Creation, so he opens his narrative with a description of what happened in the beginning. As indicated earlier, al-Tabari often neglects to note from what source(s) he drew his information, and that is the case here. One would have to conclude from the nature of his account that he did not accept, or was ignorant of, the story in Genesis, and that he received some inspiration from the Koran.

Following this excerpt about the Creation, there come two that deal with the reign of Haroun Ar-Raschid, Islam's most illustrious caliph. The first describes his accession to the throne, the second, the rise and tragic fall of the family of the Barmecides. While scholars have no means of checking the accuracy of al-Tabari's account, they accept its general reliability. The noted Arab historian Ibn Khaldun did reject as without credibility al-Tabari's portrayal of al-Abbasah, the sister of Haroun Ar-Raschid, as having a son by the lowborn Ja 'far. What is especially significant about Ibn Khaldun's argument, however, is that he did not appeal to other historical evidence to refute al-Tabari's story—there was none other extant—but simply to his reasoning that a woman of al-Abbassah's noble ancestry could not have stooped to such behavior. Evidently al-Tabari had no such reservations, although one suspects that he introduced the episode of al-Abbasah and Ja'far as much to entertain as to inform the reader.

The fourth excerpt contains material from the reign of Chosroes Anushirwan, the greatest of the Sassanid Persian monarchs and a contemporary of the Byzantine emperor Justinian against whom he waged intermittent warfare. While al-Tabari's account reveals some Islamic bias, it conforms generally with what we learn from Byzantine sources. Anything completely objective would be too much to expect from a writer who probably had only Islamic sources to draw upon. Because the modern historian can find adequate information about the wars between Chosroes and Justinian from Byzantine sources, what he values most in al-Tabari's history are references to Chosroes' suppression of a religious sect founded by the "hypocrite" Zaradhust and to the historian's description of Chosroes' tax system, together with such interesting items as those concerning the usurper Sahrbaraz, Queen Boran, and Queen Azarmidocht, "one of the most beautiful Persian women."

The final excerpt from al-Tabari's history describes relations between the Byzantine and Islamic empires during the period 779 to 830. It represents a splendid illustration of the historian's annalistic style of writing.

Discourse of Mohammed, Son of Djarir, Tabari, Who Is the Author of This Work[17]

Know that this is what Mohammed, son of Djarir, son of Yezid, Tabari, narrates at the beginning of this work.

God formed the creatures without their creation being necessary to him. He created them to test them. He ordered them to adore him in order to learn which ones would adore him and which would not, who would be the ones to carry out his orders and who would refuse to do so. His wisdom required that he create them so that their actions might reveal what he knew by his foreknowledge. He says in the Koran (Sur. LI, verses 56–58): "I have created jinn and men only that they might serve me. I do not ask them for food, nor do I ask them to nourish me. God is, indeed, the one who nourishes men. He is gifted with an irresistible power." This is the sense of these words: I have formed these creatures, men and *Peris,* so that they might adore me and obey my orders. I do not ask them for daily nourishment; it is I who gives this to them. I do not derive any advantage from their actions or from their conduct, and they receive from me the value and recompense for their actions. Had I not created them that would have done me no injury. Now that I have created them, if they do not do what I have ordered them to do and refuse to carry out my instructions, this will entail no loss to me; and if they do obey my orders, I derive no utility therefrom. . . .

God first created the world and then its creatures. He gave them eyes so that they might see his marvels and all his power, he gave them ears that they might hear knowledge and wisdom, he gave them hearts in order that they might understand, and he placed intelligence in their hearts that they might be able to distinguish truth from lies and discern that which is useful from that which is injurious. He gave them the earth as a rug that they might build their homes there. He spread out the sky above them, and the clouds below the sky so that the rain might pour out, that the plants might spring up from the earth, that men might eat, that they might realize that they have a creator, and that they might know and adore him and only him. . . .

God said: "I placed the sun and the moon in the sky because the world was created in darkness, and if the sun or the moon did not exist, there would be no light in the world." In the beginning when God created the world, both the sun and moon possessed the same brightness. If they had remained thus, no one would have been able to distinguish the night from the day, no one would have known the number of days, months, or years. People who performed the five required prayers would not have known the time of the prayers. God sent Gabriel to rub his wing against the face of the moon so that the light of the moon should become less than that of the sun, in order that the night would become distinct from the day, and so that the years, months, and all calculations of time might become manifest. This is indeed a great good.

The Reign of Haroun Ar-Raschid[18]

They say that Haroun had accompanied Hadi to Isa-Abad and there, after he had prayed over his body, he was immediately proclaimed [caliph]. It is also reported that Ya'hya, the son of Khalid, vizier of Hadi, was in prison at the time and that Hadi planned to kill him. Once Haroun had been invested with the insignia of the caliphate by Harthama, the son of A'yan, the same night that Hadi died, he released Ya'hya, the son of Khalid, and appointed him his vizier. When Haroun ascended the throne he was twenty-two years old. He was born at Rei, when Mahdi was in this city. He was the foster brother of Fadhl, the son of Ya'hya. Hadi wished to make his son Dja'far heir presumptive to the throne and he had already received the oath of several generals in the army, but then he abandoned the idea. After Haroun had assumed power, he forced Dja'far to make a public declaration freeing from their oaths all those who had sworn to support him, and to agree instead that the authority belonged rightfully to his uncle. The next day Haroun sent letters to all the provinces which announced his coming and his demand for oaths of loyalty. The same night that he ascended the throne it was announced to him that a son had been born to him. He considered this event a good omen and called his son 'Abdallah which is the same as Mamoun's. When Haroun returned to Baghdad he went with his entourage to the bridge and said to Ya'hya: "Mahdi made me a present of a ring of rubies whose value was 100,000 dinars. One day when he found me at the home of Hadi he saw this ring on my finger and coveted it. After I left, he sent someone after me to ask me for it. I was on the bridge when his messenger accosted me and, furious at his request, I took the ring and threw it into the Tigris. Let the divers come to find it." The ring had been in the river five months already and no one believed it could be found. The divers went in the water and found it at the place where he had thrown it. Haroun was very happy over this event of good omen. . . .

This same year there was born to Haroun his son Mo'hammed al-Emin whom he preferred to Mamoun who was older, because the latter was born of a slave, while the mother of Mo'hammed was Zobaida, daughter of his uncle Dja'far, son of Mancour. Haroun chose Ya'hya, son of Khalid, as his vizier and entrusted him with full authority over all his affairs.

The Family of the Barmecides and Their Disgrace

Ya'hya, son of Khalid, had four sons: Fadhl, Dja'far, Mousa, and Mohammed. Fadhl and Dja'far jointly exercised the functions of the vizierate in the place of their father who was old. Haroun called now Fadhl, then Dja'far, to discharge the duties of the office. Mousa and Mohammed were not ministers, but they had the rank of emir. They had children and Ya'hya also had cousins, all of whom held the rank of emir. Through the influence of Ya'hya the entire family of Barmak rose to a very high rank. Of all the sons of Ya'hya, Dja'far was the one whom Haroun loved the most. Fadhl, who was the foster brother of the caliph, always felt the greatest repugnance when he was present at Haroun's parties, when the caliph amused himself with drinking in the company of women, slaves, and musicians. He finally decided to remain away altogether from these gatherings and made a vow to abstain from then on from wine.

When Ya'hya was old, he asked Haroun leave to retire to Mecca where he might pursue his devotions. Haroun refused him permission and said: "Fadhl and Dja'far, your sons, are both in a position to carry out the functions of the vizierate. Appoint whichever one you wish and he will report to me. I shall let him know my decisions, which he will then submit to you, and after having taken your advice, he will then carry them out." Thereupon Ya'hya chose his son Fadhl who was older than Dja'far, had more experience, and had more skill in public affairs. He entrusted him with the seal of the caliph and invested him with the duties of the vizierate. Haroun made no objection although he preferred Dja'far whom he loved above all because of his beauty and his talents in the arts of writing and speaking. For two years Fadhl handled the responsibilities of the vizierate in place of his father. Then Haroun assigned these to Dja'far. Some time later he took the seal from him and returned it to Ya'hya, saying: "Give it to the one of your sons whom you wish since you are the best judge in the matter. I do not wish to interfere with your choice." Ya'hya kept it himself and remained in charge of affairs unto the moment of his fall.

One cannot name any vizier, either of the ancient kings of the Persians or of the Muslim caliphs, who occupied a position close to a prince the parallel of that of Ya'hya and his sons. But they became vulnerable upon the concurrence of two or three serious circumstances, of which the first was the long time during which they held power. For whoever governs an extended period will always make many enemies because it is impossible for any one man to please everyone. Ya'hya was not ignorant of this circumstance, and it was for this reason that he frequently sought permission to retire.

The second circumstance which contributed to the fall of the Barmecides was the following. Abou-Rabi'a Mo'hammed, son of Abou-'l Laith, a theologian of Raqqa, a very devout man whose voice was popular with the people, was displeased with the influence enjoyed by Ya'hya, and presented Haroun a letter with this message: "Prince of Believers, what will you say to God on the day of the resurrection, and how will you justify placing Muslims under the authority of Ya'hya ben-Khalid, his sons and his parents, and entrusting the empire of believers to atheists? For Ya'hya, his sons, and all the members of his family are atheists and secretly espouse the doctrines of atheism. They have no religion!"

When Ya'hya learned of this letter, he kept silence. One day Haroun ar-Raschid asked him what he thought of Mo'hammed, son of Abou-'l Laith. Ya'hya replied that he was a hypocrite, a wicked Muslim, a man without religion, who deceived the people with his discourses, who spoke badly of everyone, etc. Haroun who was angry with Mo'hammed put him in prison, although the letter he had written left an impression with him. He oftentimes inquired whether the Barmecides practised religion and he sought information about their beliefs. All persons who were resentful of them spied upon them and reported their shortcomings to the caliph, the record of which kept growing in his heart.

Haroun had still a third complaint against the Barmecides. Ya'hya, the son of 'Abdallah, the 'Hasanide, had come to the court with Fadhl, son of Ya'hya, following his revolt in Taberistan, and had then been incarcerated by Haroun and entrusted to the special care of Dja'far. When Dja'far received the order to kill him, Ya'hya spoke to him: "You, a man of such eminence, you wish to kill me, you who know who my ancestors are? They had, indeed, given me a surety, but now that they have led me here they violate their oaths." Dja'far replied: "I give you your freedom. Go where you wish. Should Haroun ask me about you, I shall tell him what is necessary." Ya'hya immediately fled. Haroun was informed of the matter by his chamberlain. One day when he was at table with Dja'far he asked him what had become of Ya'hya. Dja'far explained that he was still in prison. "Swear," ordered the caliph, "by my head and by my life." Dja'far was silent, then spoke up: "Prince of Believers, I do not wish to swear by your head and by your life. I was convinced that Ya'hya was a good man, that we had nothing to fear from him, and that he could not recruit any partisans. I have therefore set him free." Haroun, without revealing any displeasure, said to him: "You have done well; I had the same intention; my mind is in agreement with yours." Although he spoke no more of the matter, the incident left him with a feeling of great resentment.

The fourth circumstance which contributed to the fall of the Barmecides was the following. Haroun ar-Raschid had a sister named 'Abbasa, the daughter of Mahdi, who was a year older than Hadi. When the latter had wished to resort to violence against Haroun, 'Abbasa sought to dissuade him and said: "Do not do this: he is your brother: he must reign after you. One does not know what will happen." For this reason, when Haroun came to occupy the throne, he showed his sister the greatest deference and affection. He confided some of his secrets to her, enjoyed himself in her company with drinking, and lived with her in the greatest intimacy. The caliph invited Dja'far to these banquets which he shared with his sister and her slaves. Dja'far who was fearful of committing some impropriety toward 'Abbasa by look or words, would have preferred not to attend these parties any longer. Haroun understood the reason for his discretion, and said to him: "I want you to marry 'Abbasa, with the understanding that you do not see her except in my company, that your body never approaches hers, and that you will have no conjugal intercourse with her. You will then be able to attend our parties of pleasure without fear." Dja'far answered that he was at the command of the caliph. Then Haroun gave him 'Abbasa in marriage. The married couple met in the company of Haroun and spoke at a distance. In the palace of Haroun there was neither a woman among the free women nor the slaves who was more beautiful than 'Abbasa. Dja'far was himself also a man of great beauty. Both of them, therefore, sought to see each other in secret without the knowledge of Haroun, and [in time] 'Abbasa found herself with child by Dja'far. She gave birth to a male child whom she sent to Mecca in the care of two of her slaves to whom she gave considerable money. A year had passed since this incident when 'Abbasa had a quarrel with one of her slaves. She struck her and threatened to have her killed. The slave sought out Haroun and revealed to him the birth of the child to 'Abbasa and Dja'far. Haroun directed her to tell no one and he took her into his own house.

After Ya'hya, the son of 'Abdallah, had secured his freedom, Haroun made efforts to locate his retreat. Once the caliph had learned with a certainty that he was in Khorasan, he sent 'Ali, son of 'Isa, son of Mahan, to this province with instructions to find and seize Ya'hya. From this time his feelings toward the Barmecides were completely altered. He showed coldness toward Ya'hya and Dja'far. Ya'hya daily commented about the unfriendly attitude of

the caliph toward himself, but he did not dare ask to be
dismissed. 'Ali, son of 'Isa, having succeeded in arresting
Ya'hya, sent him by a trusted agent to Raqqa. Haroun put
him to death.

Now that he had reassured himself in this matter, he
resolved to move against the Barmecides. He announced
his intention of making a pilgrimage and he left taking
with him Ya'hya and the other Barmecides. After he had
completed the pilgrimage ceremonies at Mecca, he had the
son of 'Abbasa, who was a very beautiful child and who
resembled 'Abbasa and Dja'far, brought to him. He had
had the intention of slaying him, but now he said that the
child was quite innocent and he changed his mind. He then
began his return journey to Raqqa. At a station near An-
bar named 'Omr he put up for several days. On the fourth
day after his arrival, he summoned Ya'hya and his sons
Fadhl, Dja'far, and Mousa, gave them robes of honor, and
showed them many kindnesses. These made them feel very
happy and fully reassured. At the hour for the afternoon
prayer Haroun said to Dja'far: "I would not permit you to
leave this evening if I did not wish to amuse myself by
drinking with my slaves. You also amuse yourself with
yours." He then returned to his harem and began to drink.
After some time he dispatched a messenger to see if
Dja'far was doing the same. When he learned that Dja'far
was in low spirits, he had the messenger tell him: "It is
absolutely essential, I swear by my head and by my life,
that you prepare a banquet and that you give yourself over
to celebrating since I will have no pleasure in drinking
unless I know that you are also drinking." Dja'far prepared
a banquet but his heart was full of distress and fear. He
had in his service a blind musician named Abou-Zakkar.
After he had drunk for some time, he said to the musician:
"My spirits are very low tonight." Abou-Zakkar replied: "O
vizier, the prince of believers has never shown such good
will to you and your family as he has this day. You ought to
rejoice." "I have sad presentiments," said Dja'far. "Drive
these follies away," replied Abou-Zakkar, "and give yourself up to pleasure."

Near the hour of the evening prayer, a servant of Haroun's brought Dja'far sweets, dried fruits, and perfumes from the caliph. About the hour of the night prayer Haroun sent more, then again still more a third time. Toward midnight the caliph left the tent of his women. He summoned Mesrour the eunuch and said to him: "Go this instant to find Dja'far. Lead him to your tent, cut off his head, and bring it to me." When Mesrour presented himself at Dja'far's, the vizier shuddered. Mesrour said to him: "The prince of believers summons you." "Where is he?" asked Dja'far. "He has just left his women," replied Mesrour, "and he has returned to his place." Dja'far said: "Let me enter the tent of my women to leave instructions." "That will not be possible," answered Mesrour "leave your instructions here." Dja'far obeyed. Then Mesrour led him away and when he reached his tent, he drew his sabre. Dja'far asked him what the order was that he had received. Mesrour said: "The caliph ordered me to bring him your head." Dja'far said: "Take care. It is possible he gave this order when he was drunk and he may regret it later." Then he besought Mesrour, recalling to him their old friendship, that he return to the caliph. Mesrour consented. Haroun was seated on his prayer rug and was awaiting the eunuch. When he saw him enter he immediately asked him: "Where is the head of Dja'far?" "Prince of believers," replied Mesrour, "I have brought Dja'far." "It is not Dja'far that I demanded," declared the caliph, "but his head." Mesrour returned to Dja'far and cut off his head. When he presented it to Haroun, the latter said: "Keep the head and the body until I ask you for them. Now go in to the camp and arrest Ya'hya, his three sons, and his brother Mo'hammed, son of Khalid, and bring them to your tent and put them in chains. Then take possession of all their goods."

Mesrour carried out all these orders. At dawn Haroun sent the head of Dja'far to Baghdad. The next day he left for Raqqa. Ya'hya and his brother were closely guarded in prison, subjected to torture, and ordered to surrender all their possessions. After Ya'hya died in prison, the caliph gave Mo'hammed, son of Khalid, his freedom since he had nothing to reproach him with nor anything to fear from him since Mo'hammed was the best of the Barmecides. As for the others, they remained in captivity. After all their possessions had been seized Haroun had the throats of Fadhl, Mo'hammed, and Mousa cut in his presence. All the members of the family of Ya'hya and their associates were executed. Of all the Barmecides there remained only Mo'hammed, son of Khalid, and the young children of Fadhl and Dja'far who were spared. The head of Dja'far remained attached to a gallows in Baghdad until the time Haroun made his journey to Khorasan. Being then at Baghdad, he gave orders to Sindi to burn the head.

The behavior of Haroun in this episode was generally condemned. People said that had the matter not concerned his sister, all that he had done would have appeared justified. Now he had dishonored himself by his conduct. Had he been patient, the affair would scarcely have become known to his contemporaries. Because of his cruelty and the excessive punishments he had meted out, everyone was talking of the affair. And when they speak of the terrible fate of the Barmecides and ask the reason, they will say that this was the affair of 'Abbasa, sister of Haroun ar-Rashid. The memory of it will perpetuate itself until the day of the resurrection, and all will know that the punishment inflicted upon the Barmecides was neither an act of wisdom nor of prudence.

People condemned the conduct of Haroun for another reason. Because of the disappearance of the Barmecides, the security of the state was seriously endangered and Haroun repented of having had them destroyed. Everywhere he faced troubles and revolts, neither was he equal to the task of governing the empire. The province of Khorasan which was under the despotic administration of 'Ali, son of 'Isa, revolted, and Haroun was obliged to go there in person. He marched from Iraq with 50,000 men and left his son Mo'hammed al-Emin at Baghdad to whom he entrusted the regency of all parts of the empire located between the frontiers of Maghreb and the heights of Holwan. He stopped for some time at Kirmanschahan where a general meeting of the troops was arranged. He addressed them and ordered them to take a new oath to his son Mamoun to whom he gave the government of all the provinces situated beyond Holwan, that is, Kouhistan, Hamadan, Rei, Gorgan, Taberistan, Khorasan, Transoxiana, and Turkestan. Mamoun began marching with 30,000 men, while Haroun followed him with the rest of the army. When he reached Tous he died.

In the speech which he made at Kirmanschahan, he declared: "There were troubles in the west and in the east. The west is pacified. I will be able to pacify the east as well, although Ya'hya, son of Khalid, and his family are no longer there. Since I had no one to whom I was able to entrust this mission, I came myself." People disapproved of these words. They said that Haroun should not have publicly confessed his regrets nor the need he felt for the Barmecides.

Poets composed more elegies on the death of the Barmecides than they had made panegyrics during their lifetimes.

Dja'far was decapitated the night of Saturday, the first day of the month of cafar, in the year 187.

The Reign of Chosroes Anushirwan[19]

Thereupon Chosroes Anushirwan, son of Kobad, became king, etc. After he became king he sent letters to the four *padhospans,* each of whom administered a part of Persia, and to their associates (subordinate officials), of which the letter addressed to the *padhospan* of Azerbaijan read as follows: "In the name of God, the Merciful! From King Chosroes, son of Kobad, to Zadhoe(?), the uner-*ergan,* the *padhospan* of Azerbaijan, Armenia, and that region, and to his associates, greetings! Nothing affords men such just cause for anxiety than the situation that has them lacking something the absence of which gives them reason to fear their prosperity will come to an end, violence erupt, or that some injury strike one of those they hold dearest, then someone else, either in his own person, his servants, or his property or what he holds to be valuable. But we know of no source of anxiety nor any want by which the people might be more sorely grieved than the need for a good king."

Once Chosroes was firmly on the throne, he extirpated a sect which had been founded upon the Magian religion by a hypocrite from Pasa by name Zaradhust, the son of Choragan. A large number of people had accepted this heresy and it had accordingly grown quite powerful. One of his apostles near Pöbel was a man from Madharija by name Mazdak, son of Bamdadh. He ordered and enjoined the people that property and families be held in common. He assured them that this was an act of piety which God approved and for which he reserved the richest reward; in fact, even if the religious precepts which he recommended to them were not really binding, still the genuinely good fortune which God's mercy made manifest would already exist in their mutual support of one another. It was by this means that he incited the common people against the aristocracy. The low-born of all sorts mixed with the best blood, and it was a simple matter for those who envied the property of others to seize it, for evildoers to work their evil, and for adulterers to satisfy their lust and to approach the most noble women about whom they could earlier not even have dreamed. All people found themselves in the same distress. Never before had one heard of anything like it. So Chosroes prohibited the practice of any of the innovations which Zaradhust, son of Choragan, and Mazdak, son of Bamdadh, had introduced. He suppressed the entire heresy and executed many who adhered to it and who refused to respect his prohibitions concerning it. In addition to these he also executed several Manichaeans and restored to the Magians the religion which they had previously confessed. . . .

Men appreciated the virtues of Chosroes, that is, his intelligence, learning, understanding, courage, and prudence, as well as the gentleness and kindness which he showed to all. As his crown was being placed on his head, the magnates and nobles pressed forward and with all earnestness presented their petitions. Once they had finished with their requests, he stood up to give an address. First he spoke of the goodness which God had shown his creatures in that he had created them. Next he spoke of his confidence that God would guide them and would provide them sustenance. And so he omitted nothing (necessary) in his speech. Then he reminded them of the misfortunes they had suffered through the teaching of Mazdak, including the loss of their possessions, the destruction of their faith, and the utter confusion which existed in all matters concerning their children and their property. He promised, however, to see to it that the matter would be thoroughly remedied and he asked the people to cooperate with him in this. Then he had the leaders of the Mazdakites beheaded and their possessions distributed among the needy, while many of those who had taken property from the people were also executed and the possessions restored to their rightful owners. He further ordered that every child about whose parentage there remained some doubt, should be assigned to that family with which he was then living, and that he should receive that portion of the inheritance of the man to which he was entitled when this man recognized him. To each woman who had submitted to another (man), the violator was required to pay the marriage fee in order to reconcile himself fully with the family. She would then have the option of either remaining with him or of marrying another. If she already had a husband, she was to be returned to him. He further decreed that whoever had damaged the property of another or had deprived him of anything, should pay full damages immediately, then suffer further punishment in keeping with his crime. He permitted the children of the nobility whose guardians were dead to be recorded as his own, their daughters to be married to members of that class and provided with dowries from state funds. He gave the young men in marriage to women of the aristocracy, for whom he furnished dowries, then made them wealthy but obliged them to remain at court in order that he might invest them with high offices. To the wives of his father he left the choice of either remaining with his own wives, to live with them and receive the same allowances as they did, or to have him marry them again in keeping with their station.

He had canals dug, constructed aqueducts, and advanced loans to farmers and assisted them in other ways. He had every wooden bridge rebuilt that had been destroyed, also stone ones which had fallen into ruin, and every village which had been laid waste he restored to a condition it had scarcely ever had before. He also inspected the horsemen, and whoever lacked the means he supplied with a gift of horses and equipment, and assured them a regular pay. He further appointed overseers for the fire temples and made provision for good roads. Along these roads he erected castles and fortresses as protection against robbers. He chose capable governors and prefects and to all of these he issued strict instructions. He studied the life of Ardashir, his letters and judgments, took him for his model and admonished his people to do the same.

Now that he was firmly established in power and had subjected the entire country – he had already reigned several years – he marched against Antioch. He captured the city and the emperor's generals stationed there. Then he had a map made of Antioch which carefully indicated the extent and number of its houses, streets, and all other circumstances. Next he had a city built near Media which was exactly the same. The place, which was called Rumija (the Roman), was laid out in strict accordance with the plan of Antioch. Then he had the inhabitants of Antioch moved to the new city. They all came in through the gate, then each went to a dwelling which was so much like the one he had occupied in Antioch that he might well have believed he had never left that city.

After this he attacked and captured Heracleia. Next he captured Alexandria and what lay on this side of that city. He left a part of his troops as a garrison in the land of the Romans after the emperor had yielded to him and had paid him ransom. After his return from the Roman territories, he marched against the Khazars and took the bloody revenge upon them he had hoped to do for the injury they had done him by their violence against his people. He turned next to Aden, barricaded by means of large ships, boulders, iron posts, and chains a part of the sea that lay between two mountains, in the vicinity of Abyssinia, and executed the nobility of the country. Then he returned to Media once the Roman territory on this side of Heracleia and Armenia had become his, and in addition to this all that lay between these lands and the sea, that is, the country of Aden.

Then he appointed Mundhir b. Nu'wan king of the Arabs and bestowed honors upon him. After this he remained in his own domain in Media and attended to all those matters which required his attention. Afterwards he marched against the Haital in order to avenge the death of his grandfather Peroz. But before this he arranged a marriage alliance with the Chakan, informed him before his attack of what he planned to do, and bade them to join him against the Haital. So he reached their country, slew their king, and exterminated his entire house. He marched on over Balk and what lay beyond, and had his troops encamp in Ferghana. Then he returned home from the east, but after he had reached Media, people came to him to seek his help against the Abyssinians. So he sent them one of his generals with troops from Delem and the neighboring lands. These slew the Abyssinian Masruq and remained there.

Thus was Chosroes constantly victorious and feared by all peoples, so that there could always be found numerous ambassadors at his court from the Turks, Chinese, Khazars, and similarly distant peoples. He paid honor to scholars. His reign lasted for forty-eight years. The birth of the Prophet took place during the latter part of the reign of Anushirwan. According to Hisam, Anushirwan reigned for only forty-seven years. He says, moreover, 'Abdallah b. 'Abdalmuttalib, the father of the Messenger of God, was born in the twenty-fourth year of his reign and died in the forty-second.

Hisam says further: when Anushirwan had grown powerful, he sent to Mundhir, the son of Nu'man the Elder, whose mother was Ma'assama, a wife from the family Namir, and set him up as king of Hira and that region which Harith, the son of 'Amr the Murar-Eater had possessed, and he held that position until he died.

Hisam relates further that Anushirwan marched against the Burgan, then returned and caused the great gates to be erected (in the Caucasus).

[The history according to Hira.] Hisam writes: The king who ruled the Arabs in the name of the Persian kings after

Aswad b. Mundhir was his brother Mundhir b. Mundhir b. Nu'man, whose mother was in the same manner Hirr, daughter of Nu'man. He reigned seven years. After him Nu'man b. Aswad b. Mundhir ruled for four years. His mother is Umm al Malik, daughter of 'Amr b. Hogr, sister of Harith b. 'Amr Kindi. His successor Aba Ja'fur b. 'Alcama b. Malik b. 'Adi b. Dhumail b. Thaur b. Asas b. Arba(?) b. Numara b. Lachm ruled for three years. Then Mundhir, son of Amraalqais al Bad', that is, Dhulqarnain, became king. He was called that because he had two locks of hair. His mother is Ma'assama, that is, Marija, daughter of 'Auf b. Gusam b. Hilal b. Rabi'a b. Zaid-Manat b. 'Amir Dahjan b. Sa'd b. Chazrag b. Taimallah b. Namir b. Qasit. In all he ruled for forty-nine years. Then his son 'Amr b. Mundhir became king. His mother was Hind, daughter of Harith, the son of 'Amr, the grandson of Hogr the Murar-Eater. He ruled for sixteen years. After he had reigned for eight years, eight months, the Messenger of God was born. That was during the reign of Anushirwan, in the year that Asram Abu Jaksum marched with the elephant against the temple in Mecca. . . .

As they relate, there was peace and a truce between Chosroes and the Roman emperor Justinian. But now there arose a dispute between the Arab whom Justinian had appointed king of the Arabs in Syria, a man by name Chalid b. Gabala, and a man, named Mundhir b. Nu'man, of the family Lachm, whom Chosroes had made king over the territories of Oman, Bahrain, Jamama to Taif, and the other parts of Hedjaz and over the Arabs living there. So Chalid b. Gabala attacked the territory of Mundhir, slaughtered many of his subjects, and captured numerous kinds of booty from him. Mundhir complained about this to Chosroes and asked him to write to the Roman emperor in order to secure satisfaction from Chalid for himself. Chosroes did indeed remonstrate with Justinian that there was peace and a truce between them, informed him, too, what had happened to Mundhir, his governor of the Arabs, at the hands of Chalid, and asked him to instruct the latter to restore all the booty he had seized in his territory, pay the wergeld for the Arabs he had slain, and to see that Chalid gave full satisfaction to Mundhir. And he warned him that he should mark well what he had written, otherwise that would be the end of the truce between them.

He repeatedly sent similar letters to Justinian to see that justice be done to Mundhir, but he paid no attention to them. So Chosroes prepared for war, attacked the territory of Justinian with some 90,000 soldiers, captured Dara, Edessa, Mabbog, Qinnesrin, Haleb, Antioch which was the most important of all the cities of Syria, Apamea, Hems, and many neighboring places, and carried off all the money and other things he found in the cities. He led the inhabitants of Antioch away to Sawad where, as I indicated above, he had erected near Ctesiphon a city entirely similar to the plan of Antioch, where he directed them to live. That is the city which is called Rumija. He set up for them a circle of five jurisdictions: the upper, middle, and lower Naharwan, Baderaja, and Bakusaja. From the prisoners of Antioch whom he settled in Rumija he demanded fixed military service and turned the administration of their affairs over to a Christian of Ahwaz, by name Baraz, whom he had earlier appointed to the governing committee of his workmen. He did this out of sympathy for the prisoners and because he wanted them to give their confidence to Baraz as a fellow-believer. But the other cities of Syria and Egypt the emperor ransomed for a large sum which he paid to him. He also pledged himself to pay an annual tribute to secure his promise not to attack his territory. He gave Chosroes a written document to this effect which he and the leading Roman officials signed, and thereafter each year he paid him the tribute.

Before the reign of Chosroes Anushirwan the kings of Persia were in the habit of requiring from each of the circles a land-tax which amounted to a third, a fourth, a fifth, or a sixth of the produce depending on the amount of irrigation and the agriculture in the circle, and a head tax of a fixed amount. After this Kobad, the son of Peroz, toward the end of his reign had directed that the land, both plain and mountainous, be surveyed in order that the land-tax from them might be properly determined. This survey was

carried out, although the project had not been fully completed at the time of Kobad's death. Now that his son
Chosroes had come to the throne he had the survey completed, also the date palms and olive trees as well as the
taxable inhabitants counted, and then the total amount
established by his scribes. Next he sent out a general summons to his people and had the tax assessors inform them
of the amounts upon which the *Areal* was reckoned, based
upon the different kinds of farm produce; further the number of date palms, olive trees, and heads (taxable). When
this had been announced to them, Chosroes explained: "We
have made allocations and arrangements concerning the
estimated totals of the now surveyed cropland, also of the
date palms, olive trees, and heads, in order that these
might be annually paid in three installments. In this way
money will accumulate in our treasury with which we shall
find ourselves prepared to act should we receive news from
one of our frontier fortresses or frontier districts about a
disturbance or anything evil, for the settlement or suppression of which money is needed. For we do not wish in
such instances first to publish a new tax assessment. Now
what do you think of our plan and decision?"

But to his question no one had any suggestion to offer
and no one uttered a syllable. Then after Chosroes had
repeated his question three times, a man stood up in the
crowd and said to Chosroes: "Will you, O king — may God
give you long life! — impose eternal taxes on perishable
things: a grape vine that will die some day, a seed that
withers up, a canal that dries up, a spring or water-pipe
that runs out of water?" To this Chosroes exclaimed: "You
cursed, impudent fellow. To what class of men do you belong?" "I am one of the scribes," he answered. Then
Chosroes exclaimed: "Hack him to pieces with the *Dinte-
geschirr*." They fell upon him immediately until he was
dead, the scribes in particular since they wished to disasso-
ciate themselves completely from his point of view.

Then the people announced: "O king, we are in agreement
with what you have imposed upon us as land-tax." Then
Chosroes selected several responsible and well-intentioned
individuals and directed them to ascertain the amount of

the different kinds of produce, the number of palms, olive trees, and individuals who were taxable, and on the basis of these figures to determine the rate of assessment according to a standard which would permit his subjects, in their judgment, to live well and without worry. They were to give him a report about the matter.

Then each one declared how high in his opinion his assessment should be, and they then, after careful deliberation, worked out an agreement about the land-tax to be imposed on the field produce which nourished man and beast, namely, wheat, barley, rice, vines, lucerne, date palms, and olive trees. A tax of one dirham was laid on each *garib* of land in which wheat or barley was sown; on a *garib* of vineyard eight, on a *garib* of lucerne seven, on every four Persian date palms one dirham, on every six common date palms the same amount, and the same on every six olive trees. The tax was to apply, however, only to date palms which grew in plantations or in large numbers, not to those which grew by themselves. All remaining products with the exception of the seven indicated were left tax-free, and upon these the people could well support themselves. The head tax was imposed upon all with the exception of the nobles, the magnates, soldiers, priests, scribes, and those who were otherwise engaged in the royal service. They assessed the different classes twelve, eight, six, and four dirhams according to the amount of property each held. All who were not yet twenty years of age or above fifty were excused from the head tax.

Those who had been given fixed assessments presented these to Chosroes. He accepted the same, directed them to bring in the tax, and thenceforth to pay each year's taxes in three installments, a different payment every four months. He called it *Abrastar,* which means "the thing with which people in general are satisfied." Such were the assessments which Omar b. Chattab copied after he had conquered the Persian lands, and according to which he ordered the associates to be assessed, except that he levied a tax upon each *garib* of productive soil in proportion to its productivity, as on land actually sown, and on a *garib* of grain-growing land still one or two *Qafiz* of wheat in addition which he needed for the support of the troops. Otherwise Omar observed the assessment, particularly in Iraq, which Chosroes had imposed upon each *garib* of land, on the date palms and olive trees, and he exempted the same foodstuffs from the tax.

Then Chosroes had the assessments recorded and various samples made of them, of which he kept one in his chancellery and sent one to the tax-collectors and the judges of each circle so that they might acquaint themselves with the matter. He instructed these officials to prevent the administrators from collecting more land taxes in their districts than what was stated in the register, of which a sample had been sent to them. He also left instructions that anyone whose planting or otherwise (taxable) produce had suffered misfortune, was to be excused from the land tax in proportion to the amount of his loss; furthermore, that no head tax was to be required of persons who had died or who were more than fifty years old. They were to report such tax-exemptions to him, so that he might send the necessary instructions to the tax-collection officials. They should, furthermore, prevent the officials from collecting the head tax from those who were under twenty years of age.

Chosroes had a scribe named Pabak, son of Berawan, who was distinguished for his good descent, common sense, and ability, to whom he had entrusted the administration of the military stores. One day he said to Chosroes: "My job can only be accomplished if I am freed from every requirement which has been placed on the troops for the good of the king." The king granted him this. Then Pabak had a platform erected at the place where the army was encamped, covered it with rugs and blankets, and had cushions brought for him to lie on. After he had settled himself upon these, his herald summoned all the troops then in the camp to pass in muster before him, the horsemen with their mounts and weapons and the foot-soldiers with their required arms. Thereupon all the troops presented themselves before him with their proper equipment, although he did not see Chosroes among them. Then he dismissed them.

On the second day the herald issued the same summons and again all the troops passed muster before him. Again he directed them to return home but to come back on the following day since he had not seen Chosroes among them. On the third day he had his herald announce that no one who was in the camp should absent himself, even were he to hold the honor of the crown and throne, for it was a serious matter that permitted of no furlough or excuse. When Chosroes heard this he put off his crown, armed himself like the soldiers, and came before Pabak in order to pass inspection. The items of equipment which were required of the horseman included horse armor, a shirt of mail, corselet, greaves, lance, shield, a club fastened to a belt, axe or mace, quiver with two bows with the strings attached and thirty arrows, and, finally, two twisted cords which the rider fastened to the rear of his helmet. In this manner did Chosroes also present himself in full armament before Pabak, except for the two cords which he should have fastened to his helmet.

Pabak did not permit his name to pass by, but said: "You, O king, you stand before me in precisely the same condition which allows me to make no exception or mitigation. Therefore present yourself with all weapons which are required!" Then Chosroes realized that the two cords were lacking, and he fastened them on. Thereupon Pabak's herald called out with a loud voice: "The champion, the first of the champions, receives 4001 dirhams," and then Pabak announced all the names. After this the king returned home. He had given the monarch, therefore, exactly one single dirham more in pay than the soldier who had received the most. Now after Pabak had risen from his place, he came to Chosroes and explained: "The oversight which I pointed out to you today, O king, served only the purpose of enabling me to perform with efficiency the office with which you entrusted me. For one of the factors which will most assuredly accomplish the purpose of the king consists in this, that he make my position as secure as possible." Chosroes replied: "Let nothing appear as negligence to us which has as its purpose the well-being of our subjects. . . ."

It was during the reign of Chosroes Anushirwan that the
Messenger of God was born; indeed the year when Abraha
Asram Abu Jaksum marched with the Abyssinians
against Mecca and brought an elephant with him, for the
purpose of destroying the holy house of God, that is, after
forty-two years of the reign of Chosroes Anushirwan had
elapsed. That same year came the attack Gabala which is
celebrated in the Arabic Battle-Days. . . .

Then Ardashir, son of Seroe, became king, etc. He was a
small child; he is said to have been only seven years old, but
there were no longer grown members of the royal house.
For this reason the Persian magnates made him king. A
man by the name of Meh-Adhar-Gusnasp who held the
office of High Steward, undertook his upbringing. He directed the realm well and gave it such authority that people did not notice the youthfulness of Ardashir. But there
now appeared Sahrbaraz on the Roman frontier with the
troops which Chosroes had given him and which he called
"the Fortunate." Chosroes and Seroe had written to him
about all important matters and had asked him for his
advice. Since the Persian magnates had neglected to do
this when they elevated Ardashir to the throne, he used
this now as a pretext for voicing remonstrances and violent protests against them, indeed for shedding blood, and
made of this an occasion to seek the royal dignity for himself and to raise himself from the lowliness of a subject to
the height of royal power. For he despised Ardashir because of his youth, marched in autocratic fashion against
the magnates, and decided to call the people together in
order to arrange a conference concerning the occupation of
the throne. Then he pushed forward with his troops.

Meh-Adhar-Gusnasp had for his part worked hard to
strengthen the walls and gates of Ctesiphon, and brought
Ardashir to the city as well as the other remaining members of the royal dynasty together with their wives, and
beyond this all the money in Ardashir's treasury and all
remaining supplies and livestock. The troops with which
Sahrbaraz advanced numbered six thousand Persians
which had been stationed on the Roman frontier. So he

took up his position near Ctesiphon, encircled the inhabitants, and fought them about the city. He also brought up siege works against it, but was unable to effect its capture. When he saw that he could not take the city by force, he resorted to cunning, and for a long time plotted deceitful attacks with a man by name New-Chosroes, the commander of Ardashir's bodyguard, and with Namdar-Gusnasp, the son of Adhar-Gusnasp, the *spahbedh* of Nimroz, until they agreed to open the gates of the city for him. He marched inside, captured a number of the magistrates, killed them, seized their possessions, and raped their women. Upon Sahrbaraz's directions some men slew Ardashir, son of Seroe, this in the second year of his reign, in the month of Bahman during the night of the day Aban, in the palace of Chosroes-Sah-Kawadh. His reign had lasted one year and six months.

Then Sahrbaraz, that is, Ferruchan, became king for the month *spendarmadh*. He was not of royal descent but nevertheless called himself king. But as he was sitting on the throne, he suffered an attack of diarrhea, and this was so severe that he could not make it to the latrine, but had a vessel brought and placed in front of the throne, upon which he then took care of his need. A man from Istachr by name Pusferruch, the son of Mah-Chorsedhan, and his two brothers had become very angry over the fact that Sahrbaraz had slain Ardashir and had himself seized the authority. In their bitterness they solemnly swore that they would murder him. All three happened to be members of the royal bodyguard. When the king came on his horse, it was then the custom for them to line up in two rows, equipped with armour, helmet, shield, and sword, and with a lance in the hand. When the king passed next to anyone, that one would place his shield on the edge of the royal saddle and place his forehead on it as though he would touch the ground with it before him. So when one day soon after his accession Sahrbaraz came riding out, there stood Pusferruch and both his brothers all near each other in a row. As soon as he (the king) found himself opposite to them, first Pusferruch struck and then immediately his brothers after him. This happened on the day Dai ba Din in the month *spendarmadh*. He immediately fell dead from his horse. They tied a cord about his leg and dragged his body here and there. Assisting them in this (the king's) murder was a magnate by name Zadhan-Ferruch, the son of Sahrdaran, another man by the name of Mahjar, a trainer of horsemen, and still many other magnates and nobles. They also cooperated with them in hunting down different individuals who had attacked Ardashir, the son of Seroe, and slew a number of magnates. Then they raised Boran, the daughter of Chosroes, to the throne. In all Sahrbaraz had reigned forty days.

Then Boran, the daughter of Chosroes Parwez, ascended the throne, etc. According to report, on the day of her accession she announced: "I will hold myself to virtuous behavior and shall dispense justice." She gave Sahrbaraz's title to Pusferruch and invested him with the office of vizier. She ruled her subjects well, extended justice over them, had coins minted, and stone and wooden bridges repaired. She excused the people their tax arrears and issued open letters for the most part in which she explained that she wished them well and praised the deceased members of the dynasty. In these [letters] she also said that she hoped God would assist her in her solicitude and her determination in the matter, to prevent the country from being prostrated before the fury of men, the camps from being stormed by their violence, the victory from being lost through their attacks, and a conflagration lighted; rather that all should be as God willed. She instructed them further to be obedient and urged them to show themselves loyal. Thus her letters included all that was necessary. Through negotiations with the Catholicus Isojabh, she restored the wooden cross to the Roman empire. Her reign lasted one year and four months.

After her a man by the name of Gusnaspdeh became king, a very distant cousin of Parwez, who ruled for less than a month.

Next came the reign of Azarmidocht, the daughter of Chosroes Parwez, etc. She is said to have been one of the most beautiful of Persian women, also to have promised upon her accession to the throne: "We shall conduct our-

selves entirely as did our father Chosroes the Victorious,
and should any one oppose us, we shall have his blood."
According to common belief, the most important of the
Persian magnates at the time was Ferruch-Hormisdas, the
spahbedh of Khorasan. He sent to ask her to be his wife. As
her answer she sent him the following message: "It is not
proper for a queen to marry. But since I realize your hope
in this matter is simply to satisfy your lust with me, come
to me on such and such a night." And that is what Ferruch-
Hormisdas did, and he rode to her on the designated night.
Azarmidocht had earlier instructed the commander of her
bodyguard that on the night she had appointed for the
rendezvous, he should waylay and kill him. So this man
carried out her orders, and she had the body dragged out
by the feet and thrown in the courtyard of the palace.
When they discovered Ferruch-Hormisdas dead the next
morning, they removed his corpse. But they knew that he
could not have been slain except for some weighty cause.
Meanwhile Rustem, the son of Ferruch-Hormisdas, the
man whom Jazdegerd later sent to fight the Arabs, served
as deputy for his father in Khorasan. When he learned the
news, he advanced with a large army, encamped in Media,
and blinded Azarmidocht. According to other [writers] she
was poisoned. She reigned six months.

Extracts from Al-Tabari Concerning Relations between the Byzantine Empire and Islam during the Years 779 and 830.[20]

And Aaron[21] went on till he encamped at a village in the
land of the Romans in which was a fortress called Samalu;
and he stayed before it thirty-eight days, and he set up
siege engines against it until God took it, after he had done
destruction in it, and after its inhabitants had been smitten with thirst and hunger, and after slaughter and
wounds among the Moslems. And its capture was on conditions which they made for themselves that they should
not be killed or removed or separated from one another.
And they were granted these terms and surrendered, and
he kept faith with them. And Aaron returned with the

Moslems safe and sound except those who had been smitten there. . . .

And among the events [of the year 780–781] was the raid
of 'Abd Al Kabir the son of 'Abd Al Hamid the son of 'Abd
Al Rahman the son of Zaid the son of Al Khattab by the
pass of Adata. And Michael the patrician advanced
against him, as is recorded, with ninety thousand men,
among whom was Tazadh the Armenian, the patrician.
And 'Abd Al Kabir was afraid of him and prevented the
Moslems from fighting, and returned. And Al Mahdi[22]
wished to cut off his head, but intercession was made for
him, and he shut him up in prison.

Among [the events of the year 781–782] was the
summer-raid of Aaron the son of Mahomet Al Mahdi; and
his father sent him, as is recorded, on Saturday 18 Gu-
mada II to make a raid upon the country of the Romans,
and he appointed Al Rabi' his maula to accompany him.
And Aaron entered the country of the Romans and took
Magida. And the horsemen of Niketas, Count of Counts,
met him; and Yazid the son of Mazyad went out against
him. And Yazid waited for a time and then fell upon Niketas unawares; and Yazid smote him until he was routed.
And the Romans were put to flight, and Yazid took possession of their camp. And he went to the domestic at Nikufu-
diya [Nikomedeia] (and he is commander of the forces).
And Aaron marched with 95,793 men; and he carried from
them in gold 193,450 denarii, and in silver 21,414,800
drachmai. And Aaron marched until he reached the Khalig
of the sea, which is over against Constantinople, and the
ruler of the Romans at that time was Ghustah [Augusta],
the wife of Leo; and that because her son was a child, his
father having died, and he was under her guardianship.
And messengers and ambassadors passed between her
and Aaron the son of al Mahdi, seeking peace and accom-
modation and the payment of ransom. And Aaron accepted this from her, and stipulated for the payment by
her of what she in fact paid him, and that she should supply
him with guides and markets on his way, and that because
he had come by a road that was difficult and dangerous to
the Moslems; and she agreed to what he asked. And the

sum for which peace was established between him and her was ninety thousand or seventy thousand denarii, which she was to pay in April every year and in June. And he accepted this from her, and she supplied him with markets on his return, and with him she sent an envoy to Al Mahdi with what she gave, the terms being that she was to pay as ransom such sum as she could provide in gold and silver and goods. And they drew up an agreement for a truce for three years, and the prisoners were handed over; and the number which God delivered into the hands of Aaron until the Romans submitted to pay tribute was 5,643 persons; and there were killed of the Romans in the battles 54,000, and there were killed of the prisoners in bonds 2,090 prisoners. And the number of beasts trained to bear burdens which God delivered into his hands was 20,000 beasts, and there were slain of cattle and sheep 100,000 head. And the regularly paid troops exclusive of the volunteers and the traders were 100,000. And a horse was sold for a drachma, and a mule for less than ten drachmai, and a cuirass for less than a drachma, and twenty swords for a drachma. . . .

And among the events [of the year 782–783] was a rupture made by the Romans in the peace which had been made between them and Aaron the son of Al Mahdi, which we have recorded above, and their perfidy; and that was in the month of Ramadhan [17 March–15 April] of this year. And between the beginning of the peace and the perfidy of the Romans and their breach of it were thirty-two months. . . .

And in it [the year 802–803] Al Rashid sent his son Al Kasim on the summer-raid; and he gave him to God and made an oblation for himself and a propitiation; and he appointed him wali of Al 'Awasim. . . .

And in this year Al Kasim the son of Al Rashid entered the land of the Romans in Sha'ban [25 July–22 August] and besieged Kurra [Koron] and blockaded it; and he sent Al 'Abbas the son of Ga'far the son of Mahomet the son of Al Ash'ath, and he besieged the fort of Sinan until they were sore distressed. And the Romans sent to him offering him 320 Moslem prisoners if he would retire from them. And he accepted their offer and retired from Kurra and the

fort of Sinan in peace. And 'Ali the son of 'Isa the son of
Moses died on this raid in the land of the Romans and he
was with Al Kasim.

And in this year the ruler of the Romans broke the peace
made between his predecessor and the Moslems, and
refused what their previous king had undertaken to pay.

And the reason of this was that peace had been made
between the Moslems and the ruler of the Romans (and
their ruler at that time was Rina, and we have recorded
above the reason of the peace made between the Moslems
and her); and the Romans turned against Rina and deposed her and made Nikephoros king over them. And the
Romans record that this Nikephoros was a descendant of
Gafna of Ghassan, and that before his accession he was
comptroller of the revenue-accounts. Then Rina died five
months after the Romans had deposed her. And it is recorded that when Nikephoros became king and the Romans were confirmed in allegiance to him, he wrote to Al
Rashid:

"The queen considered you as a rook, and herself as a
pawn. That pusillanimous female submitted to pay a tribute, the double of which she ought to have exacted from
the barbarians. Restore, therefore, the fruits of your injustice, or abide by the determination of the sword."[23]

And when Al Rashid read the letter, his wrath was
roused so much that no one could look at him, much less
speak to him; and his household separated, fearing to increase it by any speech or action on their part; and the
wazir was in doubt whether to give him advice or to leave
him to his own deliberations without him. And he called for
an inkpot and wrote on the back of the letter:

"In the name of the most merciful God, Harun al Rashid,
commander of the faithful, to Nicephorus, the Roman dog.
I have read thy letter, O thou son of an unbelieving
mother. Thou shalt not hear, thou shalt behold, my re-
ply."[24]

Then he set out the same day and marched until he
reached the gate of Herakleia; and he made captures and
took spoil and carried off the best of everything and slew

and wasted and burnt and extirpated. And Nikephoros asked for a treaty on condition of paying annual tribute, and he accepted his offer. And, when he had returned from his raid and reached Al Rakka [Kallinikos], Nikephoros broke the treaty and violated the compact. And the cold was severe, and Nikephoros made sure that he would not return against him. And the news came that he had gone back from the conditions which he laid upon him, and it was not easy for any one to tell him this through fear of returning at such a season on his account and their own. And an artifice was used by him by means of a poet. . . .[25]

And, when he had finished his recital, he said, "The action of Nikephoros has kindled this"; and he knew that the wazirs had used an artifice with him in this matter. And he retraced his steps amidst the greatest hardships and the sorest fatigues, until he encamped in his possessions, and he did not return until he was satisfied and went as far as he wanted. . . .

And among the events of the year [803–804] was the summer-raid of Abraham the son of Gabriel and his invasion of the land of the Romans by the pass of Al Safsaf.

And Nikephoros came out to meet him, but there was brought to him from behind the news of an event which caused him to turn aside from coming to meet him, and he fell in with a party of Moslems and received three wounds and was routed. And there were slain of the Romans, as is recorded, 40,700 men, and four thousand beasts of burden were captured. . . .

And in this year [804–805] was the ransoming between the Moslems and the Romans, and no Moslem remained in the land of the Romans who was not ransomed, as is recorded. And Marwan the son of Abu Hafsa said of this:

And through thee were the captives freed, for whom high prisons were built, wherein was no friend to visit them, for so long as the price of their redemption passed the Moslems' power to pay. And they said, 'The prisons of the polytheists are their graves!'

And in this year [805–806] Al Rashid made the summer-raid. . . .

And in it the Romans went out to Anazarbos and Kanisa Al Saudaa and overran the country and took prisoners; and the men of Mopsouestia recovered all that were in their hands. And in it Al Rashid took Herakleia and dispersed his troops and his horsemen over the land of the Romans; and he entered it, as is recorded, with 135,000 regularly paid men besides the camp-followers and volunteers and those who were not registered. . . .

Then Al Rashid went to Tyana and encamped there. Then he removed from it and left 'Ukba the son of Ga'far in command of it and ordered him to build a station there. And Nikephoros sent Al Rashid the contribution and tribute for himself and his successor-designate and his patricians and other inhabitants of his country, fifty thousand denarii, of which 4 denarii were for his own person and 2 denarii for that of his son Stauracius. And Nikephoros wrote a letter and sent it by two of his chief patricians about a female slave among the captives of Herakleia, which I have copied: "To God's slave, Aaron, Commander of the believers, from Nikephoros, king of the Romans. Peace to you. To proceed, O King, I have a request to make of you that will not injure you in your religious or your worldly life, a small and easy matter, that you will give my son a female slave, one of the inhabitants of Herakleia, whom I had sought as a wife for my son; and, if you think good to perform my request, do so. And peace be to you and God's mercy and blessing."

And he also asked him for some perfume and one of his tents. And Al Rashid ordered the slave to be sought, and she was brought and decked out and seated on a throne in his tent in which he was living; and the slave was handed over, and the tent with all the vessels and furniture in it, to the envoy of Nikephoros.

And he sent him the scent which he asked, and he sent him some dates and figs and raisins and treacle. And Al Rashid's envoy handed over all this to him, and Nikephoros gave him a load of Islamic drachmai upon a bay horse, the amount of which was 50,000 drachmai, and one hundred silk garments and two hundred embroidered garments and twelve falcons and four hunting dogs and three horses. And Nikephoros had stipulated that he should not lay waste Dhu'l Kila or Samaluh or the fort of Sinan; and Al Rashid stipulated with him that he should not restore Herakleia, and that Nikephoros should undertake to pay him 800,000 denarii.

CHAPTER 4

Otto of Freising

OTTO OF FREISING, "the leading philosophical historian of the twelfth century,"[1] was born about the year 1110 into the great German family of Babenberg. His father was Leopold III, margrave of Austria, his mother Agnes, the daughter of the German emperor Henry IV. Most prestigious were the associations he had through his mother whose first husband had been Frederick of Hohenstaufen, duke of Swabia. This link made Otto the half-brother of the reigning Conrad III (1038-52) and an uncle of Frederick I Barbarossa (1152-90), who succeeded Conrad. Otto's brother Henry, who was duke of Austria, had married a Byzantine princess. This connection may explain Otto's considerable interest in Byzantine history.

In 1127 or 1128 Otto journeyed to Paris to secure an education befitting a prelate, a position that his political connections assured him. (He was a younger son and probably marked for the church from his early youth.) Who his teachers in Paris may have been he does not say. The attention he gives to Abelard and to Gilbert de la Porrée in his writing suggests that he may have studied under one

127

or the other. Otto may also have heard the mystic Hugh of St. Victor lecture for he was clearly influenced by his thought. Probably about the year 1133, after some five years in Paris, he set out for home but broke his journey at the Cistercian abbey of Morimond in eastern Champagne. So impressed was he by the spiritual character of the community that he remained with the monks there, and several years later was chosen abbot. In 1137 he was consecrated bishop of Freising, which is in western Bavaria.

Otto appears to have visited Italy in the fall of 1145 and made the acquaintance of Pope Eugenius III. He accompanied his half-brother Conrad III on the ill-fated Second Crusade (1147–49), and though he leaves no history of the expedition – as he explained, it was his purpose "to write not a tragedy but a joyous history,"[2] – he does describe several incidents, including a sudden flood that overwhelmed part of the crusading army as it was nearing Constantinople. He was among the fortunate few who managed to make it to Jerusalem, entering the city on Palm Sunday, April 4, 1149. Little else remains to tell of his life. He pleaded ill health in 1154 and did not accompany Frederick I Barbarossa to Italy. Four years later, with some premonition of his approaching death, he paid a visit to the abbey of Morimond. He died there on September 22, 1158 and was buried near the high altar in the cathedral in Freising.

We have this sympathetic description of Otto from the pen of Rahewin, the bishop's secretary and continuator (of the *Deeds*).

> He had no common or ordinary education in the field of letters, being considered the first, or among the first, of the bishops of Germany. This was so far true that apart from his knowledge of Holy Writ, in whose cryptic and hidden meanings he was notably well versed, he was virtually the first to bring to our land the subtlety of the philosophers and the Aristotelian books of the *Topics, Analytics,* and *Elenchics.* Because of these and many other accomplish-

ments, and sure of his knowledge of secular affairs and of his most eloquent tongue, he frequently spoke with great assurance on ecclesiastical matters before kings and princes. His consequent fame won him praise, and the praise — as is usually the case — aroused no little envy; yet unperturbed, he avoided the traps of his adversaries and escaped their slanderous remarks unscathed, being a thoroughly good man.[3]

Otto's distinction as a writer of history rests upon two works. The more famous of the two, which the author referred to as *History of the Two Cities*,[4] was a chronicle of universal history that extended from the Creation to the year 1146 A.D. The author composed this work between 1143 and 1147. The second work, *The Deeds of Frederick Barbarossa*, which reaches back to 1076 A.D., stops with the author's death in 1158. His secretary Rahewin added a continuation to the year 1160. The authenticity of several philosophical treatises attributed to Otto, also a history of Austria, is so dubious that scholars customarily ignore them. Otto's Latin is good, although not classical; his style is clear and flowing. Save for an occasional quotation from some classical author, it is for the most part unembellished with any rhetorical devices or display of erudition. In the prologue of the *Deeds,* which Otto addresses to his nephew Frederick, he does, however, reserve the privilege of rising above the humble level of historical narrative to a loftier height more suited to speculative thought.

> Nor will it be regarded as inconsistent with a work of this sort if the style is exalted, as the opportunity for a digression presents itself, from the simple diction of history to loftier — that is, to philosophic — heights. For this very practice is not at variance with the prerogative of the Roman empire: to intersperse the simpler with loftier affairs. For Lucan and Vergil and all the other writers of the City frequently elevated their style of expression so as to touch certain intimate secrets of philosophy, in recording not only historical events but even fables, whether modestly in

the manner of shepherds or peasants or in the more exalted style of princes and lords of the earth. For thus not only those whose pleasure consists in hearing the record of achievements, but also those to whom the refinement of the subtle reasoning affords greater delight, are attracted to read and to study such a work.[5]

One may ask how a bishop as actively engaged in diocesan and imperial affairs as Otto managed to find time to write history. The answer may lie in Otto's deep faith and his otherworldly philosophy of life. Of these he gives the reader constant reminders. There is no question that he found the spiritual message of the Cistercians powerfully attractive, as did so many other men of that period when the order enjoyed the height of its popularity. Otto joined the Cistercian community at Morimond, served as abbot, and returned to the abbey to die. He must always have considered himself a Cistercian, and to the true Cistercian all this world had to offer was the opportunity to prepare for the next. This conviction must have motivated Otto to write history. No theme appears more frequently in his *Two Cities,* his major work, than that of the transitory nature of this world with its miseries and the inevitability of death and judgment. So after writing of the destruction of those two powerful and prosperous cities of the Mediterranean, Carthage and Corinth, he muses:

The misfortunes that we have set down are sufficient to prove the mutability of human affairs. Hence since much has been said concerning the citizens of the world I think we should hurry on to the citizens of Christ and to Christian times. For I desire the reader to remember that, in accordance with my promise, I ought to record the conflicts of this world in order to demonstrate the wretchedness of changing events; that by pondering upon such events we may be led to pass by the eye of reason to the peace of Christ's kingdom and the joy that abides without end.[6]

Or again, after mentioning that the vestal virgin Popilia was buried alive for her unchastity, about the same time that Xerxes suffered disastrous defeat at the hands of the Greeks, he observes: "It is wearisome to weave together here the tangled network of woes, yet I wish to touch upon them briefly to point out the miseries of mortals."[7]

Otto believed that such miseries were precisely what God intended. In the prologue of the *Two Cities,* after listing the chief sources he had consulted in the preparation of this study, he declares:

In those writings the discerning reader will be able to find not so much histories as pitiful tragedies made up of mortal woes. We believe that this has come to pass by what is surely a wise and proper dispensation of the Creator, in order that, whereas men in their folly desire to cleave to earthly and transitory things, they may be frightened away from them by their own vicissitudes, if by nothing else, so as to be directed by the wretchedness of this fleeting life from the creature to a knowledge of the Creator.[8]

Otto was willing, withal, to satisfy the more conventional curiosity many individuals had about the past. "I have undertaken to speak of the Two Cities," he wrote, "that the studious and painstaking investigator may find a record of past happenings free from all obscurity."[9]

Otto declares it was also to deter ambitious men from making war that he was writing of past events. So he wrote of "wars and tottering kingdoms, not to arouse others to war by the example of those who considered that they had played the man, but to reveal the miseries in wars and in the various hazards of changing, unstable events."[10] Beyond this, the motive that has traditionally prompted men to write history appears also to have had his approval.

This, I think, has been the purpose of all who have written history before us: to extol the famous deeds of valiant men in order to incite the hearts of mankind to virtue, but to

veil in silence the dark doings of the base or, if they are
drawn into the light, by the telling to place them on record
to terrify the minds of those same mortals.[11]

In his dedication of the *Two Cities* to the emperor Frederick, who had requested a copy of the book, Otto addresses himself in a more personal manner to this question
of motivation.

> I have . . . obeyed your command willingly and gladly, so
> much the more devotedly as I regard it as thoroughly in
> accord with your royal preeminence that you desire to
> know what was done in olden times by kings and emperors,
> and to know this not only for the better protection of the
> state by arms, but also for its better molding by laws and
> statutes.

And he warns Frederick that since he was a king, these
words of the Bible had a direct application for him.

> Hear, ye kings, and understand, learn, ye judges of the
> ends of the earth: give ear, ye that have dominion over
> many peoples, and make your boast over multitudes of
> nations, because your power was given you by the Lord,
> and your strength by the Most High, who shall search out
> your works, and shall make inquisition of your counsels.[12]

Then Otto becomes more explicit concerning the motive
that led him to write the *Two Cities*, his major work. This
goal was to instruct Frederick and other rulers, first in the
performance of their day-to-day duties, next in the necessity to remember always their last end. In his present role
as emperor Frederick will find the *Two Cities* useful.

> The knowledge of history . . . will be proper and advanta-
> geous to Your Excellency, for thereby, considering the
> deeds of brave men and the strength and power of God,
> who changeth monarchs and giveth thrones to whomso-
> ever He will, and suffereth changes to come to pass, you
> shall live ever in His fear, and, advancing in prosperity,
> shall reign through many circling years.[13]

Still this life, even should the king conduct himself in a God-fearing manner, promises little happiness and much woe. For this reason he should never forget his inevitable end.

> Accordingly, let Your Nobility know that I wrote this history in bitterness of spirit, led thereto by the turbulence of that unsettled time which preceded your reign, and therefore I did not merely give events in their chronological order, but rather wove together in the manner of a tragedy, their sadder aspects, and so ended with a picture of unhappiness each and every division of the books even down to the seventh and the eighth. In the latter books the rest of souls and the double garment of the resurrection are shadowed forth.[14]

To turn now to an examination of Otto's qualifications as a writer of history, let us consider first the sources he drew upon for the information he presents. Their nature and scope will tell something about the breadth and objectivity of Otto's search and his concern over accuracy. Early in the prologue of the first book of the *Two Cities*, he informs the reader which earlier writers he had consulted, namely, "the famous works of Pompeius Trogus, Justin, Cornelius [Tacitus], Varro, Eusebius, Jerome, Orosius, Jordanes, and a great many others of our number, as well as of their array, whom it would take too long to enumerate."[15]

For the centuries nearer his own he relied upon the chronicle of Frutolf of Michelsberg (d. 1103) and its continuation to the year 1106 by Ekkehard of Aura, whom Otto may have known. And he made constant reference to such non-Christian writers as Suetonius and Josephus. Above all others he confessed his dependence upon the two leading "historians" of the early Middle Ages, Orosius and St. Augustine.

> In this work I follow most of all those illustrious lights of the Church, Augustine and Orosius, and have planned to

draw from their fountains what is pertinent to my theme
and my purpose. The one of these has discoursed most
keenly and eloquently on the origin and the progress of the
glorious City of God and its ordained limits, setting forth
how it has ever spread among the citizens of the world, and
showing which of its citizens or princes stood forth preemi-
nent in the various epochs of the princes or citizens of the
world. The other, in answer to those who, uttering vain
babblings, preferred the former times to Christian times,
has composed a very valuable history of the fluctuations
and wretched issues of human greatness, the wars and the
hazards of wars, and the shifting of thrones, from the foundation of the world down to his own time.[16]

Although the sources that Otto had at his disposal may
have been adequate for the preparation of a general history of mankind, the goal he set for himself was such that
he could ignore much of what had been written. His purpose was chiefly to instruct, less to inform, his readers.
His hope was to convince them of the misery of this world
and the fleeting character of the little happiness it might
vouchsafe its human sojourners. So as he moved forward
from his starting point in the Creation, he introduced and
elaborated upon those episodes that he believed would
contribute to his major theme while skirting or giving
short shrift to others that he felt carried no moral lessons.
He frequently concludes a topic abruptly with the observation that because other writers had fully covered the
matter, he saw no need to pursue it further. Even on the
events of the Roman Republic he will touch "only lightly
. . . because they have been related eloquently and at
length by many writers."[17]

Yet there are times when Otto introduces material the
reader finds difficult to justify either on the basis of its
general historical importance or its pertinence to the
higher theme of the *Two Cities.* Such is the episode concerning the Sicilian tyrant Phalaris. No doubt Otto found
the story interesting and must have hoped his reader

would likewise, and it does have a moral. He tells how Phalaris

> was tormenting innocent people with many varied forms of torture, a certain Perillus, a worker in bronze, desiring to please his prince and to offer him an instrument for his cruelty thoroughly suited to him, made a brazen bull in whose side he fitted a door, to the end that, when those to be tortured had been admitted by this door and were in agony from the fires set underneath the bull, they might appear to give voice not to the groan of a human being but to the bellowing of a beast. The tyrant graciously accepted this image, and placing its inventor himself inside it punished him with his own device.[18]

Once Otto begins writing about his own time he feels more secure in his role of historian. He appears to agree with those ancient writers who deemed it proper to leave the recording of events to contemporaries.

> For it is said to have been a custom of the ancients that those who had perceived with their senses the actual events as they took place should be the ones to write about them. Whence also it is customarily called "history" from *hysteron,* which in Greek signifies "to see." For everyone will be competent to speak more fully of the things which he has seen and heard. Being in need of no man's favor, he is not carried hither and thither in search of the truth, dubiously anxious and anxiously dubious. Truly, it is hard for a writer's mind to depend on another's judgment, as though incapable of making an investigation of its own.[19]

When Otto reached the year 1106, he announced with a measure of relief that he was now on his own, as it were. "Thus far we have set down extracts from the books of Orosius, of Eusebius, and of those who wrote after them, even to our own time. What follows, since it is still fresh in men's memories, we shall record as it has been related to us by credible men or seen and heard by ourselves."[20]

In the use of his historical sources Otto reveals a degree

of objectivity and prudence remarkable in medieval writers. If he appears to take some pride in the virtues of the Germans, as will be seen, it is too subtle to grate upon the reader's sensibilities – and he is not wholly oblivious of their deficiencies. He handles the delicate subject of church and state with an unusual degree of detachment. The observation with which he concludes his discussion of the manner in which the German emperor Otto I deposed Pope John XII illustrates his desire to remain neutral. He writes: "Whether all these things were done lawfully or otherwise it is not the purpose of the present work to say, for we have undertaken to tell, in writing, what happened, not to pass judgment on what happened."[21]

Otto observes a similar prudent objectivity when introducing contemporaries he happened to know. In his discussion of the process taken against Gilbert de la Porrées by Bernard of Clairvaux and other ecclesiastics he refuses to take sides. When Gilbert succeeded in the end in clearing himself of the charge of heresy, Otto comments: "Whether the aforesaid abbot of Clairvaux in consequence of the frailty of human weakness, being a mere man, was deceived in this matter, or the bishop, being a very learned gentleman, escaped the condemnation of the Church by shrewdly concealing his view, it is not our task to discuss or to decide."[22]

In his character as both bishop and royal vassal, Otto frequently found himself caught up in the controversy between those who pressed the superior rights of the church vis-à-vis the state and those who argued otherwise. One of the bases upon which the champions of the church rested their claims was the so-called Donation of Constantine. Historians since the fifteenth century have recognized the document as a forgery. In Otto's day many people accepted both its authenticity and validity, some accepted its authenticity but denied its force, and only a few denied its authenticity. Otto treads carefully when discussing the matter. He points out that once Constantine had extended toleration to the Christians, the emperor

> so greatly exalted the Roman Church that he handed over the imperial insignia to Saint Sylvester, pope of that city, and withdrew to Byzantium and there established the seat of his realm. This is why the Church of Rome claims that the Western realms are under its jurisdiction, on the ground that they had been transferred to it by Constantine, and in evidence thereof does not hesitate to exact tribute to this day – except from the two kingdoms of the Franks. But the advocates of the empire affirm that Constantine did not hand over his kingdom in this way to the Roman pontiffs, but out of reverence for the Lord accepted them as fathers – thinking of them as priests of the most high God – and consented that he and his successors should be blessed by them and sustained by the protection of their prayers. And to prove this they adduce the fact that Constantine himself, when he divided the kingdom among his sons, handed over the West to one, the East to the other; and thus Rome with the West fell by lot to Theodosius and to others in succession, not merely to heretics but also to religious princes. They say that never would so devout a ruler have left to his sons what he had previously handed over to the Church, nor would so Catholic an emperor as Theodosius have appropriated what was not his, if it belonged to the Church. To settle definitely all these matters is not the purpose of the present work.[23]

The reader will be curious how Otto, a bishop on the one hand and a grandson of a German king on the other, presents his version of the most memorable incident involving Germany and the papacy in the Middle Ages, that is, the clash between Pope Gregory VII and Henry IV. Otto writes as a historian. He holds himself to a factual description of what he believed actually happened.[24] If the principles that governed his pen as a historian did not rule out any evaluation of the incident, his wish not to offend either the ecclesiastical authorities or his relatives, among these his nephew the emperor Frederick I Barbarossa, would have recommended silence.

When, under Emperor Henry . . . the realm had seriously disintegrated and, as the majority of the nobles were in rebellion against their prince, almost the whole extent of the kingdom was being devastated by sword and flame, Gregory VII, who then held the pontificate in the city of Rome, determined to strike this emperor with the sword of excommunication, as one already deserted by his own followers. The novelty of this action aroused all the more indignation in the empire, because it had never before this time known a sentence of this kind to be pronounced against an emperor of the Romans. Therefore the emperor called together many bishops from Italy, Gaul, and Germany at Brixen, a city of Bavaria situated in the heart of the Pyrenees,[25] not far from the valley of Trent, and held a great council. When all had arrived, he complained bitterly of the injuries inflicted upon him by the Roman Church, namely, that without consulting him (who, as king and patrician, ought to be first at the election of the bishop of his city) the people of Rome had themselves chosen a pontiff, although many had been enthroned there by his father when he was emperor, seemingly without election. By this complaint the feelings of all could the more readily be turned against the Roman Church as not only the laity, inflamed by considerations of secular honor, but also the bishops, instigated by their clerics to whom marriage had recently been forbidden by the same pontiff, acceded to the wishes of the prince. Therefore, as all exclaimed that in their judgment the aforesaid election must be annulled, Guibert, archbishop of Ravenna, called Clement (or rather, Dement!)[26] was elected bishop of the City with the assent of the king, and Gregory VII, termed by them a false monk and a necromancer, was deposed . . . . After this, the king collected a large army and invaded Italy. Advancing as far as the City, he ejected Gregory, with the approbation of the Roman people, established Guibert there, and received from him the titles of emperor and Augustus. But the venerable priest, fleeing persecution, betook himself to the safer mountainous regions of Tuscany, to the land of Countess Matilda, who was a relative of the emperor. There he remained for some time, renewing the sentence of excommunication in letters which are extant in many places, and aroused the princes of the realm against their emperor. Then, entering Campania and Apulia, he withdrew to a city of the Normans who under the leadership of Robert Guiscard had recently invaded those provinces . . . . There he awaited the day of his death.[27]

Although Otto might trim his sails in the interest of prudence in matters as sensitive as the above, he was fully aware of his responsibilities as a historian to tell the truth. He says as much in a letter he addressed to Rainald of Dassel, Frederick I Barbarossa's chancellor. He asked Rainald to be sympathetic in his interpretation of certain matters set down in the *Two Cities* should these occasion the king any displeasure. For, as he writes,

the art of the historians has certain things to clear away and to avoid and others to select and arrange properly: for it avoids lies and selects the truth. Therefore let not your Discreet Highness be offended or (as I have said before) interpret the matter in an unfavorable light in the hearing of the emperor, if it shall appear that in our history certain matters have been spoken in criticism of his predecessors or ancestors, that the truth may be held in esteem, inasmuch as it is better to fall into the hands of men than to abandon the function of a historian by covering up a loathsome sight by colors that conceal the truth.[28]

This is a truly noble statement and worthy of the most courageous historians. It is possible that Otto himself did not always measure up to it. In the *Deeds*, for example, he omits mention of events during the years 1127–35 that did little honor to the house of Hohenstaufen.[29] Still he does this in the book he wrote specifically for his nephew Frederick Barbarossa, and only the most carping critic would protest his withholding information there that might have proved offensive. In general one would have to accept the substantial truth of Otto's statement that no one can "rightfully accuse me of falsehood in matters which—compared with the customs of the present time—will appear incredible, since down to the days still fresh in our memory I have recorded nothing save what I found in the writings of trustworthy men, and then only a few instances out of many."[30]

In keeping with that principle, Otto reveals some uneasiness on occasion concerning the reliability of certain information by adding a qualifying "they say" or "it is said." An illustration of such hesitation appears in his report regarding that legendary figure Prester John. A certain Syrian bishop had come to Antioch to discuss various matters with the patriarch, and while there he told

> that not many years before a certain John, a king and priest who dwells beyond Persia and Armenia in the uttermost East and, with all his people, is a Christian but a Nestorian, made war on the brother kings of the Persians and Medes, called Samiardi, and stormed Ekbatana (the seat of their kingdom) of which mention has been made above. When the aforesaid kings met him with an army composed of Persians, Medes and Assyrians a battle ensued which lasted for three days, since both parties were willing to die rather than turn in flight. Prester John, for so they are accustomed to call him, putting the Persians to flight with dreadful carnage finally emerged victorious. He said that after this victory the aforesaid John moved his army to the aid of the Church in Jerusalem, but that when he had reached the river Tigris and was unable to transport his army across that river by any device, he turned toward the north where, he had learned, this stream was frozen over. . . . It is said that he is a lineal descendant of the Magi, of whom mention is made in the Gospel, and that, ruling over the same peoples which they governed, he enjoys such great glory and wealth that he uses no scepter save one of emerald. Inflamed by the example of his fathers who came to adore Christ in his manger, he had

planned to go to Jerusalem but by the reason aforesaid he
was prevented – so men say.[31]

Otto displayed an ability to judge evidence with a critical eye in his description of the death of Tiemo, the archbishop of Salzburg. Although he accepted as authentic the
report of the prelate's martyrdom, he dismissed as false
some of the testimony relating to his death. The Byzantine emperor Alexius had captured the archbishop as he
was making his way through Asia Minor on the way to
Jerusalem and turned him over to the king of Memphis.
Here is Otto's account of the incident.

> The venerable bishop Tiemo . . . was ordered, as they say,
> to worship idols. Having asked for a respite [and secured
> it], he entered the shrine and, since he possessed most vig-
> orous strength of mind and body, broke to pieces the idols
> which he was to have worshipped, showing thereby that
> they were not gods but the work of men's hands. For this
> he was led forth and, after suffering exquisite torments
> and all sorts of torture, was crowned with glorious martyr-
> dom. That he suffered for his faith in Christ a most reliable
> tradition affirms, but that he demolished idols is difficult
> to believe because, as is well known, the Saracens univer-
> sally are worshippers of one God.[32]

Otto clearly appreciated that his sources, even when
willing to report truthfully, frequently gave different versions of the same incident, depending upon their loyalties
and prejudices. He cites the case of Celtic and Frankish
writers who recorded varying versions of what happened
following the death of Conrad I in 918. Their "conflicting
accounts," Otto explained, occurred because "the writers
extolled each his own state as much as he could." For his
part, he promised to keep to "a middle course in these
matters . . . and holding fast the thread of truth . . . [to]
strive by God's grace to turn aside neither to the right
hand nor to the left."[33]

That Otto shows less than complete objectivity in the

Deeds, which he addressed to his nephew Frederick I Barbarossa, is what one might expect of even the most scrupulous historian. His aim in this work, however, was undoubtedly as much that of instructing his nephew in his responsibilities as in informing him about the past. One may therefore assume that some of the encomia Otto bestowed upon Frederick were intended to encourage him in what he had done and to suggest the line of conduct he should pursue if he wished to continue in his uncle's – and God's – good graces. In the fall of 1154 Frederick led his army across the Alps into Italy. Due largely to the mountains, his army ran out of provisions near Verona, and the soldiers looted some of the shrines in the area. Otto gives this report of the matter.

> In short, the army, being unable on its passage through the mountain barriers to find things necessary for the support of life, on account of the barrenness of the country, while suffering great want (a thing that is always very grievous for troops) had violated certain holy places. To atone for this – although they seemed to have the aforesaid excuse of necessity – the king ordered a collection to be taken from the entire army. He decided that the not inconsiderable sum of money thus amassed should be taken back by certain holy men to the two bishops (of Trent, that is, and of Brixen) and divided among the various places of the saints which had suffered loss. Thus he provided nobly for the common good, fulfilling nobly a leader's task. For being about to enter upon very great undertakings, he decided that before all else he must placate the Ruler and Creator of all, without Whom nothing is well begun, nothing successfully completed, and that His wrath must be averted from his people.[34]

If Otto permits himself a measure of favoritism when writing about his nephew Frederick, he also yields to the animosity his family entertained toward the Wittelsbach clan, the traditional enemies of the Babenbergs. So he identified Otto, the count palatine, as "heir not unlike his treacherous and iniquitous father, and a man who surpasses in malice all his predecessors, even to the present day ceases not to persecute the church of God."[35] But such vituperation is rare with Otto. Perhaps the only other individual who suffered such denunciation was Arius, "the vilest of all men."[36] And, although Otto's condemnation of the Roman emperor Nero was equally harsh,[37] it was what all Christian and pagan writers reserved for that ruler.

The moderation Otto showed in general when writing of men he disliked or whose policies he opposed was matched by the detachment with which he spoke of his fellow Germans and members of his family. He never mentions himself except in passing. He gives in full the letter Pope Eugenius sent to Germany in which he attacked the German bishops, Otto included, for approving the action of King Conrad when he appointed his own man to the see of Magdeburg.[38] He tells with candor and frank disapproval of the tyrannical conduct of his brother Leopold, the margrave of Austria. Leopold "forcibly occupied" Bavaria and "had moved with an armed force as far as the Lech and there destroyed the strongholds of certain of his personal enemies, laid waste all the surrounding country and returned through our territories, doing great damage to our church."[39]

Otto is careful to avoid giving special prominence to his ancestors or to members of his family. The reader will have difficulty identifying the name of his father among those whose deaths he recorded for the years 1136–37.[40] One suspects that it was with some satisfaction, nevertheless, that Otto wrote of the victory that Hermann (Arminius), one of his "ancestors," won over the Romans in the Teutoberg forest in 9 A.D.

At that time Varus, while acting insolently and avariciously – as was the habit of the Romans – toward the vanquished, was annihilated by the Germans, together with three legions. Augustus is said to have taken this disaster to the Roman arms so to heart that he very frequently dashed his head against a wall and repeatedly said, in the extremity of his grief, "Quintilius Varus, give me back my legions." Suetonius records that this war between the Romans and Germans – a very serious and bitter contest, the greatest since the African wars – was waged for three years by fifteen legions. Hence we may infer how great was the strength of the aforesaid tribe of Germans, since at the time of the greatest power of the Roman Empire it wrought such great havoc with the Roman army.[41]

Otto's view of the universe and of man's place in it determined his interpretation, or philosophy, of history. His view was substantially the one St. Augustine set forth in the *City of God.* This in turn echoed the theme implicit in the Gospels, namely, that because men are God's creatures, God keeps their actions under control, at times immediately, more often permissively, as they move on their way to death and judgment. Not only are all men headed ineluctably in that direction, but so also are the universe and the course of history. Otto accepts the six ages Augustine proposed as dividing the different eras of history, that is, Age I, from Adam to the Flood; Age II, from the Flood to Abraham; Age III, from Abraham to David; Age IV, from David to the Exile; Age V, from the Exile to the Incarnation; Age VI, the age of grace. Otto agrees with Augustine in beginning the Sixth Age with Christ's birth, also in his conviction that this last age was already far spent and that the end of the material world was almost in sight. "For we who live in the closing days of that kingdom," he wrote, "are experiencing that which was foretold concerning it, and expect that what we have yet to fear will soon take place."[42]

Otto does not adopt the precise division of the six ages in terms of world empires, which Augustine favored, but prefers the modified version offered by Jerome. He writes:

I shall briefly explain the order in which this history proceeds, that, when this is known, the nature of the work may be the more readily apparent. That there were from the beginning of the world four principal kingdoms which stood out above all the rest, and that they are to endure unto the world's end, succeeding one another in accordance with the law of the universe, can be gathered in various ways, in particular from the vision of Daniel. I have therefore set down the rulers of these kingdoms, listed in chronological sequence: first the Assyrians, next (omitting the Chaldeans, whom the writers of history do not deign to include among the others) the Medes and the Persians, finally the Greeks and the Romans, and I have recorded their names down to the present emperor, speaking of the other kingdoms only incidentally, to make manifest the fluctuations of events.[43]

Otto pays less attention to these world empires than the above statement would lead the reader to believe. He also employs a technicality in order to maintain the accuracy of his position that the world would come to an end during the period of Roman rule. According to Otto, the Romans transferred their rule to the Greeks in Constantinople, who in turn handed it over to the Franks (and Germans) in the west.

Throughout the course of his major work, which he aptly entitled *The Chronicle or History of the Two Cities*, Otto continually appeals to Augustine's division of mankind into two groups or camps, the City of God and the City of Evil, or the Earth. In the prologue of the first book he announces this to be the compulsive factor that will guide him in his writing of universal history.

In pondering long and often in my heart upon the changes and vicissitudes of temporal affairs and their varied and irregular issues, even as I hold that a wise man ought by no means to cleave to the things of time, so I find that it is by the faculty of reason alone that one must escape and find release from them. For it is the part of a wise man not to be whirled about after the manner of a revolving wheel, but through the stability of his powers to be firmly fashioned as a thing foursquare. Accordingly, since things are changeable and can never be at rest, what man in his right mind will deny that the wise man ought, as I have said, to depart from them to that city which stays at rest and abides to all eternity? This is the City of God, the heavenly Jerusalem, for which the children of God sigh while they are set in this land of sojourn, oppressed by the turmoil of the things of time as if they were oppressed by the Babylonian captivity. For, inasmuch as there are two cities – the one of time, the other of eternity; the one of the earth, earthy, the other of heaven, heavenly; the one of the devil, the other of Christ – ecclesiastical writers have declared that the former is Babylon, the latter Jerusalem.[44]

In the first seven books of the *Two Cities* Otto concerns himself with the history of mankind from the Creation down to his own time. During this long period the two cities of God and the Devil were, and remained, intermingled because they were composed of both good and wicked people. The City of God began its earthly sojourn with Adam, but there soon appeared individuals among the Promised People who were not God-fearing men. And God also chose to place citizens of his city outside of Israel. In Old Testament times there were Jewish kings who were not members of the City of God, just as there have been unworthy popes since the Incarnation who were reprobates. In a narrow sense there has been but one city since the year 313 when Constantine extended toleration to the Christians, that is, the City of God, and from that year it is only this city that receives Otto's attention. Still in terms of individual men, both cities will continue to exist on the earth until the end of the world, until final judgment. Then, those who loved God will be permanently separated from the damned – the first to occupy the City of God, the latter the City of the Devil. Otto explains:

Furthermore, enough has been said above, I think, regarding the two cities: how one made progress, first by remaining hidden in the other until the coming of Christ, after that by advancing gradually to the time of Constantine. But after Constantine, when troubles from without had finally ceased, it began to be grievously troubled at the instigation of the devil by internal strife even to the time of the elder Theodosius; Arius was the author of this and the lords of the world, the Augusti, were his coadjutors. But from that time on, since not only all the people but also the emperors (except a few) were orthodox Catholics, I seem to myself to have composed a history not of two cities but virtually of one only, which I call the Church. For although the elect and the reprobate are in one household, yet I cannot call these cities two as I did above; I must call them properly but one – composite, however, as the grain is mixed with the chaff. Wherefore in the books that follow let us pursue the course of history which we have begun. Since not only emperors of the Romans but also other kings (kings of renowned realms) became Christians, inasmuch as the sound of the word God went out into all the earth and unto the ends of the world, the City of Earth was laid to rest and destined to be utterly exterminated in the end; hence our history is a history of the City of Christ, but that city, so long as it is in the land of sojourn, is "like unto a net, that was cast into the sea," containing the good and the bad. However, the faithless city of unbelieving Jews and Gentiles still remains, but, since nobler kingdoms have been won by our people, while these unbelieving Jews and Gentiles are insignificant not only in the sight of God but even in that of the world, hardly anything done by these unbelievers is found to be worthy of record or to be handed on to posterity.[45]

Despite the lofty title of Otto's principal work and the fame he has earned for his philosophy of history, he pays relatively little attention to the theme of the two cities in the course of his historical narrative. For the most part he restricts his speculating along that line to the prologues of the different books and to the brief observations with which he concludes these divisions. The above quotation is representative of the prologues; the following excerpt, which concludes Book Two, illustrates the manner in which he brings each such section to a close.

> At this point we are constrained to cry out against the wretchedness of life's vicissitudes. For lo! we see at what cost, not only to its enemies but even to its own citizens, the Roman Republic grew. For by alternating changes, after the manner of the sea – which is now uplifted by the increases that replenish it, now lowered by natural loss and waste – the republic of the Romans seemed now exalted to the heavens by oppressing nations and kingdoms with war and by subduing them; now in turn was thought to be going down again into the depths when assailed by those nations and kingdoms or overwhelmed by pestilence and sickness, and – what is more significant even than such matters – after they had arranged everything else well and had set it in fine order, they were miserably disemboweled by falling upon one another in internal civil strife. All these calamities springing out of unstable events and (so to speak) the daily deaths of mortal beings should have had the power to direct men to the true and abiding life of eternity. But as we have said above, when the city of the world was afflicted by these and like misfortunes the rising of the true Light was drawing nigh as though following the darkness of murky night. And so, since after hurrying over the instances of fluctuating disasters that affected the Medes and the Persians, as well as the Greeks and the Romans, we are now approaching the coming of Him, who, being truly the peacemaker, pacified all things "whether things upon the earth, or things in the heavens," even Christ Jesus himself, let us set an end to this second book, inasmuch as we are hastening on to speak of that peace which was secured to the whole world under Augustus at the coming of Christ's nativity.[46]

In Book Eight Otto brings to conclusion both his *Two Cities* and the contest between the two cities as well. These two cities had passed through their earlier stages, that before grace and that during the period of grace. Now comes the third stage when the two will be permanently separated and continue in that manner through eternity, one wholly good, the other wholly evil. But before this comes to pass Anti-Christ will appear who will bring with him violent persecution for the purpose of chastening the faithful. The Anti-Christ is the devil. Being a consummate hypocrite, he will be able to deceive many people, especially many Jews, but in time he will be slain. Then will follow "a time of repentance ... a time whose length is hidden from all mortals."

> Then when all those things which have been foretold shall have been brought to completion, and strange signs shall have been revealed in the sun, the moon, the stars and the sea – when all men shall be fainting for fear, and for expectation of the things which are to come upon the whole world – then the destruction of the evil city, and the increase of the City of Christ, and the day of the Lord are at hand, in accordance with the word of truth which, sweetly consoling God's own people, says: "When ye see these things coming to pass, know ye that the kingdom of God is nigh."[47]

Few theologians, no historians, would dare to carry their narrative to the end of time. Yet Otto presumes to go even beyond time, although with admitted diffidence. He confesses his lack of competency to speak of eternity, but he feels this is incumbent upon him, and with God's grace he will make an attempt to look at the hereafter. So he discusses the resurrection of the dead and their final judgment, which will be swift.

> It is needless to say how swiftly this judgment will be accomplished when all subterfuges and all sophistry, such as we are accustomed to endure in court trials in this world, shall be swept away by the clear perception of the judge and the keen insight of the searcher of reigns and of hearts. In this world of ours where, in accordance with court proce-

dure, in the case of an accused person the prosecutor brings suit, the advocate makes a defense, the witness endeavors to convince, the judge, since he is ignorant of the hearts of men, because he is but mortal, is often deceived and frequently a criminal who ought to be condemned is acquitted. Because this cannot happen in the court where each man's own conscience accuses or defends him, we must believe that the judgment in that court is consummated with a swiftness beyond belief.[48]

All that now remains to be said, Otto explains, is "to inquire concerning the end of both cities, the end which follows the resurrection and judgment." The reprobate will be buried in hell, the blessed welcomed to the glories of heaven to share there the happiness of the angels. For all his ambitious speculation concerning the kind of eternity which the incomprehensible deity has prepared, Otto closes on a humble note. He acknowledges that his work is not definitive, and, addressing himself to his reader (Frederick), he concludes:

It will be your task to supplement what has been said insufficiently, to correct what has been said imperfectly, to prune away the superfluous and as, laden with sins, I struggle in this wide sea of the world, to aid me by the solace of your prayers.[49]

If there persists any doubt by whose will the world turns, this is dispelled here in Book Eight where God's word brings an end to all things. Of this fundamental fact of life Otto keeps reminding the reader throughout the course of the *Two Cities*. He discerns the working of divine providence as a constant factor in all ages, whether contemporary or ancient, Christian or pagan. One may assume that Otto considered it to be his responsibility as a historian to emphasize this constant operation of the divine will. Only in thus serving a spiritual need can the reading and writing of history justify themselves. For this reason, and, of course, to press the theme of the *Two*

Cities, Otto opens and closes each of the eight books with
reflections upon the hidden meaning of events and their
ultimate application to the eternal plan. All things that
happen, all men who live, fit into God's plan of salvation.
Even for events that might appear to fall outside the concern of God, Otto manages to find a place. "I think," he
writes,

> it must be ascribed not to mere accident, but to the provi-
> dence of God who divideth the light from the darkness,
> that at about the time of the going out of the children of
> Israel from Egypt – or, according to others, during the
> time of their sojourn in the land of promise – the world
> seethed with new and unheard-of crimes (as I have just
> related). For even as we read that Herod, a king of this
> world, was troubled when Christ, the King of Heaven, was
> born, so quite naturally, when the Lord descended into
> Egypt and led his people forth from that country, the devil
> was disturbed, and incited to iniquitous ventures and most
> vile deeds the city that had been entrusted to him. For the
> same reason to this day we frequently see the world shaken
> and disturbed when the Lord calls his servants from the
> Egypt of the world to his own kingdom. For a like cause
> therefore, such events took place at a time of the entrance
> of the people of God into the land of promise and of the
> ejection of the tribes that had dwelt there.[50]

Otto attributes the final decisive victory of the Romans
over Carthage to the working of divine providence. "What
the Romans attributed to their gods as defenders of the
City," he declares, "that we indeed may ascribe to the secret and awful judgments of God, without whose nod not a
leaf falls to the ground."[51] Even more manifest was the
hand of God in the emergence of Constantine and his success in eliminating other contenders for the imperial
throne.

> When therefore the Lord willed to exalt His Church, which
> had been exhausted by many trials and persecutions, He
> chose, in preference to all others, a personage through

whom He might the more readily accomplish this exalta-
tion. Accordingly He commissioned the emperor of the
Romans, to whom the whole world at that time paid honor,
to effect it. . . . And that you may know that all this was
brought to pass not by chance, as haphazard, but through
the profound and righteous judgments of God, behold a
man who but yesterday was skulking in hiding and fleeing
from every man (of even the lowest condition) become
speedily of so great authority that he rules kings, judges
kings; behold him held in so great veneration by the world
that the lords of the earth come to bow before him and
worship the soles of his feet as he sits upon the throne.[52]

In the *Deeds* Otto accords divine providence the same
positive role in human affairs as he does in the *Two Cities.*
After describing how Conrad III and his large host set out
from Nuremberg in 1147 on the Second Crusade, passed
on to Regensburg, then down the Danube, he tells of the
tragic storm that struck the crusading army near the
town of Cherevach (Catalca). The army had finished pitch-
ing its tents—"never had a pleasanter camp," Otto
writes—when a violent storm arose that brought about
the loss of many lives and horses and the destruction of
much equipment.

Suddenly such a tempestuous storm of rain and wind en-
sued that it caused the tents to sway, tore them loose, and
dashed them violently to the ground, arousing us from our
beds, to which we had retired after matins. A tumult arose,
filling all the air round about. For the little stream—
whether from the backwash of the neighboring sea or the
downpour of rain or a cloudburst betokening the vengeance of the Majesty on high is uncertain—had swollen so
greatly and in consequence of its swollen waters had so
overflowed beyond its custom that it covered the entire
cantonment. What were we to do? Considering this a divine punishment rather than a natural inundation, we were
the more dismayed. Nevertheless, we hurried out to our
powerful steeds, each one seeking to cross the river as best
he could. You might have seen some swimming, some

clinging to horses, some ignominiously hauled along by ropes to escape the danger, some dashing in disorder into the river and sinking because they were heedlessly entangled with others. A great many, believing they could wade across, were swept away by the rush of the river, injured by the rocks, and, swallowed up by the force of the eddies, lost their lives in the river. Some, who had not learned how to swim, laid hold of those who were swimming and clung to them in order that they might escape and exhausted them, so hampered, until they ceased the motions of their arms and, flat on their backs, both alike were submerged and drowned.

On the morning after the tragedy,

when the waters had subsided and the face of the land appeared, all of us being scattered here and there, you might have obtained as sad a picture of our encampment as on the preceding day you could have seen it glad. So that, not inappropriately, it appeared clearer than light how great is the power of the high Deity, and how human happiness is unstable and passes quickly.[53]

Still Otto does not present the working of divine providence as a kind of blind, inexorable force that punishes and rewards, or simply makes its presence known to convince men of the brevity of life and the importance of eternity. God permits suffering only because of man's sins, and he is always ready to hold back his anger when man repents or when the prayers of the faithful interpose themselves, particularly the petitions and sacrifices of holy men. Thus of the pillaging in France that accompanied the hostilities between Louis VII and Theobald, count of Blois, Otto writes, "that if peace had not recently been restored through the merits, the prayers and the counsel of the holy men who dwell there the land would, it is believed, have been utterly ruined."[54]

That a man with Otto's reverence for the omnipotence of God and the pervasiveness of the divine will believed in miracles is not surprising. But God gave such manifest demonstrations of his power only rarely, Otto appears to have believed. The Almighty preferred to permit events to take their natural course in accordance with the laws he had built into the universe. For this reason Otto finds space for very few miracles. Several of these he credits to the saint Corbinian, who had himself been a bishop of Freising. Of Corbinian Otto writes:

> It is told of him that on one occasion, when he was on his way to Rome to satisfy the needs of his church, a bear killed his pack horse. The man of God caught the bear, placed his packsaddle upon the beast, and ordered him to carry it; and the word of the Lord, rendered "sharper than any sword," compelled that wild animal to obey the behests of the man of God. On that same journey, while his companions were suffering from hunger in a desert place, an eagle suddenly brought them a fish. All that were present ate of the fish and were, in consequence, both amazingly refreshed and greatly exalted.[55]

What was Otto's position concerning pagan myths? It seems he was willing to grant such legends a basis in fact, although he dismissed all preternatural elements in these stories except in so far as they might have been the work of demons. The manner in which Otto handles the story of Romulus and Remus, a favorite with the early Romans, illustrates his general attitude toward such legends. He tells how after Amulius had succeeded Procas as king of Italy, his brother Numitor discovered his own daughter Rhea Silvia, although a vestal virgin, had become the mother of twin boys. He had them both thrown into the Tiber. Otto writes:

> These are the twin brothers Remus and Romulus, founders and builders of the city that was destined to be the capital of the world. The writers of Rome, assuming that Rome was destined to rule the whole world by martial prowess, claim that they were also the sons of Mars, and in proof of

this assert that they were nursed and nurtured, contrary to nature, by a she-wolf – the beasts, at any rate, of Mars. But whether they were really nourished by a wolf, as those writers say, or (as others have it) by some harlot or other called "Wolf" on account of her vile manner of living – as we call the houses of such women *lupanaria,* after that same word, *lupa,* wolf – is no concern of mine. I merely make this statement, that they were the sons not of Mars but of some man and, according to certain reliable authorities, a priestess.[56]

Otto suggests that the stories about Odysseus, who had ten years of spectacular adventures before finally returning to his faithful Penelope in Ithaca, may simply have been legends or their incredible aspects the work of demons. "Whether they (the Greeks and Romans) invented all these stories out of love for their gods," he writes, "or such things can really be brought to pass by the mocking action of demons and certain hidden forces of nature, does not concern the present work."[57]

A subject to which Otto kept adverting in both the *Two Cities* and the *Deeds* was the relationship between church and state. For this he had good reason. As both bishop and royal vassal, he found himself in the most sensitive of all positions in the perennial controversy that had been born almost the moment Constantine granted Christians toleration. A circumstance that made Otto's position even more delicate was that his nephew Frederick I Barbarossa was the Holy Roman emperor, and as it proved, both an unusually ambitious and able monarch. Although Frederick's ambitions had netted him significant successes in Germany in improving his position vis-à-vis the church, without greatly annoying the advocates of ecclesiastical supremacy, it was his trips to Italy and his actions there that brought him into direct conflict with the pope, the head of the church. The initial meeting between pope and emperor went reasonably well, and Otto is happy to provide his reader an illustration of the harmonious manner the two rulers of church and state should deal with one another. The setting was Frederick's first expedition to Italy when he had resolved one of Pope Adrian IV's most vexing problems by seizing Arnold of Brescia and having him executed.

> Now on his way to the City the king encamped near Viterbo. Thither came the Roman pope, Hadrian, with his cardinals, and was received with the honor due to his office. He was given a deferential hearing as he uttered bitter complaints against his people. For the aforesaid people, since their endeavor to reinstate the order of senators, in their rash daring did not shrink from inflicting many outrages on their popes. There was this additional aggravation of their seditious conduct, that a certain Arnold of Brescia, of whom mention has been made above, under guise of religion and – to use the words of the Gospel – acting as wolf in sheep's clothing, entered the City, inflamed to violence the minds of the simple people by his exceedingly seductive doctrines, and induced – nay, rather seduced – a countless throng to espouse that cause.[58]

Otto next introduces a sketch of Arnold's career, together with a summary of his "revolutionary" views that had helped inspire the revolt leading to Pope Adrian's flight from the city. But Arnold's foes, conservative elements among the hierarchy and aristocracy for the most part, eventually succeeded in capturing Arnold with the assistance of Frederick, after which he was tried and executed. Otto continues his account.

> But that my pen may come back to the topic whence it has digressed, after the supreme rulers of the world had been united amid their retinue, they advanced together for several days, and pleasant converse was exchanged as between a spiritual father and his son. Both ecclesiastical and secular matters were discussed, as though a single state had been created from two princely courts.[59]

As it proved, this spirit of cooperation between pope and

emperor did not long endure, and it was fortunate for Otto that he terminated his account of the *Deeds* before real trouble developed.

In the prologue to Book IV of the *Two Cities* Otto discusses the problem of church-state relations at some length. He notes the position of the one group that insisted the church possessed the two swords "read about in the story of the passion of the Lord" (Luke, 22.38). As they interpreted this biblical passage it justified the priestly order's employing both spiritual and secular weapons in carrying out its duties, even to the prejudice of the civil authorities. The opposing group argued, also quoting the Bible, that Peter had used but one sword (John, 18.10), and on the basis of this scriptural reference maintained that the church lacked the right to issue orders to civil authorities in what were considered secular matters.

> Accordingly, just as it is not permissible for the person who bears the material sword to deal with those things that are spiritual, so it is not fitting that the other should usurp those powers which are not properly his. Men adduce many passages of Scripture to establish what I have just said. In fact they adduce the example of our Lord himself and of the saints, as for instance the well-known gospel command: "Render unto Caesar the things that are Caesar's, and unto God the things that are God's."[60]

Still Otto does not leave the matter here where the advocates of the supremacy of the state would have preferred. He declares that God surely invested his church with royal powers befitting such a sublime institution, and he notes that holy men, including popes Sylvester and Gregory the Great, and St. Boniface, the "Apostle of Germany" as well, all employed powers outside the strictly spiritual. Then he gives his position.

> I admit that I am absolutely ignorant whether the exaltation of His Church which is so clearly visible today pleases God more than its former humiliation pleased Him. In-

deed, that former state seems to have been better, this present condition more fortunate. However, I agree with the holy Roman Church, which, I doubt not, was built upon a firm rock, and I believe that what she believes must be believed and that what she possesses can legitimately be possessed.[61]

He nevertheless confesses his inability to speak with complete confidence about so difficult a matter, and he leaves his reader, more specifically Frederick, with the reminder that the question remained unresolved. Inasmuch as he seems to have favored the champions of ecclesiastical supremacy, this was being prudent. He writes:

Let what has been said concerning the righteousness of the priesthood and of the kingship suffice. But if anyone wishes to reason about it more subtly and profoundly, he will by no means submit to having the matter prejudged by me.[62]

To evaluate Otto of Freising as a historian is no simple matter. His two works are of so diverse a character. In the *Two Cities* he assumes the role of a moralist. His aim there is to convince his reader, on the basis of history, that life is brief and filled with uncertainty and misery. Yet these "evils" are permitted by a loving God for the purpose of convincing men to pay less attention to the short pleasures of this life and more to the permanent values of eternity. Otto's aim was "to compose a history whereby through God's favor I might display the miseries of the citizens of Babylon and also the glory of the kingdom of Christ to which the citizens of Jerusalem are to look forward with hope."[63] In the *Deeds* Otto assumes the garb of a chronicler, although not wholly putting behind him the theme of the *Two Cities*. Thus he observes in closing his description of the terrible storm that wrecked the crusaders' camp near Constantinople, "how human happiness is unstable and passes quickly."

Otto showed no concern for secular history as such, nor

did he write to entertain, even though he appreciated the importance of introducing interesting material in the hope of holding his reader's attention. The episode concerning Perillus and the bronze bull would fall into this latter category. True, this story did contain a moral, as was the case with that concerning Regulus, one of the Roman heroes during the Punic Wars.[64] Otto must have felt his readers would enjoy reading about Regulus, although if pressed as to why he included the story he would probably have justified it on the basis of the moral it taught, that a person must be true to his word. He writes:

> Do you see in how many ways we are incited in these words to follow a pattern of endurance and through love of virtue to despise death and pain? For what else is the declaration that it is characteristic of valor to fear nothing, to hold all things in contempt, and the fact that neither love of country nor love of his dear ones or even torture, the racking of his body, diverted Regulus from his promise – what else is this than contempt for the present world, renunciation of parents, of possessions, and finally of one's very own self.[65]

The space Otto devotes to Regulus points up the leading consideration that determined the kind of material he selected for the *Two Cities*. While he must furnish the reader enough general information about the past to qualify as a writer of universal history, the material he selects is rarely without its moral. For this reason he moves with relative speed through ancient history from the Creation to the Incarnation, from which point the rise of Christianity provides him many more opportunities for moralizing. At first glance the nearly four pages he devotes to Alexander the Great appear excessive. What explains this amount of attention is that Orosius, upon whom Otto depended for his information, devotes that conqueror twice as much space. Furthermore, it is significant that both Orosius and Otto capitalize on the early death of this world conqueror, presumably at the hands of a treacherous attendant who gave him poison, by expatiating upon the miserable lot of us mortals.

In the *Deeds*, where Otto was under no compulsion to moralize, he felt free to elaborate upon any incident he might find interesting. This is what most medieval chroniclers were apt to do. Otto writes how Roger II of Sicily sent a fleet of "triremes and biremes (which are now ordinarily called galleys or *sagitteae*) and other vessels carrying war equipment" against Greece. After the fleet had captured a number of cities, they found Corfu so powerful that they had to resort "to craft and trickery."

> Accordingly, having sent ahead (as the story goes) certain men to pretend that they were bringing a corpse for burial — for there is in the aforesaid stronghold a congregation of clerics or monks, as is customary among the Greeks — they burst into the town, seized the fortress, and, ejecting the Greeks, stationed their garrisons there. Next, advancing into the interior of Greece, they took by storm Corinth, Thebes, and Athens, renowned for their ancient glory. There they carried off a great amount of booty and, as an insult to the emperor and in compliment to their own prince, they led away captive even the workmen who are accustomed to weave silken goods. Establishing them in Palermo, the metropolis of Sicily, Roger bade them teach his craftsmen the art of silk weaving. Thenceforth that art, previously practiced only by the Greeks among Christian nations, began to be accessible to the genius of Rome.[66]

Otto showed as much ability to judge past information critically as did any of his medieval contemporaries. That he accepted the existence of angels, demons, and the supernatural in general is what the modern reader must expect of any medieval writer. But his approach to ancient myths affords an excellent illustration of his reasonable approach to the preternatural. As in the case of the Greek hero Odysseus, he divested such stories of their supernatural overtones and sought to explain their origin in human terms. He must have been among the few who rejected the authenticity of the story concerning Emperor Constantine's leprosy. This disease was supposed to have prompted the grateful Constantine to relinquish control of the west to Pope Sylvester when he found himself miraculously cleansed. Otto writes: "what we read in the Life of Saint Sylvester about his leprosy and his conversion is seen to be apocryphal."[67]

Otto's record on the score of that prime canon that requires historians to tell the truth would be above question except for a tendency to laud Frederick in the *Deeds* and to withhold information Frederick, his nephew, might find disagreeable. His position on the investiture controversy between church and state, wherein he frankly found something to be said for both sides, does him credit. Although he appears to have sided with his nephew over the appointment to the see of Magdeburg,[68] he leaves the impression in the end that the church's ascendancy in his day must have been what God wanted.

Unusual for a medieval chronicler of the twelfth century was Otto's appreciation of natural beauty. Time and again he breaks his narrative to make some observation about the beauty of the topography. When Conrad III set out on his Crusade, "the rigor of the winter cold had been dispelled, as flowers and plants came forth from the earth's bosom under the gracious showers of spring and green meadows smiled upon the world, making glad the face of the earth."[69] He also described less attractive scenes, such as that after the making of peace between Frederick and Tortona. The citizens, long under siege and suffering, finally made their way out of the city. The "wretched townsmen . . . came forth . . . from the pitiful prison house of the fortress to the freedom of the mild spring air, by their deathly pallor resembling corpses coming from their tombs."[70]

Few writers of so early a period attempt to portray character, and Otto does so only rarely. But the reader is able to form a mental image of the kind of man Abelard must have been, at least in the eyes of Otto, from that Otto has to say.

> This Peter [Abelard] . . . from an early age had been de-
> voted to literary studies and other trifles, but was so con-
> ceited and had such confidence in his own intellectual
> power that he would scarcely so demean himself as to de-
> scend from the heights of his own mind to listen to his
> teachers. . . . Then he became a teacher and went to Paris,
> showing great capacity by his originality in discovering
> matters not only of importance for philosophy but also
> conducive to social amusements and pastimes.[71]

If this concluding observation refers to Abelard's affair with Heloise, it is the only occasion when Otto waxes sarcastic.

A final glance at the historical value of Otto's two works is apt to be puzzling. Of the two, the *Deeds* is more useful to the modern historian, the *Two Cities* the more important. The *Deeds* has been called the best biographical study of the twelfth century, which means less than it suggests – the Middle Ages produced few studies of this kind. Yet the *Deeds* does contain valuable information about Frederick Barbarossa and his reign, as well as important asides concerning such significant figures as Arnold of Brescia, Peter Abelard, and Gilbert de la Porrée. And perhaps nowhere else can the modern historian discover more convincing evidence to help him gauge the impact of rising scholasticism. At one point in the *Deeds*, for example, when Otto is writing of the examination of Gilbert de la Porrée, he introduces a four-page discussion of his own for the purpose of clarifying the problem of universals as it applied to the Trinity.

Had Otto written only the *Deeds* he would receive little more than mention among other writers of his century. It is the *Two Cities* that gives him prominence and qualifies him for membership in that select circle of philosophers of history. Without doubt the *Two Cities* represents the most balanced story of mankind in which history is presented as a record of what nations and individual men have done on their miserable march toward eternity, with God looking on and now and then interposing his divine will. Of pure historical information the scholar will find little except in the sixth and seventh books, which deal with France and Germany in the period before Otto. The book does confirm the persistence of the theme of St. Augustine's *City of God*, also the ability of Western Europe to produce prelates in the twelfth century who were dedicated to both learning and to their spiritual responsibilities. To characterize Otto as a philosopher of history may be an overstatement. One must grant him, however, the distinction of being the most reflective writer of history during the whole of the High Middle Ages.

CHAPTER 5

Matthew Paris

L ITTLE OF A PERSONAL nature is known about Matthew
Paris, the best known of English chroniclers. Because
he entered the monastery of St. Albans in 1217, probably
at the age of seventeen, one may assume he was born
around the year 1200. But where he was born and to what
social class, no one ventures to guess. Even the Paris in his
name is puzzling; it may have been a patronymic. His
attendance at the university of Paris, at any rate, is ruled
out for lack of any reference in his writings to his having
been there, nor would anyone suggest the word Paris be-
spoke his love of the French. For his neighbors across the
channel he harbored a dislike as positive as that he entertained for the Greeks.

Until the year 1247 when Matthew visited Westminster
Abbey, he appears to have lived a cloistered life at St.
Albans. He probably made the acquaintance of different
English cities and monasteries during these early years,
although only hints of this remain in his writings. Some
time before 1236 he became the assistant of Roger of Wendover, the chronicler of the abbey, for it was in that year,

the year of Roger's death, that he assumed his superior's responsibilities. His new duties probably kept him close to St. Albans for the remainder of his life except for occasional visits to London and other neighboring communities. For one who revealed such great interest in news from the continent, it is strange that he made but one trip outside of England and that, on his own admission, "unwillingly."[1] In 1246 King Haakon IV of Norway sought his good services for the abbey of St. Benet Holm on the island of Nidarholm in Norway, which was in financial difficulties with the money-lenders (Cahorsins) of London. Why Haakon enlisted Matthew's aid is not clear, but the chronicler must have handled the matter successfully. Two years later, in 1248, when the abbey again found itself in difficulties, this time with its archbishop, it requested that Matthew be sent to give it advice, a request that occasioned Matthew's solitary trip to a foreign land. One circumstance that attended this visit deserves comment — the letter that Louis IX of France had Matthew take to Norway in an effort to induce Haakon to join his crusade. That Matthew was the bearer of this letter says something about the nature and variety of his associations, considerations of prime importance to a medieval chronicler.

Beyond these few facts, little is known about Matthew's life. Even the year of his death remains uncertain, although scholars place it in 1259 because his chronicle comes to an abrupt halt in May of that year. Following his last entry in the manuscript there appears the announcement by Matthew's successor — in his modesty this monk withholds his name as unworthy of mention with that of "so great a predecessor" — that the famous chronicler had completed his work. Immediately below this announcement one of his fellow monks sketched a likeness of Matthew on his deathbed and added the brief notice *Hic obit Matheus Parisiensis.*[2]

The period from 1236, when Matthew took up the task of chronicler, until 1259 when he died, were busy and productive years. His writing fills the greater part of twelve volumes in the *Rolls Series*.[3] Of the original manuscripts the majority are in his own hand. Many of these are decorated with sketches and illustrations, in all probability Matthew's own work. These pictorial representations include shields, swords, crossbows, mitres, croziers, as well as more ambitious subjects such as the siege of Damietta and an elephant, with a man to furnish scale. He placed these sketches in the margins to give point to his narrative (an inverted mitre and crozier to mark the death of a bishop, for example). It may be no exaggeration to say that Matthew's illustrations entitle him to a place in the history of medieval painting, his maps to a place in the history of cartography, and his shields and coats of arms to a mention in the history of the science of heraldry.

The products of Matthew's prolific pen include the *Chronica Majora*, which was his *opus magnum*, the *Historia Anglorum* (an abridged version of the *Chronica Majora* with most of the matter omitted not directly concerned with England), the *Abbrevatio Chronicorum* (an abridgment of the *Historia Anglorum*), the *Liber Additamentorum* (a collection of documents to which he makes reference in the *Chronica Majora*), the *Gesta Abbatum* (a sketch of the history of St. Albans through the lives of its abbots), the *Vitae Offarum* (the lives of the two Offas whose names were associated with the founding of the abbey), the *Flores Historiarum* (a work once ascribed to a Matthew of Westminster), and a genealogical chronicle of the kings of England beginning with Alfred.

The *Flores Historiarum* appears to be in Matthew's own hand from 1241 to 1249, from 1249 in those of other scribes. While it is based on the *Chronica Majora*, its lively tone suggests that the author intended it to serve as a popular version of the larger work. Matthew Paris also produced some hagiography including a life of Stephen Langton. Some controversy continues over the authenticity of several of these writings.

Matthew Paris's principal work, the *Chronica Majora,* opens with the *Flores Historiarum* of Roger of Wendover as slightly revised by Matthew, after which his own chronicle follows as a continuation from the year 1236. (The *Flores* begins with the Creation.) Why Matthew undertook to make sundry revisions in Roger's narrative before embarking on his own narrative is not known. Because his revisions went beyond the correction of errors, he no doubt believed his changes would make for a more balanced and informative account. (Matthew made errors of his own, however, in the process of correcting Roger's.) He introduced stylistic changes to add spark to the narrative. To further its appeal, at least in his judgment, he interpolated words, even entire passages, which would leave the reader better informed about the events of the past. These interpolations also served to make it evident that the activities were the work of individuals, some virtuous, most of them sinners!

The following passages will demonstrate Matthew's approach in his emendation of Roger's chronicle. Roger had recorded in a wholly impersonal manner how Henry III returned to England in the fall of 1230 after arranging for the defense of Poitou. To this bland statement Matthew supplied the additional information that Henry had done so "after having expended an enormous amount of money and having suffered the loss of an innumerable number of men, either dead or wasted away by disease and hunger or reduced to abject poverty."[4] A second example of Matthew's editing introduces the pope, who with Henry III shared the dubious distinction of frequently experiencing the venom in Matthew's pen. Roger of Wendover noted without comment in his annal for 1230 that John of Brienne had fled to France. To this simple statement Matthew appended the observation that John had done so "with his mercenaries whom the pope enriched with ecclesiastical plunder and honored with booty taken whencesoever from the poor he had captured."[5]

Once Matthew reached the annal for 1236 he brought an end to his revision of Roger's chronicle and commenced his own account. It appears he had initially planned to terminate his work with the annal for 1250, then changed his mind and continued his narrative to May 1259. Meantime as he continued with his own writing he stole odd hours to review what he had already written to correct errors and to clarify obscure passages. That he should have wished to improve his work in this fashion is understandable, particularly since his chronicle remained in his possession and invited polishing.

What was unusual, however, was that Matthew's emendations did not stop with correcting errors and stylistic infelicities. They extended in several dozen instances to softening the sharp language of the original. Most frequently what was modified was the asperity of the language he had employed in the original account, when castigating Henry III for his tyrannical exactions, for example, or the papacy for its venality. One of the most striking illustrations of the manner in which Matthew altered his earlier language in the process of emending the original narrative is furnished by these two passages concerning the friars. The chronicler wasted no love on the mendicant orders. One of the first passages in which he expressed his views of the friars reads as follows:

> At this time the Dominicans and Franciscans applied themselves diligently to their preaching which was now lucrative, and worked industriously for the success of the crusade. They preached and harangued until they were hoarse, then proceeded to sign with the cross people of all ages, sex, or condition, regardless of their health. But the following day, or even immediately thereafter, they took back for a price the cross the people had accepted and released from their vows those who had promised to go.

The money they deposited in the treasury of some influential person. All of which appeared improper and ridiculous to simple souls, and the devotion of many people cooled since as sheep they had been sold for their fleeces.[6]

Some years later Matthew Paris pasted over the first account, replacing it with a statement concerning the activities of these same friars. It reads quite differently:

At this time the Dominicans and Franciscans exerted themselves, as did others who were trained and learned in the art of preaching, and produced manifold fruit by their preaching and sowing useful seed in the field of the Lord. And lest any faithful Christian be prevented in any way from gaining the indulgence which they had promised those who took up the cross on this crusade, they graciously accepted a redemption in accordance with each person's means, so that by virtue of the immense beneficence of God a ready willingness might be judged as worthy as the act itself. For they concluded that women, children, the sick, and even poor and unarmed people would accomplish little against the multitude of the infidels.[7]

Matthew's task of expurgation, if this is not too strong a term to use, appears to have been still under way when the chronicler died. One can only wonder whether he modified the language of the earlier narrative under pressure from his superiors, because he had changed his opinion and felt his original statements incorrect, or because he judged them simply in bad taste and imprudent. A probable explanation is that as he grew older he realized, in rereading his narrative, how harshly he had expressed himself on occasion, not an uncommon experience with writers who write with strong feeling. Equally possible is the explanation that his own subsequent experience, such as greater acquaintance with the friars, caused him to alter earlier views that he had based on reports from prejudiced men.

In the task of simply reporting information, as opposed to the role of analyst that Matthew Paris ordinarily es-

chewed, no writer rises above the sources of his information. For this reason the first consideration pertinent to an
evaluation of Matthew as a chronicler raises the matter of
these sources. Surely a common question readers of his
work ask is how could a cloistered monk have attempted
anything more ambitious than a simple recording of
events that directly affected his monastery or took place
in its immediate vicinity? That Matthew earned an envi-
able reputation as a chronicler of European history renders the question of his information all the more intrigu-
ing.

Undoubtedly a large portion of the information that
Matthew recorded in his chronicles came to him by way of
visitors who put up at the abbey. From the point of view of
the chronicler, St. Albans' location about a day's journey
on the road leading to the north and northwest of London
could not have been more advantageous. In an age when
inns were few, many people availed themselves of the abbey's hospitality. Matthew is himself the authority for the
statement that the stables the abbey reserved for guests
could accommodate three hundred horses. The poor and
the pilgrim came on foot.

The most distinguished visitor to drop in at St. Albans
was King Henry III. No fewer than nine times, as noted in
Matthew's chronicle, did the king stay at the abbey, once
for as long as six days. And it was Matthew's good fortune
to have personal access to the king, so that he was not
dependent on learning secondhand from the abbot or
others what news the king might be bringing with him. Of
the king's visit to the abbey in March 1257 Matthew wrote
that he "prolonged his stay . . . for a week, and as the
writer of this book was his constant companion in the
palace, at table, and in his chamber, he dictated to him
with care and affability."[8]

On what must have been one of Matthew's infrequent
visits to Westminster, this one in the fall of 1247, Henry
summoned the chronicler to take a seat near the throne,

where he conversed with him and afterward invited him to have lunch with him.[9] On another occasion Matthew mentions that the pope had offered to place Henry's son on the German throne to replace Frederick II, but Henry had refused. "And this the said king declared to me, Matthew, who wrote these pages."[10]

Other notables who visited the abbey included Queen Eleanor, Richard, the earl of Cornwall, who was Henry's brother, King Haakon IV of Norway, members of the royal council, barons, and bishops, among the latter Robert Grosseteste, the bishop of Lincoln, noted scholar and scientist. Of singular importance to Matthew was his association with members of the exchequer. No fewer than fourteen documents recorded in the *Liber Additamentorum* are copies of originals from the Red Book of the Exchequer.

Visitors of lesser rank who appeared in large numbers — almost daily, Matthew writes[11] — included Dominicans and Franciscans. Because of the mobility of the friars and the extensive use popes made of them as papal emissaries, their knowledge of events on the continent and beyond must have been unmatched. How circuitous might be the source of Matthew's information is revealed in the report from the Holy Land that reached him in 1252 from "monks of the Cistercian order, who returning from their general chapter . . . having obtained their information from Cardinal John, an Englishman, commonly called the White Cardinal, because he was a monk of the Cistercian order, who sent letters to his chapter by a monk of the same order."[12]

. Yet how suspect this roundabout information might be is suggested by the nature of the report that "a venerable man, a master of the brethren of St. Thomas' Church at Acre," brought with him to St. Albans in 1257. He reported

that a sort of infernal lightning, which, however, descended from the skies, had suddenly set fire to and destroyed the temple of Mahomet, together with his statue; and that again a second explosion, similar to the first, had reduced the said temple to small bits; and that a third had, as we believed, thrust the ruins into an abyss in the earth. After this, he said, this fire, which burned with a most devouring heat, though it did not give a bright light, crept along under the earth, like the fire of hell, consuming even rocks in its way, and could not even yet be extinguished. And thus the whole city of Mecca, and the country in its vicinity, were consumed with inextinguishable fire.[13]

The reader ventures the hope that Matthew recorded this and similarly fantastic items with the same open mind with which Herodotus noted sundry yarns he passed on to posterity.

Of some of the information recorded in Matthew's chronicle he was himself an eyewitness. It is rare he ever mentions his presence at any given event described in his chronicle, however, and it is only by accident that the reader can be sure he saw what he relates. One such instance was the awesome occasion when what many believed to be Christ's own blood was brought to Westminster Abbey on St. Edward's Day in 1247. The chronicler describes how the king, with the entire clergy of London in attendance, bore the sacred vessel from St. Paul's to Westminster where mass was celebrated and the bishop of Norwich preached a sermon. During the discussions after the ceremonies the question was asked how Christ could have risen from the dead "full and entire in body" yet leave his blood on the earth. According to Matthew, the bishop of Lincoln, Robert Grosseteste, answered all doubts "to a nicety," and the chronicler adds that the bishop's argument "is written in the book of *Additaments,* as the writer of this work himself heard and put down carefully word for word."[14]

The vividness with which Matthew Paris describes many incidents tempts the reader to assume he must have been present. One can almost spot him among the notables and other guests who assembled to attend the wedding of Henry's daughter Margaret to Alexander, king of Scotland, at York on Christmas in 1252.

> There had assembled there an immense multitude of the clergy as well as of knighthood, that the splendour of this grand nuptial ceremony might shine far and wide. For there were there present the king and queen of England, with their nobles, whom it would take long to enumerate by name; there were also present the king of Scotland and the queen his mother, who had been summoned from the continent for the occasion, in whose train were many nobles, not only of Scotland, but also of France, where she was born, whom she had brought with her. For she having, as was the custom with widows, obtained a third part of the revenues of the kingdom of Scotland, which amounted to five thousand marks and more, besides holding other possessions, which she had received as a gift from her father Engelram, appeared abroad with a numerous and pompous train of attendants. When they had all arrived at York, those who had come with the king of the Scots were lodged in one street, without mixing with any others, by way of caution. But whilst certain officers of the nobles, whom we call mareschals, were providing lodgings for their lords, they engaged in fights amongst themselves, first with fists, afterwards with staves, and finally with their swords; some of them were severely wounded, one fell slain, and others who were wounded never afterwards recovered. The kings, however, by means of prudent and temperate guards, whom they had there, skillfully restrained the strife of the lords as well as the servants.[15]

It is unlikely that Matthew actually witnessed these events at York, although the personal manner he constantly employs in describing such incidents leaves the reader that impression. He also delights in interpolating statements in the first person, even speeches, ostensibly made by the principals involved, a practice that heightens the illusion of his having been present.

An important source of Matthew Paris's information,

particularly when this came from foreign countries, was by letter, either addressed to him personally, more frequently passed on to him by the addressee. When the sender was a person as important as Frederick II of Germany and the addressee Henry III, Matthew might be excused for accepting the letter as eminently trustworthy, at least when its intent was non-political. At first glance the letter that Frederick sent to Henry and that Matthew inserted in the annal for 1241 would fall into this category. Frederick wrote to Henry, who was his brother-in-law, in the hope of securing his cooperation against a dreadful danger that "threatens general destruction to the whole of Christianity," specifically against the Tartars who were swarming into eastern Europe. Frederick confessed that he had no knowledge of whence this people came, but that it had "lately emerged from the regions of the south," had multiplied like locusts, and was bent on slaughtering all peoples and extending its fearful sway over the entire world. To punctuate the ferocity of these Tartars and the gravity of the danger they posed for the Western world, the emperor went on to describe them and their mores.

The men themselves are small and of short stature, as far as regards height, but compact, stout, and bulky, resolute, strong, and courageous, and ready at the nod of their leader to rush into any undertaking of difficulty; they have large faces, scowling looks, and utter horrible shouts, suited to their hearts; they wear raw hides of bullocks, asses, and horses, and for armour, they are protected by pieces of iron stitched to them, which they have made use of till now. But, as we cannot say it without sorrow, they are now, from the spoils of the conquered Christians, providing themselves with more suitable weapons, that we may, through God's anger, be the more basely slain with our own arms. . . . They are incomparable archers, and carry skins artificially made, in which they cross lakes and the most rapid rivers without danger. When fodder fails them, their horses are said to be satisfied with the bark and

leaves of trees, and the roots of herbs which the men bring
to them; and yet, they always find them to be very swift
and strong in case of necessity.[16]

Among other information the emperor included in his
letter to Henry was a critical reference to the papacy, to
the point that while the gravity of the situation warned all
Christians to unite against so terrible a peril, the pope was
stubbornly refusing Frederick's peace overtures. Matthew must have shared the reservations others entertained concerning the entire accuracy of Frederick's
words. He mentions that those men who hated the emperor had charged him with inciting the Tartars to ravage
these peoples, then with sending out this letter simply to
cover up his own complicity. For his part Matthew singles
out certain errors in the emperor's letter. He doubts, for
instance, whether so populous a nation as the Tartars
could have escaped the notice of travelers, as Frederick
had declared. "Where," Matthew asks, "have such people,
who are so numerous, till now lain concealed?" Whatever
Matthew may have thought about the reliability of Frederick's report, he was surely pleased to file the emperor's
letter with other documents concerning the Tartars that
had come into the abbey's possession. He invites the
reader who wished more information about these people to
visit St. Albans and consult this file.[17]

Information such as this concerning the Tartars, ques-
tionable though some of it may have been, constitutes one
of the major features of Matthew Paris's chronicle. He
does well recording events and is at his best when he can
do it without displaying emotion. What he writes about
England and Wales and Scotland generally appears to be
the report of an honest and reasonably accurate chronicler, except when he is castigating the king or some agent
of the pope. Even the information he supplies regarding
developments on the continent is for the most part as
reliable as any available from that period.

Our chronicler can be depended upon to present a factual, straightforward report of an incident such as the bringing to Paris the crown of thorns that many believed Christ had worn on his way to Calvary. This event occurred in 1240 and stirred Western Christians. The crown came to France because the Latin emperor of Constantinople needed money, "a common case," Matthew observes, "with those who carry on war." So the impecunious ruler approached Louis, the saintly king of France, and offered to sell him the relic "in consideration of his old ties of friendship and relationship."

> The French king, by the advice of his natural councillors, willingly agreed to this, and, with his mother's concurrence, he liberally sent a large sum of money to the emperor Baldwin, whose money had been exhausted by continual wars, and thus replenished his treasury, inspirited his retainers and his army, and inspired the said Baldwin with confident hopes of obtaining a victory over the Greeks. In return for this great benefit obtained from the king, the emperor, according to his promises and agreements, faithfully sent to him the crown of Christ, precious beyond gold or topaz; and it was therefore solemnly and devoutly received, to the credit of the French kingdom, and indeed of all the Latins, in grand procession, amidst the ringing of bells and the devout prayers of the faithful followers of Christ, and was placed with due respect in the king's chapel at Paris.[18]

That the intricacies of international diplomacy are not a phenomenon of the nineteenth century or, if one wishes to venture back so far, a game first played by the Italian despots of the late Middle Ages, is evident from the description Matthew Paris gives of the war undertaken by the count of Flanders in 1240. The count, with the permission of his overlord, Louis of France, had come to London where he was met

> not only by the king (Henry) and his courtiers, but also by an immense multitude of the London citizens on magnifi-

cently accoutered horses, with trumpets, and every demonstration of pleasure and joy, and was received . . . with much honour, and loaded with presents. The king immediately gave him five hundred (or, as some say, three hundred) marks of new sterling money, and made a grant to him of the same sum from the treasury yearly for the next twenty years, in consideration of the homage which the said count did to him. When this matter was settled, the count . . . immediately returned to Flanders . . . where he began to stir up war in his provinces, and to summon his stipendiary soldiers and followers, hired for pay; and having thus raised a numerous army . . . he attacked the bishop elect of Liége, who was of the emperor's (Frederick) party, and a relation of his, and also some others of the empire, who, by the emperor's command, had remained by the said bishop elect.

His majesty, the emperor, on hearing of this proceeding, sent word, with dreadful threats to the said count, to refrain from his rash and daring proceedings, and not—contrary to what he, the emperor, deserved from him—any longer to harass him, who was disquieted by so many arduous matters and by the annoyances of the pope, or his allies, especially the bishop elect of Liége, his friend and relation . . . and to cease disturbing the empire; he also ordered the dukes of Louvain and Brabant, and other neighboring potentates, to oppose and weaken the attacks of the count of Flanders; he then wrote also to the count of Provence, who was known to be of the emperor's party, ordering him, as his faithful ally, to check the designs and attempts of the count of Flanders, whom the former count had inspired with arrogance; but as both of these nobles, the count of Provence and the count of Flanders, neglected to obey his orders, the emperor wrote to the count of Toulouse, ordering him, under pain of his, the emperor's, just retribution, to make war against the count of Provence, who . . . refused to punish the count of Flanders; and he himself sent effectual assistance to the count of Toulouse, for the purpose of harassing the count of Provence. . . . The count of Toulouse, who was rendered more ready to obey the emperor, owing to the old injuries often inflicted on him by the French, roused himself at the summons of the emperor, and eagerly marched against the count of Provence, on whom he inflicted irreparable injuries; the latter, however, immediately flew for protection to the French king, humbly begging him . . . to give effectual assistance. . . . The king of England, hearing that the count of Provence had sustained great losses in his destructive struggle . . . wrote to the emperor in a friendly way, begging him for the sake of relationship . . . to spare the count of Provence, his father-in-law. The most potent king of the French . . . sent seven hundred knights, with a great many more retainers, to check the attacks of the enemies of the Provençals.[19]

Matthew Paris constantly astonishes the reader with the wealth of detail with which he describes, and enlivens, incidents, even when these happened many miles away. The event described in the following passage occurred across the North Sea in Germany. The excerpt also shows Matthew's fondness for classical quotations and allusions, devices he hoped would enhance the literary quality of his narrative.

In the same year [1256], William of Holland, who had been created king by the pope, and exalted by him to the high position he held over the kingdom of Germany, and who had preconceived the means and opportunity of obtaining the Roman empire, after an endless expenditure of the pope's money on him and by him, now on the offering of a slight opportunity, began to make war against the Frieslanders, a rude, uncivilized, and untameable nation of people. These Frieslanders inhabit a northern country, are skilled in naval warfare, and fight with great vigour and courage on the ice. It is of the cold regions of these Frieslanders, and their neighbours the Sarmatians, that Juvenal says, "One had better fly hence beyond the Sarmatians and the icy ocean," etc. The Frieslanders, therefore, having laid ambuscades along the sea-coast, among the rush-beds, as well as along the country, which is marshy (the winter season was coming on about the festival of the Purification of the Blessed Virgin), went in pursuit of the said William, armed with javelins, which they call "gaveloches," in the use of which they are well skilled, and with Danish axes and pikes, and clad in linen dresses covered with light armour. On reaching a certain march they met with William, helmeted and wearing armour, and mounted on a large war-horse, covered with mail; but as he rode along, the ice broke, although it was more than half a foot thick, and the horse sunk up to his flank, and became fixed deep in the mud of the marsh. The enraged rider dug his sharp spurs into the animal's sides till they reached his entrails, and the noble, fiery beast struggled to rise and free himself, but without success; crushed and bruised, he only sunk the deeper, and at length by his efforts he threw his rider amongst the slippery, rough, fragments of ice. The Frieslanders then rushed on William, who had no one to help him from his position, all his companions in arms having fled to avoid a similar accident, and attacking him on all sides with their javelins, despite his calls for mercy, pierced his body through and through, which was already stiffened with wet and cold. He offered his murderers an immense sum of money, by way of ransom, if they would spare him and allow him to escape alive; but these inhuman men showing no mercy, cut him to pieces. And thus, just as he had had a taste of empire, was the flower of chivalry, William, king of Germany and count of Holland, the creature and pupil of the pope, hurled, at the will of his enemies, from the pinnacle of his high dignity to the depths of confusion and ruin. But "to die at the option of enemies," says the philosopher, "is to die twice." When this intelligence reached the pope, his grief was [immense], at having thrown into Charybdis such an amount of money which had been gathered in all quarters, and by all kinds of means.[20]

The critical references to the pope introduce a facet of Matthew Paris's work as chronicler that does him little honor. He is unable to report information concerning the papacy with the measure of detachment, or degree of perceptivity for that matter, one would expect of so responsible a writer. His vitriolic language when writing of the papacy and the pope's agents resembles that of a Protestant polemicist of the sixteenth century rather than that of a Benedictine monk of the thirteenth. What renders Matthew's position in this regard all the more indefensible is the essential selfishness of the motivation that inspired it, namely, his objection to papal exactions and the extension of papal authority in the church. Still in taking this position he served as the spokesman, not only of his abbey, but of the English church in general, and, no doubt, voiced the sentiments of most hierarchies outside Italy.

One must admit that the English church could rationalize its objection to papal exactions on the score that the bulk of these was funneled to the pope's allies in his war with Frederick II, a war that most Englishmen considered unjustifiable. (Among other explanations of English sympathy for Frederick was that the emperor was the brother-in-law of Henry III.) The English church refused to accept the pope's argument that he was locked in a life-and-death struggle with the emperor who, he insisted, would stop at nothing short of complete domination of the Italian peninsula including Rome. Many reasonable men, including Louis IX of France, questioned the pope's analysis of the situation. Nevertheless, that every pope, whatever his political preferences before his election, pursued the same intransigent policy toward Frederick should have at least given the chronicler Matthew Paris pause. It did not.

Already in 1236, the year Matthew assumed his work as chronicler, he wrote of the "insatiable greediness of the Roman court."[21] That same year, in his first reference to the controversy between Frederick II and the pope, he took the part of the emperor.

About the same time, the pope, by mandatory letters, strictly forbade the emperor to invade Italy; for the latter had, in the summer, called together all the imperial forces

he could muster, to attack the insolent Italians, and especially the inhabitants of Milan, for that city was the recep-
tacle for all heretics, Paterines, Luciferians, Publicans, Albigenses, and usurers; and it seemed to the emperor to be
an ill advised plan for him to assist the Holy Land by the
presence of himself and such a large army of God, and to
leave behind him false Christians, worse than any Saracen.
He moreover wondered beyond measure that the pope
should be in any way favourable to the Milanese, or should
seem in any manner to afford them protection, since it
became him to be a father to the pious, and a hammer to
the wicked.[22]

Given Matthew's sympathy for Frederick in the emperor's contest with the papacy and the cities of north
Italy, one can appreciate his excoriation of papal exactions that would have been offensive enough even had
they been expended on a "worthy" cause. Illustrative of
the scores of such criticisms that Matthew scatters
throughout his writings is this one, which he inserted in
the annal for 1241:

About this time, either with the permission or by the instrumentality of Pope Gregory [IX], the insatiable cupid-
ity of the Roman court grew to such an extent, confound-
ing right with wrong, that, laying aside all modesty, like a
common brazen-faced strumpet, exposed for hire to every
one, it considered usury as but a trivial offense and simony
as no crime at all; so that it infected other neighbouring
states, and even the purity of England, by its contagion.
Although the examples of this which offer themselves
abound, I have thought proper briefly to relate one, in
order to show how justly, although tardy, the anger of God
was kindled against the said court.[23]

Even more objectionable to Matthew Paris, the English
church, and the English people than financial demands
were papal appointments of Italians to English benefices.
The pope's rationale for ordering such foreign appointments was that they enabled him to meet the cost of main-

taining the curia in Rome, which served all Christendom. In the medieval age when the bulk of revenues derived from land or benefices, it appeared only logical in the judgment of the papacy to handle the problem of financing the papal government in this manner. That the need for raising ever greater funds to prosecute the war against Frederick II was perhaps as pressing a concern of the pope's as simply that of financing the running of his curia is suggested by the following document. In this instance the pope had given orders to institute a large number of Italians to English benefices

amongst the sons and relations of the Romans at their pleasure, on condition that they should all rise with one accord against the emperor, and use all their endeavours to hurl him from the imperial throne. . . . Therefore . . . the pope sent his sacred warrants to Edmund, archbishop of Canterbury, and to the bishops of Lincoln and Salisbury, ordering them to provide for three hundred Romans in the first benefices which should be vacant; giving them to understand, that they were suspended from giving away benefices till that number were suitably provided for. . . . Edmund, archbishop of Canterbury, who had already submitted, willingly or unwillingly, to the above-mentioned hateful exactions, and paid eight hundred marks to the pope, now seeing that the English church was daily trampled more and more, despoiled of its possessions, and deprived of its liberties, became weary of living to see such evils upon the earth. He, therefore, after having asked the king's permission, and gaining nothing but evasive answers, left the country, provoked by these various injuries, and sailed to France, where, with a small retinue, he took up his abode at Pontigny, at which place his predecessor, St. Thomas, had dwelt in his exile, and employed himself in prayer and fasting.[24]

Scarcely a less frequent target of Matthew Paris's venomous pen than the papacy and Roman curia were Henry III and the royal government. No individuals or institu-

tions suffered anything approaching the measure of vilifi-
cation and scathing criticism that the chronicler heaped
upon papacy and crown. It was rare that Matthew discovered in either the pope or the king anything to commend; it
was seldom that he did not make himself a ready bedfellow
of their foes. That both targets of Matthew's ire were the
two authorities that exercised jurisdiction over St. Albans
reveals the principal source of the chronicler's hostility.
During the eleventh and twelfth centuries the abbey of St.
Albans had enjoyed an autonomous position vis-à-vis the
crown and papacy. Here in the thirteenth century this
autonomy came under attack by both king and pope.
Nothing brought home to the abbey its loss of autonomy
more than the increasing number of financial demands
both papacy and crown were making upon it, or the way
both were interfering in the selection of bishops and abbots and interposing their appointees in the filling of benefices.

Royal interference in the selection of bishops was, of
course, an ancient problem, but for Matthew writing the
annal for 1246 it appeared especially unpalatable, almost
as if it were an innovation on the part of Henry III. So he
notes that

> the canons of Salisbury, finding that no one hardly would
> be acceptable to the king, unless a person belonging to his
> court, in order to guard against peril in their church and to
> gain the king's goodwill, unanimously elected William of
> York, a most familiar clerk of the king's, and provost of
> Beverley, a man well skilled in the laws, to be their bishop
> and pastor of their souls; and as it was believed that this
> election pleased God, and was agreeable to the king, it was
> confirmed without delay.[25]

Considerably more distasteful to the chronicler was the
"election" of a favorite of Henry's as part of an arrangement with the pope. Such was apparently the case with
Ailmar, the king's uterine brother who

was confirmed in the see of Winchester by the pope, not-withstanding his youth, his ignorance of learning, and his utter incapacity for such a high station and the cure of so many souls. He was also shown such great favour by the pope, that he retained the revenues he had previously held; and all this was brought about by the watchful diligence of the king. But the pope, to prove that he had not sown seed on a barren coast, without hope of reaping benefit from the harvest, at once demanded the son of the count of Burgundy, a child, to be provided for by the grant to him of a revenue of five hundred marks.[26]

What principally evoked Matthew Paris's denunciation of the king in the chronicler's role as self-appointed spokesman of both English church and aristocracy was Henry's never-ending demands for subsidies. Historians are not in full agreement concerning the "injustice" of these demands. Until recent years they were inclined to accept Matthew's fulminations as the responsible voice of a courageous, impartial critic who stood up boldly against the crown for its sins of misgovernment and its quest for power. Now that subsequent studies have called the chronicler's objectivity as well as his perceptivity into question, the king's position and policy are receiving a more sympathetic evaluation.

Still the error, if error it was, of judging Henry too severely, was not that of Matthew so much as his modern readers. Medieval chroniclers contented themselves with covering the events of the day as these struck them, somewhat in the manner of newspaper reporters although not from such an on-the-spot vantage point. Generally speaking, those events or developments affecting the chronicler or his community adversely were to be deplored, those that benefited them were to be commended. It is unrealistic to picture Matthew Paris as an impersonal observer, capable of approaching events with the broad vision of an Ibn Khaldun who lived 150 years later and whose analytical powers were judged precocious even for his day. Matthew did not appreciate such circumstances as the rising cost of government, which might have justified Henry's repeated appeals for financial assistance. He singled out rather the king's extravagance, expended as it was on his wife's foreign relatives and on such fatuous foreign ventures as that of placing his son on the throne of Sicily. The modern historian should expect such an approach from Matthew. Without question Henry's practice of showering his wife's relatives and friends with gold and offices left him vulnerable to attack and provided his critics easy arguments by which to convince themselves that the crown's financial troubles were of its own foolish making. Beyond the baronial hostility to Henry, which Matthew expressed, lay also the fear that concessions to the crown might jeopardize the position the barons had wrung from Henry's father, John, at Runnymede.

Matthew seems to delight in reminding his readers of the frequency with which Henry enriched his French in-laws. When the king's uterine brother Guy de Lusignan left England in the fall of 1247, the chronicler notes how

> the king filled his saddle-bags with such a weight of money that he was obliged to increase the number of his horses. To his other brother William de Valence he gave the castle of Hertford, with the honours pertaining thereto, and a large sum of money . . . and to Ethelmar, the third of his brothers, he made provision out of the rich and abundant revenues which he had, by imperious entreaties, extorted from each bishop and abbot . . . so that he seemed now to exceed the Romans in audacity, and the said Ethelmar to surpass the bishops in their wealth.[27]

Matthew Paris was willing to place some of the responsibility for Henry's misgovernment on his counselors who were giving him "evil advice." Upon their encouragement and without concern for his own subjects Henry

> declared on his oath, at a conference [in 1237] to which he had called the nobles from a distance, that he was entirely

destitute of money and in a state of the greatest need; he therefore most urgently begged of them to grant him the thirtieth part of property throughout the kingdom, that the dignity of him, the king, and that of the kingdom, might be supported in a more honourable manner, and be established on a firmer foundation. The nobles were greatly troubled at hearing this, and replied that they were so often oppressed in this way, and saw so many foreigners fattening on their property, that the kingdom was weakened by poverty, and that manifold dangers were impending over it. However, after much discussion, inasmuch as the king humbled himself and promised that he would thenceforth abide by their counsels without hesitation, the thirtieth part of all moveable property was granted to him, though not without great difficulty. This he afterwards ordered to be collected, and estimated, not at the royal valuation, but according to the common values, and not to be placed in convents and castles, as had been prearranged and determined on, nor to be expended at the discretion of the nobles; but without taking the advice of any one of the natural subjects of his kingdom, he gave it to foreigners to be carried abroad, and he became like a man bewitched, as if he had no sense. A murmur therefore arose amongst the people, and the indignation of the nobles waxed hot.[28]

Despite the vehemence with which Matthew belabored the financial demands and policies of the pope and Henry, the chronicler's loyalty to neither was never in doubt. In 1238 he noted that

the archbishop of Antioch . . . presumed with rash violence to break forth into such audacity, that by an empty authority he excommunicated the pope, with the whole Roman church and court, and solemnly preaching blasphemy, he set himself and his church before his holiness the pope and the Roman church, both in age and rank; that it was and had been superior to the Roman church, because St. Peter the apostle had in the first place ruled the church of Antioch for seven years. . . . By these and other superficial arguments the said antipope concealed his scars, to his own destruction, and made excuses for sins; but that pillar of the church, the true pope and successor of the godly Peter (although not quite an imitator of him), remained unmoved, reserving all vengeance till the time of retribution.[29]

In 1255 on the occasion of Henry's visit to St. Albans in March, Matthew had these kind words to say of him:

On the ninth of March in this year, whilst his son Edward was in Gascony, the king went to Saint Alban's, and remained there for six days, during which time he daily and nightly prayed devoutly, and with tapers lighted, to Saint Alban, as chief martyr of the kingdom, on behalf of himself, his son Edward, and other of his friends. He also made an offering to God and to the blessed martyr of two costly cloaks which we call baudkins, and a handsome choral cape ornamented with gold. And it should be remarked, that no king of England, not even King Offa himself, the founder of the convent of St. Alban's, nor any of his predecessors, nor indeed all of them together, had ever contributed so many palls to ornament the walls of that church, as Henry the Third, king of England had alone given, as is entered in the small book in the said church, and in which a full account is given of the palls, rings, and costly jewels.[30]

In terms of space, Matthew devoted most attention to the papacy, to Henry III, and, somewhat strangely, to Frederick II of Germany. What explains his interest in Frederick was the emperor's marriage to Henry's sister, an association that made the two kings potential allies in any contests with the French and with the papacy. Matthew's great interest in a crusade also explains the attention he gave Frederick because he believed the emperor's avowed concern about the Holy Land to be genuine. Frederick's position as Holy Roman emperor also made him Christendom's champion against the menace posed by the Tartars. In explaining Matthew's interest in Frederick one should not ignore the simple circumstance that because of the close ties between the emperor and Henry many communications made their way to England that eventually reached him.

Such a communication was the letter Frederick sent to Richard, earl of Cornwall, in 1237 describing his spectacular victory over a large Milanese army at Cortenuova. Matthew Paris does not say how the letter or a copy came into his possession, but he gives the missive in full. Frederick is "speaking":

> By a fortunate chance . . . it happened that the Milanese with their allies were summoned to garrison Brescia, and thus a river was interposed between us and them, by which they were surrounded, as it were, by a rampart; on this we pitched our camp on the other side of the river Oglio; but here the faithful knights and people of the cities returned home, not being able any longer to endure the tediousness of the unexpected delay, and the inclemency of the season; we, however, with a chosen body of our army, directed our steps along the banks on the other side of this swift river to the bridges, by which those returning home were obliged to cross. The Milanese and their allies, not being able to stay any longer in their hiding-places, owing to the scarcity of necessaries, crossed the river Oglio by the fords and bridges, and came into the open plain, thinking to escape from us by a secret flight, and perhaps not imagining that we were so near. When, however, they knew of our proximity, fear and terror fell on them like a clap of thunder from heaven, and at the sight of the advanced guard of our imperial army, even before they could see the victorious standards, the imperial eagles, they turned to flight before us in such confusion, that, till they reached their carrochium, which they had sent forward to Nuova Croce, as fast as horses could carry it, not one of our pursuing troops could gain sight of the faces of the fugitives, and, as we believed that it was necessary for us to hasten to the assistance of the auxiliary troops, who had proceeded in advance in a small body, we marched forward after them with all speed with the strength of our army, and when we expected to find them repelled by the attacks of the fighting

enemy, we found our progress impeded by the numbers of horses which were running hither and thither without riders, and by the multitude of knights lying wounded or slain; whilst those who were alive were either standing or lying on the earth, having been bound by the esquires of the knights, who followed their lords. At length we discovered their carrochium, near the walls of Nuova Croce, surrounded by trenches, and protected by an immense body of knights, and all their foot soldiers, who fought wonderfully in its defence; we then directed our attention to the attack and capture of this standard, and we saw that some of our troops, after having forced their way over the top of the trenches, had, with commendable bravery, forced their way almost to the pole of the carrochium. The shades of night, however, coming on, which our men ardently wished for, we desisted from the attack till the following morning early, lying down to rest with swords drawn, and without taking off our armour, determined to return to gain an undoubted victory, and to get possession of the carrochium. When day broke, however, we discovered it deserted and left amidst a crowd of vile waggons entirely undefended and deserted, and from the top of the staff where the sign of the cross had been, the cross had been cut off, but appearing to the fugitives to be too heavy, it had been left half-way. The garrison and inhabitants of the castle of Nuova Croce, under protection of which we thought that they would escape our attacks, all abandoned it; their podesta, the son of the duke of Venice, under whose command they had raised their sorrowful standard, did not escape from our hands. To make a short account of the matter, almost ten thousand men[31] were said to have been taken and slain; amongst whom a great many nobles and chiefs of the Milanese faction fell. Of all these matters we send you word, to give you joy, that you may see how our empire is exalted, by the news which we now tell you. Given at Cremona, this fourth day of December, the eleventh indiction.[32]

Despite his general sympathy for Frederick, Matthew expressed disapproval of what he judged to be excessive demands that the triumphant emperor made upon Milan after this victory. He tells how the Milanese offered to surrender "all the substance they possessed in gold and silver" and as a sign of their submission "to collect all their standards and burn them at the feet of the emperor." They also agreed to supply him with 10,000 troops to accompany him in a crusade against the Infidel in Palestine.

> But the emperor proudly refused all these offers, demanding unalterably that the citizens, in common with their city and all their property, should resign themselves and their will absolutely to his pleasure. To this piece of tyranny of his, the citizens, with one consent, replied that they would on no account do this, for said they, "We have learned by experience, and fear your cruelty; we would rather die under our shields by the sword, or spear, or by javelins, than by treachery, famine, and flames." From that time the emperor began to lose favour with many, because he had become a tyrant; and the Milanese, for their humility, were extolled and gained strength. According to the words of the Gospel, "God resisteth the proud, but gives grace to the humble."[33]

What accounts for the sympathy Matthew Paris generally expressed for Frederick was probably the emperor's marriage link with Henry III, who, for all his deficiencies, was king of England. Matthew never forgot that he, too, was an Englishman. Among the earliest exponents of English national consciousness that students of that phenomenon trace to the thirteenth century appears, with good reason, the name of our chronicler. Few contemporaries matched the positive dislike he showed for the French, while no one approached the sharpness with which he assailed papal policies that were filling English benefices with Italians and drawing off English money to finance papal "political" ambitions against Frederick. The arrival of the count of Flanders from across the channel in the summer of 1244 for the purpose of aiding Henry in his war with the Scots evoked this announcement from Matthew.

> His arrival excited great indignation and derision in the
> hearts of the English nobles, for, they said, England was
> capable of utterly uprooting Scotland without him. The
> said count brought with him sixty knights, and a hundred
> retainers, well equipped with arms, and all of them eagerly
> grasping after the king's money.[34]

Matthew undoubtedly shared the resentment of the English nobles at the arrival of the count. Of this resentment and that over the feudal overlordship that John had surrendered to Innocent III in 1213, he was most explicit. When a fire in the pope's lodging at Lyons in 1245 caused considerable damage, he noted that among other articles destroyed was "that detestable charter, concerning the English tribute, which was made in the time of King John, of lamentable memory."[35]

For the Welsh Matthew expressed mixed sentiments. When they fought Henry he was inclined to sympathize with them. On other occasions the following entry is apt to better express his position.

> The faith of the Welsh is a want of faith, and they show no
> mercy when they have it in their power; and when fortune
> befriends them, they persecute those who fall into their
> power; but when defeated, they either fly or humble themselves; and such persons are never to be trusted, as the
> poet says, "I fear the Greeks, even when they bring gifts";
> and the philosopher Seneca also says, "You will never
> make a safe treaty with an enemy."[36]

Even stronger than Matthew's love for England was the affection he had for his abbey and the pride he felt in that community's leading position among English monasteries. He noted with deep satisfaction the refusal of his abbot – the only prelate who had the courage – to confirm the election of Boniface as archbishop of Canterbury, on the ground that he was unfit for that office.[37] The chronicler pointed out that because the abbot refused to approve Boniface's "election,"[38] the abbot of Westminster affixed his seal where the abbot of St. Albans should have placed his, since "St. Alban is the first martyr of England, so his abbot is the first in order and rank of all the abbots of England, therefore his seal should be appended first."[39] Again when the abbot refused a later request of the archbishop of Canterbury to confer holy orders in the conventual church lest it lead to some impingement of the abbey's exempt position, Matthew was pleased to record his superior's firm stand.[40]

The pride Matthew Paris took in his abbey and the Benedictine order, as much as his opposition to innovation, explains the animosity he showed toward the friars during his early years as chronicler at St. Albans. Except for the Cistercians, he found little good in other religious orders, none in particular in the new ones that were "daily springing up and shooting forth without end." It provoked him that so many learned men, despising the discipline of the most blessed Benedict, who was full of the spirit of all the saints, and that of the noble Augustine, should, contrary to the statute of the general council held in the time of Pope Innocent the Third, of glorious memory,[41] suddenly fly to these unheard-of and lately-invented orders.[42]

What especially embittered the older orders, and the secular clergy as well, against the friars was the unrestricted manner in which they went about preaching, accepting mass offerings, and hearing confessions. Matthew attributed the "zeal" of these friars to a combination of avarice and arrogance:

> When noblemen and rich men are at the point of death . . .
> they, in their love of gain, diligently urge them, to the
> injury and loss of the ordinary pastors, and extort confessions and hidden wills, lauding themselves and their own
> order only, and placing themselves before all others. So no

194

faithful man now believes he can be saved, except he is directed by the counsels of the Preachers and Minorites.[43] Desirous of obtaining privileges in the courts of kings and potentates, they act the parts of councillors, chamberlains, treasurers, bridegrooms, and mediators for marriages; they are the executors of the papal extortions in their sermons, they either are flatterers, or most cutting reprovers, revealers of confessions, or imprudent accusers. . . . They look upon the Cistercian monks as clownish, harmless, half-bred, or rather ill-bred priests; and the monks of the Black (Benedictine) order as proud epicures.[44]

The reader might expect a chronicler who wrote with such strong feeling about pope, king, and friars would display even sharper prejudices when speaking of Jews, for example, or Muslims. Such is happily not the case. True, Matthew appears to have shared that indigenous prejudice that many individuals and cultures entertain toward minorities. Illustrative of this trait is his ready acceptance of the myth of Jewish ritual murders, a myth whose authenticity few of his contemporaries would have denied.

In 1255, for example, he reported as a fact that the Jews of Lincoln had kidnapped a boy of eight, then sent secret summons to fellow Jews throughout England to come and take part in the torture and murder of the Christian. The boy's execution was to proceed in strict accordance with the gospel account of Christ's crucifixion, that is, they would first scourge the boy, then crown him with thorns, and finally crucify him. Some days after the alleged crime had been committed, the owner of the house where the boy had gone to play before his disappearance was apprehended and induced to make a full confession on the promise of clemency. He accordingly confessed that what "the Christians say is true: for almost every year the Jews crucify a boy as an insult to the name of Jesus." The supposed ringleaders in the crime were tried by jury and executed, including the informer, who "was tied to a horse's tail and dragged to the gallows, where he was delivered over body and soul to the evil spirits of the air."[45]

Matthew Paris makes a point of assuring the reader that the perpetrators of this deed were all properly tried and convicted, and he castigated the Franciscans for having pleaded the cause of these Jews when the Jews had appealed to them for assistance. Matthew felt that these friars should have realized that there could be, or should be, no hope, either in this life or in the next, for such wretched criminals, and as a deserved punishment for their taking the part of the Jews he mentions that the lower classes had turned against the Franciscans "and would not bestow alms on them as formerly."[46]

Yet Matthew, for all his prejudice, now and then expresses his pity "for the most unfortunate Jews." In the annal of 1243 he refers to them as the perennial victims of royal avarice and tyranny. In 1254 he noted that so heavy had grown the weight of royal exactions that the Jews "appeared to be entirely and irreparably impoverished."[47] He also treated news about the Muslims with a reasonably tolerant pen although his abhorrence of Muhammad himself and the Prophet's teachings was a different matter.[48]

In his writing Matthew Paris reveals what many scholars consider a peculiarly medieval interest in natural phenomena, particularly when these were of an unusual or destructive nature. No doubt the origin of that special curiosity was the Gospel's warning about signs and wonders presaging the end of the world, and, in addition, the belief of many Christians that God constantly employed evils such as storms and plagues to punish men for their sins. The chronicler reports a terrifying number of major conflagrations for the year 1248 that "we do not remember ever to have seen the like before." Fires raged in a number of countries, even in Norway where three of the principal communities, one of them Bergen, were nearly destroyed. It was evident that God had sent these fires as a sign of

divine anger, and this was surely true of the fire at Bergen
where the

> sin-avenging flame flew, like a fire-vomiting dragon drag-
> ging its tail after it, to the king's castle, which is about five
> arrow flights distant from the city; wherefore nothing ap-
> peared more certain and manifest to the inhabitants than
> that the severity of the divine vengeance caused this mis-
> fortune.[49]

Matthew also reported an earthquake that struck Chil-
tern and St. Albans in 1250 and frightened the pigeons,
jackdaws, sparrows, and other birds so greatly that they
"suddenly expanding their wings, took to flight, as if they
were mad, and flew backwards and forwards in confusion,
exciting fear and terror in those who saw the occurrence."
But what especially aroused people's anxieties was the
conviction that this phenomenon announced "the end of
the world was at hand."[50]

So careful is Matthew in reporting the appearance of
comets that the modern astronomer might well depend
upon his chronicle in preparing a record of their frequency
at that time. The eclipse that Matthew reported for October 6, 1241, was the second within a period of two years, an
event, he declares, "hitherto unheard of."[51] He wrote of a
bright star that made its appearance on the eve of St.
James in 1239, then moved toward the north, "not swiftly,
but as a hawk usually flies." It eventually vanished from
sight behind a cloud of smoke and sparks. The chronicler
identified the phenomenon as either a comet or a dragon,
"greater to the eye than Lucifer, having the form of a mul-
let, very bright at the front, but at the hind smokey and
sparkling." No one had any satisfactory explanation of the
phenomenon, although "one thing is certain, that afterwards, the crops which had been almost all choked by
protracted rains, the season was at this very hour changed
into one of a most remarkable fertility."[52]

Matthew left the explanation of the phenomenon that

occurred the night of July 26, 1243, to "scientists." Here is his description of the marvel.

> And in the same year . . . the night was most serene, and the atmosphere very pure, so that the Milky Way appeared as plainly as it is accustomed to do on the most placid winter night, the moon being eight days old. And behold, stars were seen to fall from heaven, swiftly darting to and fro. But, contrary to what usually happens, not little sparks shooting after a manner of stars (which is stated as a natural phenomenon in Aristotle's book on *Meteors*), like lightning, produced by thunder; but, in one instant, thirty or forty were seen to shoot about or fall, so that two or three at once appeared to fly in one train. Thus, if they were real stars (which no wise man can think), there would not have been one left in the heavens. Let astrologers declare what this kind of thing may portend, which appeared strange and miraculous to all beholders.[53]

The enormous loss of life attributed to the Black Death of 1348–1350 tends to obscure the fact that plague and pestilence in less virulent forms struck Europe from time to time during the preceding millenium. Matthew notes that in the fall of 1247 casualties were so great "that nine or ten corpses were buried in one day in the cemetery of one church, namely, that of St. Peter in the town of St. Alban's."[54]

Because this happened in Matthew's neighborhood, the reader may accept the relative accuracy of Matthew's statistics. One hesitates to credit his statement, on the other hand, that in 1258 some fifteen thousand poor people died from starvation in London. In the summary he leaves for that year Matthew notes that so many people died "that the gravediggers were overcome with weariness and threw several bodies into one grave."[55]

Strange animals have always aroused curiosity and at no time more so than in the Middle Ages, when zoos were almost unknown. Matthew must have found no animal more fascinating than the elephant that Louis IX sent to

Henry III as a token of his goodwill. The chronicler observes: "We believe that this was the only elephant ever
seen in England, or even in the countries on this side the
Alps; wherefore the people flocked together to see the
novel sight."[56] About the same time Matthew wrote of a
strange animal that the sea had cast up off the coast of
Norwich, "an immense sea monster, which was disturbed
by the violent commotions of the waves and was killed, as
was believed, by the blows and wounds it received. This
monster was larger than a whale, but was not considered
to be of the whale kind."[57]

The summary noted in the second paragraph above with
which Matthew Paris concluded the annal for 1258 may be
considered something of an innovation on his part. The
medieval chronicler seldom furnished his reader a summary; his responsibilities ceased with recording events.
Even Matthew's summaries, which appear regularly from
1241, fall short of what the modern reader would regard as
anything approaching a digest of the year's events. The
majority are little more than tokens of what a summary
might be. That for the year 1244 reads:

> Thus ended this year which was throughout abundantly
> productive in fruit and corn, so much so, indeed, that the
> price of a measure of corn fell to two shillings; its events
> were most inimical to the Holy Land; marked with distur-
> bances in England; fraught with peril to the French king-
> dom; raised suspicion in the Church and turbulence among
> the Italians.[58]

The most ambitious summary that Matthew prepared
was that covering the fifty-year period ending in 1250.
That he had intended to conclude his work as chronicler
with that year may help explain the unusually gloomy
character of his account. In his judgment, during no previous half century since the birth of Christ "did so many
wonderful and extraordinary novel occurrences take
place. . . . And there are some, indeed many writers and

searchers into history, who say that not in all the other half centuries were there seen so many prodigies and astonishing novelties, as occurred in the one now ended; and even worse events than these were now expected with fear."[59]

Among other events he enumerated were the enormous conquests made by the barbarous Tartars, the capture of Jerusalem by the Infidel, England's suffering an interdict for seven years and then becoming a papal fief, the defeat of Otto IV of Germany at the battle of Bouvines (1214), the frequency of eclipses, earthquakes, and meteors (phenomena which could only presage impending ruin), Frederick II's capture of many prelates bound for a meeting of a general council, Henry III's two expeditions to France from which he "twice returned ingloriously," three popes reigning within an interval of two years, papal appointment to English benefices of Italians "who never troubled themselves about a charge of souls," the rise of many new religious orders including the Beguines, even a decline among the Benedictines the degree of which had never been so great during any preceding fifty-year period, the suppression of the Albigenses (probably the only development Matthew could consider a blessing!), the occupation of Canterbury "by an incompetent person thrust in by the king," the destruction of the crusading army of Louis IX in Egypt, the terrible war between the papacy and Frederick, and the death of this Frederick, "the wonder of the world."[60]

Critics may consider Matthew Paris's practice of interjecting moral judgments as his most reprehensible weakness as a writer of history. He surely liked to do this. Personages as highly placed as the archbishop of Canterbury were not safe from his biting pen. When the archbishop arrived in England in 1244, Matthew wrote that "no one rejoiced . . . for each and all recalled to memory how extraordinarily and how cruelly he acted at London, when he there exacted from religious men the right of visiting them; how, moreover, he had in manifold ways impoverished the kingdom and the church."[61] Even their deaths did not protect certain persons from censure. He noted the passing of Cardinal John of Colonna in the annal for 1244 with this entry: "At the same time of the year . . . died John of Colonna, a Roman cardinal, a vessel of all kinds of pride and insolence; who, as he was the most illustrious and powerful in secular possessions of all the cardinals, was the most efficacious author and fosterer of discord between the emperor and the pope."[62] Lay individuals fared no better than members of the clergy. In the annal of 1258 Matthew announced the death of William Heron, sheriff of Northumberland, who had been a "most avaricious man, a hammer of cruelty to the poor and a persecutor of the religious orders. From worldly avarice and thirst for wealth, he passed, as is believed, to the infernal regions, to experience the thirst of Tantalus."[63]

If Matthew trafficked in moral judgments beyond other chroniclers, he shared with them their wont of moralizing about life in general. Following his description of the splendid festivities that attended the marriage of Earl Richard to Cynthia, he left the reader a sobering thought to ponder.

> There was so much nuptial conviviality at this wedding, and such festivity among the noble guests, that nothing could be compared to the splendour of the entertainment – it would require a long and tedious treatise to describe it. That I may say much in a few words, in the cook's department there were thirty thousand dishes got ready for those who sat down to dinner. . . . Worldly pomp, and every kind of vanity and glory was displayed in the different bodies of gleemen, the variety of their garments, the number of dishes and the multitude of feasters; but these only proved how transitory and contemptible are such joys, how shadowy and deceptive is this world, when the morrow's dawn dissipated like a cloud all these great and varied doings.[64]

Matthew sounds very much the moralizer in his description of a tragic quarrel between two canons of the house of the Holy Trinity in London that ended in the murder of one of them. Although the guilty man attempted to hide his crime by inflicting deep wounds upon himself, his guilt was revealed and he was punished. Matthew concludes his account of the incident with this observation:

> By the agency of the devil, who planned all this proceeding, the entire religious community, which it is his principal study to defame and blacken, to our sorrow and grief, incurred scandal, disgrace, and confusion. What could these two decanonized canons, who incurred the peril of damnation, say before the tribunal of the supreme judge to the accuser of the human race? Woe to them through whom a scandal arose which defiled religion in general. Let religious men, for whom the devil more particularly lays his snares, beware and cautiously restrain their anger and hatred when quarrels and reproaches commence, for "Anger engenders strife, strife causes wars, and wars cause death." And such a death as this at first brings on a second, which is eternal.[65]

This note concerning the last judgment provides a proper moment to take leave of our chronicler. If there was even any question, the reference to death and eternity would mark him clearly as a chronicler of the Middle Ages. He likes to remind his reader of God's presence, of divine providence, of death, and judgment. These are the themes he shares with his medieval fellows. Like them, he contents himself with narrating events as they happen, almost never outside their chronological sequence. His approach is that of a simple narrator of things and the doings of people. He does not analyze; he ordinarily eschews the role of interpreter. His responsibilities stop with telling what happened, and if there were any laws other than, or above, the laws of God that guided or influenced the course of events, neither he nor his Christian contemporaries were aware of them.

Matthew also stays with his medieval fellows in the interest he shows in natural phenomena, in his concentration on things political and ecclesiastical, in his general indifference to peasants and merchants and to what passes as social and economic history. (He does, however, remind his reader with some regularity about the fluctuating price of bread.) He shares with other monastic scribes his ignorance of political theory, his acceptance of miracles and portents, and his pessimistic bent. (Because all men were sinners, how could the future be anything but dark!) And while he furnishes the reader greater insight into his temperament by the personal character of his writing than is traditional with medieval chroniclers, he remains as impersonal as they in his handling of his information. Almost humble is his tone when he makes a rare reference to himself. At the close of the annal for 1250 he writes: "Here ends the chronicles of Brother Matthew Paris, monk of St. Alban's, which he committed to writing for the benefit of posterity, out of love for God and for the honour of St. Alban, the English protomartyr, that the memory of modern events might not be destroyed by age or oblivion."[66] There is nothing more.

Matthew Paris's principal weakness as a chronicler is the lack of objectivity with which he wrote. It is an infrequent page that does not breathe his prejudices. He was a conservative in the classical sense, that is, he was wedded to the status quo or what he believed this should be. So he opposed papal and royal exactions as a devious means of enhancing the authority of papacy and crown and thereby threatening the autonomy of his abbey. For the same reason he sympathized with the barons in their struggle to maintain their dominant place in society and in public affairs. He found the appearance of the Mendicant orders distasteful because they were new, even though the church had great need for a different kind of monk. He objected to Grosseteste's visitation of the monasteries in his diocese of Lincoln, even though he must secretly have approved that prelate's motives. Still it is only in recent years that scholars have come to appreciate the full force of his prejudices. Striking proof of his influence upon their interpretations is the strongly anti-Henry, antipapal, and pro-Frederick II writing of the first half of this century.

Where Matthew Paris excels, where he is clearly the superior of his fellow chroniclers, is in the vivid language he employs and in the personal manner he handles his narrative. His descriptive and anecdotal powers were unusual for his age, also somewhat exceptional his efforts to enhance the literary qualities of his narrative with quotations from classical writers.[67] That he frequently introduced statements in the first person, also speeches and an occasional dialogue, further reveals his concern about making his chronicle a pleasure to read. Only on that basis can one justify the inclusion of many episodes that a completely official record would have excluded as trivial. However welcome the reader may find these rhetorical devices, they detract from the strict credibility of Matthew's account, especially where the chronicler permits his bias to show through. Few readers could accept as Llewellyn's own words, for instance, those which Matthew puts into the mouth of this Welsh prince when he addressed his soldiers in 1257 just before confronting the army of Henry III. The prince refers to Henry as a king, Paris writes, "who impoverishes, disinherits, and debases his natural subjects, the English."[68]

Matthew Paris showed himself ahead of his time, almost modern in fact, in his appreciation of the value of documents, of official orders, of letters, and speeches, as historical evidence. For this reason, also lest their extensive use mar the literary quality of his chronicle, he collected them in a separate volume called the *Additamentum*. He also appreciated the major problem that has confronted God-fearing historians throughout the ages.

"Hard is the case of historical writers," he observes, "who, if they tell the truth, provoke men, and if they commit to writing that which is false, they are not acceptable to the Lord."[69] It is to the credit of Matthew Paris that he showed less fear of provoking man than of offending God.

CHAPTER 6

John Froissart

J OHN FROISSART, ON HIS affirmation a historian rather than a chronicler, remains nonetheless one of the most interesting and informative of medieval chroniclers. Several circumstances conspire to make him interesting. He lived in an exciting age; he concerned himself principally with people who were causing excitement; he described these people – and events – in a personal and vivid manner. Geoffrey Chaucer, a contemporary of Froissart, was not an exciting person as the chronicler would have defined that term, so he does not appear in his *Chronicles*.[1] If the two writers met, neither would have recorded that fact. Chaucer was interested in types rather than in individuals; he also remained austerely impersonal in his writing. Froissart, while forever introducing individuals to his readers, limits his selection to members of the aristocracy or to individuals beneath that class whose prowess or political actions earned them recognition. Any mention of Chaucer would have been out of place in his *Chronicles*.

Still Froissart must have known Chaucer, just as he undoubtedly knew Petrarch and Boccaccio. All four

writers attended the marriage in 1368 of Lionel, duke of
Clarence, to Violante, the daughter of Galeazzo Visconti,
in Milan, but Froissart saw no point in mentioning this.
Several curious parallels suggest themselves between the
Italian geniuses on the one hand and Froissart on the
other. Like Petrarch, Froissart was a priest, although
both wore their clerical garb so unobtrusively that few
people were, or are, aware of that fact. Like Boccaccio,
Froissart first composed poetry, but it was their prose
which brought the two men distinction. Of the four
writers, Chaucer, Petrarch, Boccaccio, and Froissart, the
Frenchman[2] probably found himself most at ease in sophisticated society. Of the four, too, Froissart was surely
the most eager to talk to people and to listen to what they
had to say, for upon them he depended for much of the
information he wove into his *Chronicles*. Chaucer lingered
over mannerisms and over idiosyncrasies in speech and
dress to make his people live. Froissart showed little or no
interest in character portrayal. His concern was with people who were important in themselves or who performed
important or heroic deeds. His interest lay in action, not
character, and though his study is narrowly political
within the broader connotation of chivalry, the picture he
paints of the period in these respects has furnished his
readers a more accurate view of contemporary society
than did his English contemporary with his broader sweep
on the canvas.

Froissart, probably the son of a prosperous townsman,
was born in or about the year 1337, in Valenciennes, a city
of Hainaut, a county in the region of the upper Scheldt and
today a province of Belgium. He took up studies for the
priesthood and persisted in that vocation even though, as
he confesses, he found greater delight in romantic literature and song, and in girls, too, for that matter, than he did
in things spiritual. At the age of twenty he interrupted his
studies to undertake, upon the request of his lord, Robert
of Namur, the writing of the events that had recently

taken place in France. In 1361 he traveled to the English court where he presented his first historical work, a poem on the battle of Poitiers. Queen Philippa, a countrywoman of his, received the gift "to my great profit."[3] During the five years he remained in England enjoying her generous patronage, he had time for a trip north and "traveled all though Scotland"[4] in the company of King David who was making a progress about the country.

Next we find him in Bordeaux, in 1367, where he joined that city and the Black Prince in celebrating the birth of the Prince's son, the future Richard II. The following five years saw him traveling about France and Italy, his quest usually the courts of princes, including that of the pope at Avignon. In 1368, for instance, he went to Milan in the company of Lionel, duke of Clarence, on the occasion of the latter's marriage to the daughter of the despot of Milan. In 1373 he returned to Hainaut where for want of better employment he appears to have taken up the duties of a curate at Lestines — until rescued from what must have been uninspiring work for him by an offer of a post in the household of Wenceslas, the duke of Brabant. When this patron died in 1383 he moved to the establishment of Guy de Châtillon, count of Blois, who made him his private chaplain and directed him to undertake the writing of the *Chronicles*. In the fall of 1388, partly to secure additional information for his work, he journeyed to Béarn on the northern slopes of the Pyrenees and spent six enjoyable and fruitful months at Orthez, a castle belonging to Gaston Phoebus, count of Foix.

Some time later, in 1397, when his patrons, the "count and countess of Blois . . . by indulging themselves too much in the pleasures of the table, and eating too many sweet dishes . . . were become enormously fat,"[5] and, what was worse, financially straitened, he found another patron in William of Ostrevant, the governor of Hainaut. It was probably with the assistance of William that Froissart was able to pay a second visit to England. This one came in 1395, when he presented Richard II a book of lyric poems "handsomely written and illuminated, and bound in crimson—velvet, with ten silver gilt studs, and a rose of the same in the middle, with two large clasps of silver gilt, richly worked with roses in the center."[6] The king was pleased with the gift, but for Froissart the trip proved a deep disappointment. He "found no one there that I had been acquainted with in my former journies: the inns were all kept by new people, and the children of my former acquaintances become men and women."[7] He dropped out of sight after his return to Hainaut, and scholars place his death about the year 1404 or shortly thereafter.

Froissart, the chronicler of chivalry, came by that romantic role honestly. His first literary love in terms of time was poetry. His versifying gained him no great distinction, but it would have merited him mention in a history of French literature even without the *Chronicles.* He composed some fourteen thousand lines of lyric verse and a romance of thirty thousand lines in octosyllabic couplets entitled *Méliador,* or *The Knight of the Golden Sun.* Somewhat curious was his choice of Scotland as a setting for this romantic novel; that country was the least chivalrous and romantic of those with which he was familiar. In the composition of this poem he had the collaboration of his patron Wenceslas who was something of a poet himself and who interspersed the story with love lyrics of his own.

But the composition of poetry and romances was never more than an aside for Froissart. It was the writing of history that most intrigued him. His interest in history would itself have justified seeking out the company of the aristocracy, even had not patrons encouraged him to do so, for the purpose of gathering the information he required for his *Chronicles.* We have it on his own testimony that he enjoyed the writing of history. He wrote:

> To continue this noble and pleasant history . . . I John
> Froissart . . . set myself to work at my forge, to produce

new and noble matter relative to the wars between France and England and their allies, as clearly appear from the various treaties which are of this date, and which excellent materials, through the grace of God, I shall work upon as long as I live; for the more I labour at it, the more it delights me.[8]

Not only did Froissart enjoy writing his *Chronicles*, he found his writing afforded others delight as well — lords and ladies who listened to him reading what he had written. He even spoke confidently of the manner his writings would continue popular for the years to come. "I well know," he declared, "that in time to come, when I shall be dead and rotten, this grand and noble history will be much in fashion, and all nobles and gallant persons will take pleasure therein."[9]

Froissart wrote above all to entertain his readers. He also shared the motive that has ordinarily inspired earlier and later historians: leaving to posterity a record of deeds that, if noble, would serve as an inspiration, if evil, would provide a sobering influence. In this second role Froissart has less to say. He seems even to have avoided inserting stories or information that would denigrate someone's name. Alice Perrers, the "ambitious" mistress of Edward III in his declining years, fails of mention, as does the oft-repeated charge that John of Gaunt, the uncle of Richard II, was seeking to take over the throne for himself. If his *Chronicles* ocasionally mention deeds that were less than noble, it was regrettable, but the subject made their introduction necessary. His first interest was that of preserving the knowledge of memorable deeds. He writes:

That the honourable enterprises, noble adventures, and deeds of arms, performed in the wars between England and France, may be properly related, and held in perpetual remembrance — to the end that brave men taking example from them may be encouraged in their well-doing, I sit down to record a history deserving great praise.[10]

Froissart wants his reader to know that he classes himself as a historian, not simply as a chronicler. "If I were merely to say, such and such things happened at such time," he explains, "without entering fully into the matter, which was grandly horrible and disastrous, it would be a chronicle, but no history."[11] The distinction Froissart draws between chronicle and history is one he clearly bases upon the amount of information supplied. If the matter is presented in a simple narrative style, in the manner of an annalist, it constitutes a chronicle. History demands depth and detailed description, and Froissart never fails to supply these, as his tiring readers may lament.

Whether he wrote as a chronicler or historian, a more important consideration for Froissart was that of telling the truth. To him this was the first requisite of any writer and of this he reminds his reader on several occasions. One such instance concerned the execution of Sir Simon Burley, a tragedy at which "I was exceedingly vexed . . . and personally much grieved; for in my youth I had found him a gentle knight, and, according to my understanding, of great good sense."[12] Burley found himself caught up in the bitter power struggle between Richard II and the aristocratic lords who opposed him. He was charged with having embezzled 250,000 francs—a charge Froissart judged unfounded—taken to the Tower and shortly after "was carried forth . . . and beheaded, as a traitor, in the square before it." For all the anguish the subject caused him, Froissart felt obliged to record it. "Notwithstanding I thus relate his disgraceful death, which I am forced to do by my determination to insert nothing but truth in this history."[13]

An incident that touched Froissart more intimately than the execution of Sir Simon because it brought dishonor to his fellow countrymen took place in 1388. A small force under the command of the duke of Gueldres defeated a veritable army of Brabanters. At the first charge more than six score Brabanters were unhorsed. "Great confusion and dismay . . . reigned among them. They were so suddenly attacked . . . that although they were so numerous, and had many great lords, they were dispersed." Froissart recorded the incident despite the humiliation he suffered. "Scarcely can I for shame perpetuate the disgraceful defeat of the Brabanters," he wrote, "but, as I have promised at the commencement of this history to insert nothing but what was strictly true, I must detail the unfortunate consequences of this battle."[14]

If Froissart did not twist the truth or withhold information he found embarrassing, many scholars insist that he may have colored his account to suit the preferences of his patrons. The temptation to do this must have been a real one. It was the generosity of these patrons that enabled Froissart to live the life he loved, that of mixing with members of the aristocracy and preparing a chronicle of the chivalrous deeds of the times. Still if he did color his account, the reader has two reasons to excuse him. There is, first, that without this patronage there would have been no *Chronicles*, and a slanted history is better than none. Second, Froissart did not pretend to write a completely accurate, balanced history of the times. His aim was to record events and episodes that related to the aristocracy, to chivalry, and to the wars fought between the French and English and their allies.

It is generally believed that the first version of Book I reveals some pro-English bias. Froissart wrote this book at the request of Robert of Namur, a nephew of Queen Philippa, at whose court he spent some of the years covered. Part of this English sympathy may be traced to Jean le Bel, a canon of Liège, upon whose chronicle Froissart drew heavily in this early work of his. A second redaction of Book I that Froissart prepared when Guy de Blois was his patron reveals greater independence, while a third version completed in 1400 or thereabouts is devoid of any English bias. Books II and III suggest some French sympathy. This would have pleased Guy de Blois, Froissart's patron at the time, while Book IV, written when William of Ostrevant was his patron, may express a measure of Burgundian bias.

Although one might hesitate to discuss the point of Froissart's objectivity because what bias exists is insufficient to reduce appreciably the value of the *Chronicles,* it is interesting that the chronicler himself raises the issue. He does so in the course of describing an incident that involved the duke of Brittany. He writes:

> But let it not be said, that I have been corrupted by the favour of Count Guy de Blois (who has induced me to undertake, and has paid me for this history to my satisfaction), because he was a nephew of the rightful duke of Brittany. . . . It is not so; for I will speak the truth, and go straight forward, without colouring one side more than another, and that gallant prince who patronized this history never wished me in any way to act otherwise.[15]

When Froissart raises the matter of possible partiality on his part one must bear in mind that he is thinking in terms of a personal, not a national bias. Nationalism as that term is today understood was foreign to Froissart's age. It is largely a product of the French Revolution. Before the close of the eighteenth century one may speak, not of nationalism, but of national consciousness, and the further one moves back in time from 1800, the weaker does that consciousness grow. In Froissart's day there was no French or Spanish nation, and if England happened to be a unified state, most members of the English aristocracy felt a stronger tie with their fellow noblemen across the channel than they did with their "common" neighbors at home. Froissart tells that the English aristocracy received the news of the victory of the French over the Flemish at Rosebecque with satisfaction. "The nobles of England were not sorry on hearing it; for they said, that if the commonalty of Flanders had been victorious over the king of France, and his nobility had been slain, the pride of the common people would have been so great that all gentlemen would have had cause to lament it."[16]

Froissart was a native of Hainaut, one of a group of small principalities lodged between France and Germany that enjoyed strong economic ties with England. In no place in Europe except in north Italy was the spirit of autonomy so strong. In the case of Froissart, a measure of cosmopolitanism leavened his love for Hainaut. This was the result of his genuine love of chivalry wherever it might be found, coupled with his admiration of the aristocracy of any and all countries.

If the careful reader of the *Chronicles* can detect some shift of sympathy from the English, to the French, then to the Burgundians, far more evident is the writer's anxiety to bestow praise on all brave men, whatever their origin, who displayed courage in armed conflict. It is a rare page in the *Chronicles* that a Scotsman, Englishman, Frenchman, or Castillian could not have read with equal satisfaction. The manner in which Froissart describes the fierce fighting during an engagement between the English and Scots just before the battle of Ottebourne in 1388 illustrates his hope of pleasing all parties. The conflict took place between the followers of the Douglas and Percy clans, two of the most illustrious names in the long history of fighting along the border separating England and Scotland. Froissart first assures the reader that "I had my information . . . from both parties," then goes on to say that these

> agreed that it was the hardest and most obstinate battle that was ever fought. This I readily believed, for the English and Scots are excellent men at arms, and whenever they meet in battle they do not spare each other; nor is there any check to their courage so long as their weapons endure. When they have well beaten each other, and one party is victorious, they are so proud of their conquest, they ransom instantly their prisoners, and in such cour-

teous manner to those who have been taken, that on their
departure they return them their thanks. However, when
in battle, there is no boy's play between them, nor do they
shrink from combat; and you will see, in the further detail
of this battle, as excellent deeds performed as were ever
witnessed.[17]

That Froissart was generally successful in maintaining
a detached posture when describing battles between different armies does not mean that he did not see that different peoples possessed different traits. He found the Portu-
guese to be "passionate, overbearing, and not easily
pacified, and the English are spiteful and proud."[18] When
he wrote earlier about the English he met during his sojourn in Bordeaux, he also found them to be proud.

> I, the author of this history, was at Bordeaux when the
> prince of Wales marched to Spain, and witnessed the great
> haughtiness of the English, who are affable to no other
> nation than their own; nor could any of the gentlemen of
> Gascony or Aquitaine, though they had ruined themselves
> by the wars, obtain office or appointment in their own
> country; for the English said they were neither on a level
> with them nor worthy of their society, which made the
> Gascons very indignant.[19]

In view of the years Froissart spent in England it is not
surprising that some of that country's antipathy for the
Scots rubbed off on him. In one of his first observations
about the Scots he states that they were a "rude and
worthless people," and again, "In Scotland you will never
find a man of worth: they are like savages who wish not to
be acquainted with any one, and are too envious of the
good fortune of others and suspicious of losing any thing
themselves, for their country is very poor."[20] Once when
telling of an English spy whose horse had been stolen
while the man was doing some spying along the northern
border, he observed that such an incident should not be
considered unusual because the Scots "are all thieves."[21]

On the other hand, he regularly compliments the Scots for their courage. "The Scots are bold, hardy, and much inured to war."[22] The impression certain peoples of Spain and Italy made upon him was quite different. He wrote: "the Castillians and Galicians resemble a good deal the Lombards and Italians, who are always on the side of the strongest, and shout out, 'The conqueror forever!' "[23] It may be significant that Froissart has never a direct word of criticism for the French.

Given Froissart's willingness to express himself in such derogatory terms about these different peoples, it is strange he has nothing demeaning to say of the Jews. One of the few occasions when he pays them some notice was in connection with a persecution, apparently widespread, they were suffering in 1349. He wrote:

> About this time, the Jews throughout the world were arrested and burnt, and their fortunes seized by those lords under whose jurisdiction they had lived, except at Avignon, and the territories of the church dependent on the pope. Each poor Jew, when he was able to hide himself, and arrive in that country, esteemed himself safe.[24]

Because Froissart was primarily, almost exclusively, the chronicler of battles, of heroic deeds performed on the battlefield, during sieges, or in knightly combat, the question concerning the sort of philosophy of history he subscribed to has not evoked much thought. He himself has little to say that might be considered germane to this point, neither does his writing suggest the operation of principles or laws that might have influenced or guided the course of events. Had he treated the seventy-five years he covers as a unified whole and had given it a beginning and a conclusion, he might have been tempted to propose the presence of forces that directed the behavior of men in order to discover some pattern in the manner events took place. His *Chronicles* consist largely of a continuing series of episodes and incidents, chronologically handled to be

sure, but treated in a seemingly endless and unvaried sequence that would continue along the same route and in
the same manner long after Froissart had laid down his
pen.

Now and then Froissart does drop the kind of philosophical observation common to many writers, such as that
"every thing which is created must in the course of nature
have an end."[25] There are several occasions when he attributes an event to chance, to good or evil fortune, "against
which none can make head when God wills it so."[26] This
particular remark he attributes to the duke of Lancaster
when he learned that the fleet that Arundel was bringing
to the relief of the duke of Brittany had foundered in a
storm. A similar reference to supernatural powers, this
one diabolical, appears in connection with the outbreak of
fighting in Flanders. Froissart writes that the earl, "being
wise and prudent," sought to prevent its outbreak, but
failed,

> and those who read this book, or who may have it read to
> them, will say, that it was the work of the devil. You know
> wise men think the devil, who is subtle and full of artifice,
> labours night and day to cause warfare wherever he finds
> peace and harmony, and seeks by distant means, and by
> degrees, how to accomplish his ends. And thus it fell out in
> Flanders, as you will clearly see and learn from the differ-
> ent treaties and ordinances which follow relative to these
> matters.[27]

The view expressed here is, of course, that of the medieval Christian and what one would, furthermore, expect of
the priest Froissart. The reader may therefore assume
that Froissart agreed with Lawrence of Fongasse, a squire
in the service of the king of Portugal, who attributed the
good fortune of his country and of its king Don John to
that monarch's virtues. The king, he explained, "fears and
loves God, has an affection for the church which he exalts
as much as in his power . . . above all, he will have justice

administered impartially in his dominions, and the poor maintained in their rights."[28]

What the agnostic reader will find more to his liking, however, is the observation Froissart makes in the course of telling the interesting story about Amerigot Marcel, a captain of free companies. These companies were composed of unemployed soldiers who preyed on the countryside during the years following the collapse of France after the battle of Poitiers (1356). Many such ex-soldiers had joined Marcel who for a time had enjoyed unbroken success in his plundering. He had even succeeded in seizing a strong fortress called La Roche de Vendais, which he and his followers used as a base from which to ravage the adjoining countryside. But his luck finally ran out. Opposition gradually stiffened to a point where he began to fear capture, and he made the mistake of seeking the assistance of a cousin who promptly betrayed him. Froissart, who treats the episode at length, ends with this comment:

> It is thus Fortune treats her favourites: when she has raised them to the highest point of her wheel, she suddenly plunges them in the dirt: witness Aymerigot Marcel. The foolish fellow was worth, as was believed in Auvergne, more than one hundred thousand francs in money, which he lost in one day, together with his life. I therefore say, that dame Fortune played him one of her tricks, which she has played to several before, and will do the same to many after him.[29]

A critical factor in determining the credibility of a writer of history is the nature and scope of the sources of information he might have employed. Here Froissart's record is commendable and his own words on the subject reassuring.

> I may, perhaps, be asked, how I became acquainted with the events in this history, to speak so circumstantially about them. I reply to those who shall do so, that I have, with great attention and diligence, sought in divers king-

doms and countries for the facts that have been, or may hereafter be mentioned in it: for God has given me grace and opportunities to see, and make acquaintance with the greater part of the principal lords of France and England. It should be known, that in the year 1390, I had laboured at this history thirty-seven years, and at that time I was fifty-seven years old: a man may, therefore, learn much in such a period, when he is in his vigour, and well received by all parties. During my youth, I was five years attached to the king and queen of England, and kindly entertained in the household of King John of France and King Charles his son: I was, in consequence, enabled to hear much during those times: and, for certain, the greatest pleasure I have ever had, was to make every possible inquiry, in regard to what was passing in the world, and then write down all that I had learnt.[30]

Not only did Froissart go to considerable pains to gather information, but he appreciated the importance of securing the details from both sides in any controversy. Before entering upon his account of the battle fought between the English and Scots at Otterburne in 1388, he tells of his efforts to find information.

I was made acquainted with all the particulars of this battle by knights and squires who had been actors in it on each side. There were also, with the English, two valiant knights from the country of Foix, whom I had the good fortune to meet at Orthès, the year after the battle had been fought. . . . On my return from Foix, I met likewise at Avignon a knight and two squires of Scotland, of the party of Earl Douglas. They knew me again, from the recollections I brought to their minds of their own country; for in my youth, I, the author of this history, travelled all through Scotland, and was full fifteen days resident with William Earl Douglas, father of Earl James, of whom we are now speaking, at his castle of Dalkeith, five miles distant from Edinburgh. . . . I had my information, therefore, from both parties.[31]

Froissart must have made a number of shorter trips for the purpose of securing firsthand information about the different episodes he hoped to describe. In 1394 he made one such trip to Abbeville where English and French commissioners had gathered to discuss peace, so that he "might learn the truth of what was passing."[32] When the opportunity presented itself, our chronicler was not above combining business with pleasure. So he tells that in 1389 he made a trip to Paris "to learn the particulars of the conferences that were holding at Leulinghem, between the French and English, and likewise to be present at the magnificent feasts that were given at Queen Isabella's public entry to Paris."[33] The two goals of news and pleasure also brought him to the marriage of the duke of Berry that same year. "The marriage was very magnificent. . . . The feastings and tournaments lasted for four days, and I, the writer of this book, was a partaker of them all."[34]

Given the variety and informal nature of the sources of Froissart's information, it would be a gullible reader indeed who would swear to the absolute accuracy of everything in the *Chronicles*. When Froissart cites his sources, the reader may feel reasonably confident, more certain still when the chronicler declares he is relaying the information firsthand. One could scarcely demand a more precise item than the 25,000 nobles a year he says Queen Philippa realized from the large estate given her in England since he "served that queen of good memory . . . to whom I was secretary, and I then heard from many lords, ladies and knights who had received the rents of these estates, their amount."[35] Concerning the visit of the duchess of Lancaster and her daughter to the king and queen of Portugal in 1386, Froissart writes: "The whole palace was rejoiced at the arrival of these ladies; but I will not pretend to speak very particularly of what passed, for I was not there: all I know was from that gallant knight, Sir John Fernando Portelet, who was present."[36]

If the reader may not assume the accuracy of all of

Froissart's statements, he should know that the same ca-
veat applies when consulting the works of almost every
writer before Froissart's day who aspired to the role of
historian. Herodotus says that more than two million men
made up the Persian host that invaded Attica in 492 B.C., a
figure all scholars dismiss as ridiculous. Much of what the
Roman historian Livy incorporated into his history must
be classified as legend. On the other hand, scholars are
willing to accept the substantial accuracy of Froissart's
account of the battle of Crecy, for example, and even cite
his figures for the number of troops involved. The reader
must keep reminding himself of two points when reading
Froissart. First, Froissart lived before the age when the
writing of history had become a science: he did not visit
archives and study and compare conflicting accounts as is
necessary today.[37] Second, his aim was not the writing of a
balanced history of the times but that of leaving a record
of the valiant deeds performed in the wars among the
French, English, and their neighbors, and to "give a true
account" of how castles and towns were attacked and
taken. Instead of criticizing Froissart for inaccuracies,
"we shall be rather surprised at the general trustworthi-
ness of these *Chronicles* than at their particular errors."[38]

Before considering Froissart in his major role of historian of chivalry in western Europe in the fourteenth century, it will be useful to glance at other kinds of information his *Chronicles* furnish the reader. Several scholars
have gone so far in their admiration of Froissart as to
classify him as the Herodotus of the late Middle Ages.
That he surely was not. The theme of both Froissart and
Herodotus may have been wars, but where the Greek historian offers much information concerning the mores and
institutions of the different peoples he introduces, Froissart draws almost a complete blank in these respects. Still
it is unjust to fault Froissart for his lack of concern about
ordinary people, what they did and how they lived. They
simply did not come within the scope of the sights he set

for himself. His goal was to present a description of battles and acts of gallantry, against a background of political history, for the entertainment and inspiration of his aristocratic patrons and friends.

Froissart does lower his sights from time to time. When writing of battles he must, of course, include squires and men-at-arms. And there were occasions, too, when the lower classes caused their social betters trouble. The most serious such occasion was the Peasant Revolt of 1381 in England. As one might suspect, Froissart's sympathy lay with those who represented the status quo against those who would disturb it, although he does make an effort to state the case for the peasantry. His account, which he hopes "may serve as an example to mankind," strikes the reader as reasonably balanced.

> It is customary in England, as well as in several other countries, for the nobility to have great privileges over the commonalty, whom they keep in bondage; that is to say, they are bound by law and custom to plow the lands of the gentlemen, to harvest the grain, to carry it home to the barn, to thresh and winnow it; they are also bound to harvest the hay and carry it home. All these services they are obliged to perform for their lords, and many more in England than in other countries. The prelates and gentlemen are thus served. In the counties of Kent, Essex, Sussex, and Bedford, these services are more oppressive than in all the rest of the kingdom.
>
> The evil-disposed in these districts began to rise, saying, they were too severely oppressed; that at the beginning of the world there were no slaves, and that no one ought to be treated as such, unless he had committed treason against his lord, as Lucifer had done against God; but they had done no such thing, for they were neither angels nor spirits, but men formed after the same likeness as these lords, who treated them as beasts. This they would not longer bear, but had determined to be free, and if they laboured or did any other work for lords, they would be paid for it.

John Ball, a "crazy priest," had made himself the spokesman of these disgruntled peasants. Each Sunday after
mass he would harangue them in the marketplace over the
injustices they were suffering at the hands of their lords.
"My good friends," he would preach,

> things cannot go on well in England, nor ever will until
> every thing shall be in common; when there shall neither be
> vassal nor lord, and all distinctions levelled; when the lords
> shall be no more master than ourselves. How ill have they
> used us? and for what reason do they thus hold us in bond-
> age? Are we not all descended from the same parents,
> Adam and Eve? and what can they show, or what reasons
> give, why they should be more the masters than ourselves?
> except, perhaps, in making us labour and work, for them to
> spend. They are clothed in velvets and rich stuffs, orna-
> mented with ermine and other furs, while we are forced to
> wear poor cloth. They have wines, spices, and fine bread,
> when we have only rye and the refuse of the straw; and, if
> we drink, it must be water. They have handsome seats and
> manors, when we must brave the wind and rain in our
> labours in the field; but it is from our labour that they have
> wherewith to support their pomp. We are called slaves,
> and, if we do not perform our service, we are beaten and we
> have not any sovereign to whom we can complain, or who
> wishes to hear us and do us justice. Let us to the king who
> is young, and remonstrate with him on our servitude, tell-
> ing him we must have it otherwise, or that we shall find a
> remedy for it ourselves.[39]

Some critics have condemned Froissart for his callous
attitude toward the lower classes. To prove their case they
cite a passage from the *Chronicles* that describes the capture of Limoges by the Black Prince and the slaying on his
orders of the town's entire population. The news that the
city had gone over to the French had so infuriated the
prince that he "swore by the soul of his father, which he
had never perjured, that he would have it back again . . .
and that he would make the inhabitants pay dearly for

their treachery."[40] After the army had completely encircled the town, he set his miners to work to undermine the walls. In about a month they had completed their task, when they notified the Black Prince that all was ready.

> This news was very agreeable to the prince, who replied, "I wish then that you would prove your words tomorrow morning at six o'clock." The miners set fire to the combustibles in the mines; and on the morrow morning, as they had foretold the prince, they flung down a great piece of wall, which filled the ditches.
>
> The English saw this with pleasure, for they were all armed and prepared to enter the town. Those on foot did so, and ran to the gate, which they destroyed as well as the barriers, for there were no other defences; and all this was done so suddenly that the inhabitants had not time to prevent it.
>
> The prince, the duke of Lancaster, the earls of Cambridge and of Pembroke, Sir Guiscard d'Angle and the others, with their men, rushed into the town. You would have then seen pillagers, active to do mischief, running through the town, slaying men, women, and children, according to their orders. It was a most melancholy business; for all ranks, ages and sexes cast themselves on their knees before the prince, begging for mercy; but he was inflamed with passion and revenge that he listened to none, but all were put to the sword, wherever they could be found, even those who were not guilty; for I know not why the poor were not spared, who could not have had any part in this treason; but they suffered for it, and indeed more than those who had been the leaders of the treachery.
>
> There was not that day in the city of Limoges any heart so hardened, or that had any sense of religion, who did not deeply bewail the unfortunate events passing before their eyes; for upwards of three thousand men, women, and children were put to death that day. God have mercy on their souls! for they were veritable martyrs.[41]

What shocks the modern reader most about this brutal act of the Black Prince is that his age hailed him as the epitome of chivalry. Perhaps this act had best be viewed as a lapse on the Black Prince's part, surely no condemnation of Froissart. He makes it quite clear that he deplored the tragedy as wholly without justification, and he particularly condemned the slaughter of the "poor." To have referred to the massacre of the populace in harsher terms than "a very melancholy business" might have lost him his patrons and his audience – and us his *Chronicles*. And he refers to the unfortunate victims as "veritable martyrs."

For the same reason Froissart has even less to say about women than of commoners. Only by exception do they come within the purview of the matter he set himself to describe. His relative silence may not be construed as indifference to the female sex or the mark of traditional masculine prejudice. When the opportunity presents itself, he is ready to describe the exploit of any person – noble, peasant, or woman. He does so without any of the patronizing overtones a discriminated group resents. Here is his account of the manner in which the countess of Montfort, "who possessed the courage of a man, and the heart of a lion," defended the city of Hennebon in Brittany against the French. Her husband had been captured by the French. For several days the French under Lord Charles de Blois had been besieging the city. The countess, who was one of a very few who were opposed to surrendering, hurried off an appeal to England for aid, then

> clothed herself in armour, was mounted on a warhorse, and galloped up and down the streets of the town, entreating and encouraging the inhabitants to defend themselves honorably. She ordered the ladies and other women to unpave the street, carry the stones to the ramparts, and throw them on their enemies. She had pots of quicklime brought to her for the same purpose.
>
> That same day the countess performed a very gallant deed: she ascended a high tower, to see how her people behaved; and, having observed that all the lords and

others of the army had quitted their tents, and were come to the assault, she immediately descended, mounted her horse, armed as she was, collected three hundred horsemen, sallied out at their head by another gate that was not attacked, and, galloping up to the tents of her enemies, cut them down, and set them on fire, without any loss, for there were only servants and boys, who fled upon her approach.

Next she led her company to Brest where she collected some five hundred additional men. She managed to lead them back into Hennebon at midnight without the French being aware of what was going on. Despite her heroism, the city had all but decided to surrender to the French when a relief expedition under Sir Walter Manny arrived just in the nick of time. Froissart as he continues his account describes how the English then made an unexpected assault on a large tower from which the French had commanded the walls, cleared it of its defenders, destroyed it, then drove off a body of Frenchmen who had come up to attack them. When they returned to the castle, the "countess came down . . . to meet them, and, with a most cheerful countenance, kissed Sir Walter Manny, and all his companions, one after the other, like a noble and valiant dame."[42]

Froissart tells of another countess who displayed a nobility of a different sort. This woman, wife of the earl of Salisbury who was a prisoner in France, had just managed to drive off the Scots who had attacked her castle of Wark. The Scots had withdrawn from the area upon news that Edward III and his army were approaching. When the king stopped in to pay his respects to the countess, the lady

went out to meet him, most richly dressed; insomuch, that no one could cease looking at her but with wonder and admiration at her noble deportment, great beauty, and affability of behavior. When she came near the king, she

made her reverence to the ground, and gave him her
thanks for coming to her assistance, and then conducted
him into the castle, to entertain and honor him, as she was
very capable of doing. Everyone was delighted with her:
the king could not take his eyes off her, as he thought he
had never seen so beautiful or sprightly a lady; so that a
spark of fine love struck upon his heart, which lasted a long
time, for he did not believe that the whole world produced
any other lady so worthy of being beloved.

The countess showed Edward to his chamber, then went
to welcome the other guests. After she had given instructions that dinner be prepared and the hall decorated, she
returned to Edward only to find him deep in thought.
When she sought to rouse him from his pensive mood, he
explained that since he had come to the castle something
had so engrossed his mind that he could not get it out of
his thoughts. When the countess advised him to stop wor-
rying about the Scots, assuming that it was that which
was causing him his moodiness, the king explained that it
was something quite different, nothing less than his infat-
uation for her. It ran so deep, he told her, "that my happiness depends on meeting a return from you."

"Sweet sir," replied the countess, "do not amuse yourself in
laughing at, or tempting me; for I cannot believe you mean
what you have just said, or that so noble and gallant a
prince as you are would ever think to dishonour me or my
husband, who is so valiant a knight, who has served you
faithfully, and who, on your account, now lies in prison.
Certainly, sir, this would not add to your glory; nor would
you be the better for it. Such a thought has never once
entered my mind, and I trust in God it never will, for any
man living: and, if I were so culpable, it is you who ought to
blame me, and have my body punished, through strict justice."

Whereupon the countess left the abashed Edward, attended to the final preparations, then returned to Edward but with several knights in her company, to invite him to dinner. During the meal the king "ate very little, and was the whole time pensive, casting his eyes, whenever he had an opportunity, towards the countess." When after a troubled night he bade the countess goodbye the following morning, he asked her to give him a "different answer" the next time he would see her.

> "Dear Sir," replied the countess, "God, of his infinite goodness, preserve you, and drive from your heart such villainous thoughts; for I am, and always shall be ready to serve you, consistently with my honour and with yours."[43]

This did not close the matter. Froissart tells how Edward some time later arranged a series of feasts and tournaments in London to which he invited the lords and ladies of England and France. He "expressly ordered the earl of Salisbury to have the lady his wife there" (the earl had returned from prison). "The ladies and damsels were most superbly dressed and ornamented, according to their different degrees, except the countess of Salisbury, who came there in as plain attire as possible."[44] Because the chronicler has nothing more to add to this romantic episode, the reader may assume that Edward had finally gotten the message.

A major subject Froissart fairly skirted was the church and ecclesiastical affairs in general. Had he considered religion of little importance, which was not the case, the reader would not expect him to have written much on the subject. His silence here is consistent with his stated objective, that of writing about battles and about gallant men. He does give the papal schism some attention, principally because of its political ramifications, but he avoids taking sides. This again is what one might expect; he counted aristocratic friends in both camps. The English and many people in the Low Countries adhered to the

Roman pope, while those in France, Scotland, and Spain supported the one in Avignon. To have expressed sympathy for one or the other pope would have cost him some of his friends.

Though Froissart never directly addresses himself to the subject of faith and religion, he does often mention how kings, armies, and people offered their prayers to God and to the Virgin. This is what the duke of Gueldres did who succeeded in routing the army of Brabanters with his handful of knights. After the victory he insisted that, rather than riding immediately to Grave with their prisoners, they should first do as he had vowed. He explained:

> "I made a vow to our Lady of Nimeguen when I left that town, and which I again renewed when we began the combat; in obedience to which, I order, that we gaily return to Nimeguen, and offer our thanksgivings to the holy Virgin, who has assisted us in our victory." This command was obeyed: for, as the duke had given it, not one made any objection, and they set out on their return towards Nimeguen, full gallop. It was two long leagues from the field of battle, but they were soon there.
>
> On this fortunate news being told in that town, great rejoicing was made by both sexes; the clergy went out in procession to meet the duke, and received him with acclamations. The duke did not turn to the right nor left, but rode with his knights straight to the church where the image of our Lady was, and in which he had great faith. When he entered her chapel, he disarmed himself of everything to his doublet, and offered up his armour on the altar, in honor of our Lady, returning thanksgivings for the victory he had gained over his enemies.[45]

In an age somewhat romantically referred to as the "age of faith," one reads without surprise how the English, when they learned that the French were about to invade their country, made processions three times a week, "where, with much devotion, they offered up their prayers to God, to avert this peril from them." It appears Froissart credited the English aristocracy with less faith than that exhibited by the common people. He writes that Pope Urban, in order to raise an army against those who supported the Avignonese pope, promised the people "his pardons and absolutions from all crimes," but the chronicler drily observes:

> It was necessary . . . that he should have a considerable sum of ready money, if he wished to put his plans into execution; for it was well known that the nobles of England would not, for all the absolutions in the world, undertake any expeditions, unless such were preceded by offers of money. Men at arms cannot live on pardons, nor do they pay much attention to them, except at the point of death.[46]

Froissart was preeminently the historian of chivalry. He wrote about the aristocracy, of battles, tournaments, of marriages and other activities that involved members of that class. His *Chronicles,* however, do not constitute a formal history as such of the upper or ruling class. He was selective in what he considered memorable about this class. The administration of their estates, the enactment of laws, even the struggle for power between crown and aristocracy were matters that passed him by. Such subjects might have bored his readers, or he may have considered them too sensitive to discuss. In writing of the aristocracy, he introduced those subjects – stories of gallantry, heroism, and prowess – about which he was certain they would be pleased to read or to listen to.

The pages of the *Chronicles* teem with incidents and episodes that titillated the hearts of Froissart's contemporaries among the aristocracy and a legion of romantic readers since his day. Froissart was an enthusiastic admirer of the chivalric code. One of his first stories fairly oozes the idealism of knighthood. Robert Bruce, king of Scotland, was on his deathbed, a cheerless place in any circumstance but particularly so for Bruce because he had failed to fulfill his vow "to go and make war against the

enemies of our Lord Jesus Christ, and the adversaries of
the Christian faith." Had his troubled realm of Scotland
not kept him continually occupied there, he would certainly have gone to the Holy Land in person. Because that
was now impossible, he wished that his heart at least
should go there "in the stead of my body to fulfil my vow."
So he asked Sir James Douglas to undertake this mission,
"for I have that opinion of your nobleness and loyalty,
that, if you undertake it, it cannot fail of success." When
Douglas accepted the assignment, the king gave him the
following instructions:

> "I will, that, as soon as I shall be dead, you take my heart
> from my body, and have it well embalmed; you will also
> take as much money from my treasury as will appear to
> you sufficient to perform your journey, as well as for all
> those whom you may choose to have accompany you, to
> deposit it at the Holy Sepulchre of our Lord, where he was
> buried, since my body cannot go there. You will not be
> sparing of expense – and provide yourself with such com-
> pany and such things suitable to your rank – and where-
> with you pass, you will let it be known, that you bear the
> heart of King Robert of Scotland, which you are carrying
> beyond the seas by his command, since his body cannot go
> thither."

A few days after Bruce's death, Sir Douglas embarked
at the port of Montrose with his sacred charge, sailed to
Sluys, then while waiting twelve days for favorable winds,

> kept a magnificent table, with music of trumpets and
> drums, as if he had been the king of Scotland. His company
> consisted of one knight-banneret, and seven others of the
> most valiant knights of Scotland, without counting the
> rest of his household. His plate was of gold and silver,
> consisting of pots, basins, porringers, cups, bottles, bar-
> rels, and other such things. He had likewise twenty-six
> young and gallant esquires of the best families in Scotland
> to wait upon him; and all those who came to visit him were

handsomely served with two sorts of wine and two sorts of spices – I mean those of a certain rank.

On his way southward from Sluys Sir Douglas learned that Alphonso, "king of Spain," was waging war against the Infidel ruler of Granada, whereupon he decided to break his trip and do some crusading in Spain before going on. Shortly thereafter came the day when the Christian and Muslim armies were drawn up ready to do battle. When Sir Douglas

> perceived that the battalions on each side were fully arranged, and that of the king of Spain in motion, he imagined they were about to begin the onset; and as he always wished to be among the first rather than the last upon such occasions, he and all his company struck their spurs into their horses, until they were in the midst of the king of Granada's battalion, and made a furious attack upon the Saracens. He thought that he should be supported by the Spaniards; but in this he was mistaken, for not one that day followed his example. The gallant knight and all his companions were surrounded by the enemy: they performed prodigies of valour; but they were of no avail, as they were all killed. It was a great misfortune that they were not assisted by the Spaniards.[47]

This story must have pleased Froissart as much as it warmed the hearts of all his listeners, at least all but those who were Spaniards. The following anecdote is representative of the many in the *Chronicles* that do honor to both lords and knights, as well as to lowly squires. One of the valiant nobles who helped the Black Prince gain his overwhelming victory at Poitiers in 1356 was Lord James Audley. After the battle, his four faithful squires "led him ... very weak and wounded, towards a hedge, that he might cool and take breath. They disarmed him as gently as they could, in order to examine his wounds, dress them, and sew up the most dangerous." When the Black Prince returned to his camp, he asked about Audley and learned that "he is very badly wounded, and is lying on a litter hard by." The prince directed that he be brought to him if possible, otherwise he would himself go to the knight to commend him for his heroism. When the attendants brought in Audley, the Black Prince complimented him on his courage. "You have acquired glory and renown above us all," he told him, "and your prowess has proved you the bravest knight." Then as a tangible token of his esteem he announced that he was taking Audley into his own service and was granting him a revenue of five hundred marks. After the Black Prince had gone, Audley sent for the four squires who had attended him and said:

> "Gentlemen, it has pleased my lord the prince to give me five hundred marcs as a yearly inheritance; for which gift I have done him very trifling bodily service. You see here these squires, who have always served me most loyally, and especially in this day's engagement. What glory I may have gained, has been through their means, and by their valour: on which account I wish to reward them. I therefore give and resign into their hands the five hundred marcs, which my lord the prince has been pleased to bestow upon me."[48]

Later when the Black Prince learned what Audley had done, he commended him on his action but insisted that he keep another six hundred marks that he was giving him, for himself.[49]

At no time in the history of warfare were the forms and rules governing such matters as the declaration of war, even the actual fighting itself, so elaborate nor so punctiliously observed as during the high and late Middle Ages. It was considered quite irregular, for instance, when Charles V of France sent a valet to deliver a challenge to Edward III. He should have entrusted that mission to a great lord or to a prelate. Froissart tells how Charles, once he felt ready to reopen the war, sent a valet to take his "challenge" to Edward. When the valet was brought into the presence of the English king and his council, they examined his papers

> very carefully every way, as well as the seal, and clearly saw that the challenge was good. They ordered the valet to withdraw, telling him he had done his business well, and he might boldly set out on his return, for he would not meet with any obstacle to his so doing, as indeed he did not: he therefore went back to France as speedily as possible. . . .
>
> It is proper to be known that the king and his council were greatly offended that this challenge should have been brought by a valet: they said it was not decent that a war between two such great lords as the kings of France and of England should be announced and declared by a common servant; that it would not have been unworthy of a prelate, or of a valiant baron or knight, to have been the bearer of such declaration: however, nothing more was done.[50]

The rules of chivalry forbade the slaying of a knight by other than honorable means, surely not by way of a stab in the back. The following anecdote finds not only Froissart condemning the deed, but both the French and the English as well. The victim was a Welsh knight by name of Evan of Wales. He had been most successful in helping the French against the English in Aquitaine and was now directing the siege of the castle of Mortain, which was under command of Souldich de l'Estrade. "During the time of this siege, there came out of England, from the borders of Wales, a Welsh squire named John Lambe, who was scarcely a gentleman; and indeed he showed it, for no gentleman would ever have practised such base wickedness."

This John Lambe came to Poitou, ingratiated himself with Evan by speaking to him in his native Welsh and telling him that the "whole principality [of Wales] was desirous of having him for their lord. This information gained him so much the love of Evan (for every one naturally would wish to return to his own country) that he immediately appointed him his chamberlain." This proved a fatal mistake, as Froissart goes on to tell.

It was Evan's habit to rise early in the morning, take his seat before the castle of Mortain, then take his comb and plait his hair while enjoying the beautiful scenery.

> On his last visit, it was early morn and fine clear weather, and the heat of the night had prevented him from sleeping: he went thither all unbuttoned, with only his jacket and shirt, and his cloak thrown over him, when he seated himself as usual, attended by John Lambe. All the others were asleep, and no guard was kept. . . . After Evan had seated himself on the trunk of a tree, he said to John Lambe, "Go and seek my comb, for it will refresh me a little." He answered, "Willingly, my lord." On his way to seek for the comb, or when returning with it, the devil must have entered the body of this John; for with the comb he brought a short Spanish dagger that had a broad point, to accomplish his evil intentions: he stuck this dagger into Evan, whose body was almost naked, and pierced him through, so that he fell down dead.

After he had done the deed, John Lambe made his way to the castle and was conducted inside, where he told his story to the souldich.

> "My lord," said he to the souldich, "I have delivered you from one of the greatest enemies you ever had." "From whom?" replied the souldich. "From Evan of Wales," answered John. "By what means?" demanded the souldich. "By such means," said John, and then related to him the circumstances you have just heard. When the souldich heard this, he shook his head, and, eyeing him with anger, replied, "Thou hast murdered him; but know from me, that if we did not reap much advantage from thy wicked deed, I would have thy head cut off: what is done, however, cannot be undone; but such a death is unworthy of a gentleman, and we shall have more blame than praise for it."[51]

Feudal warfare could claim more conventions than that of any other period. It also left room for lighter episodes, such as the following one, that often relieved the grim business of killing. This episode describes a tilt between two contestants, one of many that Froissart finds space for in his *Chronicles*. The French squire who proposed the contest had apparently promised his beloved that he would challenge some Englishman to prove his fidelity to her. One day during the siege of a castle in Brittany, when time was heavy on his hands, this Frenchman rode out of the castle the English had under siege and challenged one of the enemy to take up his wager. "Is there among you any gentleman," he demanded,

"who for the love of his lady is willing to try with me some feat of arms. If there should be any such here, I am quite ready to sally forth completely armed and mounted, to tilt three courses with the lance, to give three blows with the battle-axe, and three strokes with the dagger. Now look, you English, if there be none among you in love."

This squire's name was Gauvain Micaille. His proposal and request was soon spread among the English, when a squire, an expert man at tournaments, called Joachim Cator, stepped forth and said, "I will deliver him from his vow: let him make haste and come out of the castle."

Upon this, the lord Fitzwalter, marshall of the army, went to the barriers, and said to sir Guy le Baveux, "Let your squire come forth: he has found one who will cheerfully deliver him; and we will afford him every security."

Gauvain Micaille was much rejoiced on hearing these words. He immediately armed himself, in which the lords assisted, in the putting on the different pieces, and mounted him on a horse, which they gave to him. Attended by two others, he came out of the castle; and his varlets carried three lances, three battle-axes and three daggers. He was much looked at by the English, for they did not think any Frenchman would have engaged body to body. There were besides to be three strokes with a sword, and with all other sorts of arms. Gauvain had had three brought with him for fear any should break.

The earl of Buckingham, hearing of this combat, said he

would see it, and mounted his horse, attended by the earls of Stafford and Devonshire. On this account, the assault on Toury ceased. The Englishman that was to tilt was brought forward, completely armed and mounted on a good horse. When they had taken their stations, they gave to each of them a spear, and the tilt began; but neither of them struck the other, from the mettlesomeness of their horses. They hit the second onset, but it was by darting their spears; on which the earl of Buckingham cried out, "Hola, hola! It is now late." He then said to the constable, "Put an end to it, for they have done enough this day; we will make them finish it when we have more leisure than we have at this moment, and take great care that as much attention is paid to the French squire as to our own; and order some one to tell those of the castle, not to be uneasy about him, for we shall carry him with us to complete this enterprise, but not as a prisoner; and that when he shall have been delivered, if he escape with his life, we will send him back in all safety."

These orders of the earl were obeyed by the marshal, who said to the French squire, "You shall accompany us without any danger, and when it shall be agreeable to my lord you will be delivered." Gauvain replied, "God help me!" A herald was sent to the castle, to repeat to the governor the words you have heard.

[A few days afterward] on the day of our Lady, Gawain Micaille and Joachim Cator were armed, and mounted to finish their engagement. They met each other roughly with spears, and the French squire tilted much to the satisfaction of the earl: but the Englishman kept his spear too low, and at last struck it into the thigh of the Frenchman. The earl of Buckingham as well as the other lords were much enraged at this, and said it was tilting dishonourably; but he excused himself, by declaring it was solely owing to the restiveness of his horse. Then were given three thrusts with the sword; and the earl declared they had done enough and would not have it longer continued, for he perceived the French squire bled exceedingly: the other lords were of the same opinion. Gauvain Micaille was therefore disarmed, and his wound dressed. The earl sent him one hundred francs by a herald, with leave to return to his own garrison in safety, adding that he had acquitted himself much to his satisfaction.[52]

A tilting contest resembled a tournament in miniature. This last by the late fourteenth century had ceased being a proving ground for war and had "degenerated" into little more than a pageant. One could conclude as much from Froissart's description of the tournament held at Smithfield in 1390, which Richard II had arranged to celebrate the public entry of Queen Isabella into Paris. He directed that

grand tournaments and feasts to be holden in the city of London, where sixty knights should be accompanied by sixty noble ladies, richly ornamented and dressed. The sixty knights were to tilt for two days; that is to say, on the Sunday after Michaelmas-day, and the Monday following, in the year of grace 1390. The sixty knights were to set out at two o'clock in the afternoon from the Tower of London, with their ladies, and parade through the streets, down Cheapside, to a large square called Smithfield. There the knights were to wait on the Sunday the arrival of any foreign knights who might be desirous of tilting; and this feast of the Sunday was called the feast of the challengers. The same ceremonies were to take place on Monday, and the sixty knights to be prepared for tilting courteously with blunted lances against all comers. The prize for the best knight of the opponents was to be a rich crown of gold, that for the tenants of the lists a very rich golden clasp: they were to be given to the most gallant tilter, according to the judgment of the ladies, who would be present with the queen of England and the great barons, as spectators.

On the Tuesday the tournaments were to be continued by the squires, against others of the same rank who wished to oppose them. The prize for the opponents was a courser saddled and bridled, and for the tenants of the lists a falcon. The manner of holding this feast being settled, heralds were sent to proclaim it throughout England, Scotland, Hainaut, Germany, Flanders, and France. It was ordered by the council to what parts each herald was to go; and, having time before hand, then published it in most countries.

Many knights and squires from foreign lands made preparations to attend it: some to see the manners of the English, others to take part in the tournaments. On the feast being made known in Hainaut, Sir William de Hainaut count d'Ostrevant who was at that time young and gallant, and fond of tilting, determined, in his own mind, to be present, and to honour and make acquaintance with his cousin, King Richard, and his uncles, whom he had never seen. He therefore engaged many knights and squires to accompany him.

The young man's decision to go to England did not please his father, the count of Hainaut, who sought to dissuade him lest he be wooed away by the English from his French associations. But the young man persisted and in time joined the grand company at Smithfield. On Sunday, about three in the afternoon,

there paraded out from the Tower of London . . . sixty barded coursers ornamented for the tournament, on each was mounted a squire of honour that advanced only at a foot's pace; then came sixty ladies of rank mounted on palfreys most elegantly and richly dressed, following each other, every one leading a knight with a silver chain completely armed for tilting; and in this procession they moved on through the streets of London, attended by numbers of minstrels and trumpets, to Smithfield. The queen of England with her ladies and damsels were already arrived and placed in chambers handsomely decorated.

The first day of the tournament saw foreign knights tilting until "night forced them to break off." Afterward many of the guests repaired to the bishop of London's palace near St. Paul's church, where the queen was lodged, for a banquet and dancing. The second day's tilting furnished the high point of the tournament.

You would have seen on the ensuing morning, Monday, squires, and varlets busily employed, in different parts of London, furbishing and making ready armour and horses for their masters who were to engage in the jousts. In the afternoon King Richard entered Smithfield magnificently accompanied by dukes, lords and knights for he was chief of the tenants of the lists. The queen took her station as on the preceding day, with her ladies, in the apartments that had been prepared. . . .

The tournament now began, and every one exerted himself to the utmost to excel: many were unhorsed, and more lost their helmets. The jousting continued with great courage and perseverance until night put an end to it. The company now retired to their lodgings or their homes; and, when the hour for supper was near, the lords and ladies attended it, which was splendid and well served. The prize for the opponents at the tournament was adjudged by the ladies, lords and heralds, to the count d'Ostrevant, who far eclipsed all who had tilted that day: that for the tenants was given to a gallant knight of England called Sir Hugh Spenser.

More tilting followed on Wednesday and more banqueting, while "the dancing lasted until day-break." The remainder of the week was given over to entertainments, the last of which was a magnificent affair furnished by the king at Windsor, "a handsome castle, well built and richly ornamented, situated on the Thames, twenty miles from London." The climax of these closing festivities came when Richard offered Count d'Ostrevant membership in the Knights of the Garter. His acceptance of this most exclusive honor led the French knights present to murmur: "This count d'Ostrevant plainly shows that his heart is more inclined to England than France."[53]

Because of Froissart's interest in feudal warfare, his *Chronicles* make a significant contribution to our knowledge of the art of war in the late fourteenth century. Here is his description of the army of Edward III on its march toward Paris in 1359.

I must inform you, that the king of England and his rich lords were followed by carts laden with tents, pavillions, mills and forges, to grind their corn and make shoes for their horses, and everything of that sort which might be wanting. For this effect there were upwards of six thousand carts, each of them drawn by four good and strong horses which had been transported from England. Upon these carts also were many vessels and small boats, made surprisingly well of boiled leather: they were large enough to contain three men, to enable them to fish any lake or pond, whatever might be its size: and they were of great use to the lords and barons during Lent; but the commonalty made use of what provisions they could get. The king had, besides, thirty falconers on horseback, laden with hawks; sixty couples of strong hounds, and as many greyhounds; so that every day he took the pleasure of hunting or fishing either by land or water. Many lords had their hawks and hounds as well as the king.

Their army was always in three divisions, and each person kept to his division: there was also a van-guard to every one of them, and their quarters were one league distant from each other, the king being with the third and largest division. This order was constantly kept on the march from Calais, until they came before the town of Chartres.[54]

The above description would fit the manner a well-supplied army might move about in Froissart's day. Because of the poverty of Scotland and the practice of frugality this forced upon its people, the Scots never enjoyed such luxury.

The Scots are bold, hardy, and much inured to war. When they make their invasions into England, they march from twenty to four-and-twenty leagues without halting, as well by night as day; for they are all on horseback, except the camp followers, who are on foot. The knights and esquires are well mounted on large bay horses, the common people on little galloways. They bring no carriages with them, on account of the mountains they have to pass in Northumberland; neither do they carry with them any provisions of bread or wine, for their custom and sobriety is such, in time of war, that they will live for a long time on flesh half sodden without bread, and drink the river water without wine. They have therefore no occasion for pots or pans, for they dress the flesh of their cattle in the skins, after they have taken them off; and being sure to find plenty of them in the country which they invade, they carry none with them. Under the flaps of his saddle each man carries a broad plate of metal, behind the saddle a little bag of oat-meal; when they have eaten too much of this sodden flesh, and their stomachs appear weak and empty, they place this plate over the fire, mix with water their oatmeal, and, when the plate is heated, they put a little of the paste upon it, and make a thin cake, like a cracknell or biscuit, which they eat to warm their stomachs: it is therefore no wonder, that they perform a longer day's march than other sol-diers.[55]

Warfare in the fourteenth century consisted ordinarily of sharp, brief battles preceded or followed by the capture of towns and castles. Even when a sizable army did begin to march, its goal may have been no more ambitious than the capture of booty and the looting of the countryside. Such was Edward's aim when he crossed over to Nor-mandy in July 1346. He plundered Caen, then led his army to the Seine, when he learned of the approach of the French. Because he had no "more than an eighth part of the forces which the King of France had," Edward sought to avoid a confrontation as long as possible. He eventually retreated to Crecy where he selected "the most advanta-geous situation" to the north of the town, divided his forces into three battalions, and waited the attack. The French arrived late in the afternoon, but being tired from their long march, Philip, the king, wisely heeded the ad-vice of his councillors and gave instructions to wait until the morning before attacking. But the orders he issued to that effect either did not reach the troops to the rear or these then found they could not halt their forward movement.

Those that were in the front halted; but those behind said they could not halt, until they were as forward as the front. When the front perceived the rear pressing on, they pushed forward; and neither the king nor the marshals could stop them, but they marched on without any order until they came in sight of their enemies. As soon as the foremost rank saw them, they fell back at once, in great disorder, which alarmed those in the rear, who thought they had been fighting. There was then space and room enough for them to have passed forward, had they been willing to do so: some did so, but others remained shy.

All the roads between Abbeville and Crecy were covered with common people, who, when they were come within three leagues of their enemies, drew their swords, bawling out, "Kill, kill"; and with them were many great lords that were eager to make show of their courage. There is no man, unless he had been present, that can imagine, or describe truly, the confusion of that day; especially the bad management and disorder of the French, whose troops were out of number.

When Philip caught sight of the English "his blood began to boil," and he cried out to his marshals, "Order the Genoese forward, and begin the battle, in the name of God and St. Denis." There were about fifteen thousand Genoese crossbowmen; but they were quite fatigued, having marched on foot that day six leagues, completely armed, and with their crossbows. . . .

During this time a heavy rain fell, accompanied by thunder and a very terrible eclipse of the sun; and before this rain a great flight of crows hovered in the air over all those battalions, making a loud noise. Shortly afterwards it cleared up, and the sun shone very bright; but the Frenchmen had it in their faces, and the English on their backs.

When the Genoese were somewhat in order, and approached the English, they set up a loud shout, in order to frighten them; but they remained quite still, and did not seem to attend to it. They then set up a second shout, and advanced a little forward; but the English never moved. They hooted a third time, advancing with their crossbows presented, and began to shoot. The English archers then advanced one step forward, and shot their arrows with such force and quickness, that it seemed as if it snowed.

When the Genoese felt these arrows, which pierced their arms, head, and through their armour, some of them cut the strings of their cross-bows, others flung them on the ground, and all turned about, and retreated, quite discomfited. The French had a large body of men at arms on horseback, richly dressed, to support the Genoese.

The king of France, seeing them thus fall back, cried out, "Kill me those scoundrels; for they stop up our road, without any reason." You would then have seen the above-mentioned men at arms lay about them, killing all they could of these runaways.

The English continued shooting as vigorously and quickly as before: some of their arrows fell among the horsemen, who were sumptuously equipped, and, killing and wounding many, made them caper and fall among the Genoese, so that they were in such confusion they could never rally again. In the English army there were some Cornish and Welshmen on foot, who had armed themselves with large knives: these, advancing through the ranks of the men at arms and archers, who made way for them, came upon the French when they were in this danger, and, falling upon earls, barons, knights and squires, slew many, at which the king of England was afterwards much exasperated.[56]

What occasioned most of Edward's exasperation was the thought of all the ransom money he lost with the death of these lords and knights. Had these men been captured and held for ransom, Edward might have realized enough to cover the cost of the entire expedition. The following description of the capture of King John the Good at the battle of Poitiers in 1356 illustrates the high value would-be captors placed upon the capture and ransoming of opposing knights. The setting finds the Black Prince, tired but triumphant after his overwhelming victory, reclining under his banner set up on a high bush to attract the attention of his scattered men. As his marshals came in he asked each in turn for news concerning King John, then when no firm information was forthcoming, he sent two of his lords to see what they could learn.

The two barons, immediately mounting their horses, left the prince, and made for a small hillock, that they might look about them: from thence they perceived a crowd of men-at-arms on foot, who were advancing very slowly. The king of France was in the midst of them, and in great danger; for the English and Gascons had taken him from Sir Denys de Morbeque, and were disputing who should have him, the stoutest bawling out, "It is I that have got him"; "No, no," replied others, "we have him." The king, to escape from this peril, said, "Gentlemen, gentlemen, I pray you to conduct me and my son, in a courteous manner to my cousin the prince; and do not make such a riot about my capture, for I am so great a lord that I can make all sufficiently rich." These words, and others which fell from the king, appeased them a little; but the disputes were always beginning again, and they did not move a step without rioting. When the two barons saw this troop of people, they descended from the hillock, and sticking spurs into their horses, made up to them. On their arrival, they asked what was the matter: they were answered, that it was the king of France, who had been made prisoner, and that upwards of ten knights and squires challenged him at the same time, as belonging to each of them. The two barons then pushed through the crowd by main force, and ordered all to draw aside. They commanded, in the name of the prince, and under pain of instant death, that every one should keep his distance, and not approach unless ordered or desired to do so. They all retreated behind the king: and the two barons, dismounting, advanced to the king with profound reverences, and conducted him in a peaceable manner to the Prince of Wales.[57]

The prospect of rich ransoms served to reduce the

amount of bloodshed during the age of feudal warfare. What further relieved the bloody character of warfare at that time was the willingness of a besieging army to accept the surrender of a town and its garrison once these had abandoned all hope of relief. One of the last French strongholds in Gascony to yield to the English during the early years of the war was La Réole. Froissart gives this description of the surrender.

> The English who were besieging La Réole, had lain before it more than nine weeks, and had constructed two large towers of great beams of wood, three stories high: each tower was placed on wheels, and covered over with prepared leather, to shelter those within from fire and from the arrows: in each story were one hundred archers. These two towers, by dint of men's force, were pushed close to the walls of the town; for, during the time they were building, they had filled up the ditches, so that these towers could easily pass over them. Those that were in them began immediately to shoot so well and quick, that none dared to appear upon the battlements unless he were well armed, or had a shield. Between these two towers were posted two hundred men with pick-axes and bars, to make a breech in the walls; which they did, and cast away the stones. The inhabitants, seeing this, came upon the walls, and inquired for some of the chiefs of the army, to speak to them. The earl of Derby, being informed of it, sent thither Sir Walter Manny and Lord Stafford, who found the townsmen willing to surrender the town, on condition of their lives and fortunes being spared.

The English accepted these terms of surrender, but the commander of the castle, Sir Agos de Bans, preferred to retire into the castle with his soldiers, where "great quantities of wine and other provisions" would enable them to continue the struggle. The English then moved against the castle and

> erected all their machines against it; but they did little mischief, for the castle was very high, and built of a hard

stone. It was erected a long time since by the Saracens, who laid the foundations so strong, and with such curious workmanship, that the buildings of our time cannot be compared to it. When the earl found his machines had no effect, he commanded them to desist; and, as he was not without miners in his army, he ordered them to undermine the ditches of the castle, so that they might pass under. This was not, however, soon done.

Still after eleven more weeks the miners had made some progress and had undermined all the walls but not those of the donjon "for it was built on too hard a rock." When the besieged became aware of their danger, they persuaded Sir Agos to approach the English about surrendering, which he did, but the English refused any terms save unconditional surrender. Further negotiations between Sir Agos and the earl of Derby eventually broke the deadlock, however, and the French were in the end permitted to leave the castle but with only their arms and horses. These "immediately armed themselves, and caparisoned their horses, of which they had only six remaining. Some purchased horses of the English, who made them pay dearly for them."[58]

Never in the history of warfare was fighting more a personal and individual contest than during the feudal period. The rules of warfare ordained that a contest of arms must be between two contestants, never two against one, for instance; that once one of the contestants had his opponent at his mercy, the latter became his honorable prisoner. The introduction of the foot soldier with his crossbow, longbow, and knife gradually altered this happy situation and warfare grew appreciably more bloody. In Froissart's day enough of the traditional atmosphere remained, especially among men on horseback, that they might approach a coming clash with almost the enthusiasm of a modern football team. Froissart's description of the approach of the English and French armies near Auray in Brittany in 1364, all resplendent in their brightly colored dress and happily expectant of meeting opponents worthy of their mettle, differs little from one a writer today might suggest concerning two football teams ready to begin their Saturday afternoon match. The English had been alerted that Lord Charles de Blois was approaching "with the finest body of men at arms, the handsomest equipped, and the best ordered that had ever left France."

> This intelligence gave great joy to the English who were there; for they were eager to fight. These companies, therefore, immediately set about putting their armour in good repair, and re-furbishing their lances, daggers, battle-axes, coats of mail, helmets, scull-caps, visors, swords, and all sorts of weapons, as they well imagined they should soon have use for them. . . .
>
> This night passed quietly. On the morrow, which was a Saturday, the English and Bretons issued forth from their quarters, marching gaily in order of battle, to the rear of the castle of Auray, where they halted, and, having chosen a situation, declared they would wait the coming of their enemies.
>
> Almost immediately after daybreak, the lord Charles and his army appeared. . . . The troops . . . were in the best and handsomest order, and drawn up in the most brilliant manner that could be seen or imagined. They marched in such close order that one could not throw a tennis ball among them, but it must have stuck upon the points of some of the lances, so stiffly did they carry them. The English took great pleasure in looking at them. . . .
>
> It was on Saturday the eighth day of October, 1364, that these battalions were drawn up facing each other in a handsome plain, near to Auray in Brittany. I must say, it was a fine thing to see and reflect on; for there were banners and pennons flying with the richest armour on both sides.[59]

While this was the side of warfare that Froissart enjoyed, he was not oblivious of its more prosaic and burdensome aspects. Here is his description of the extensive preparations the French made in 1386 for their projected invasion of England.

Greater armaments were made in France than had hitherto been done. Heavier taxes were imposed on all the towns and country than for one hundred years, and such sums had never been raised, nor were ever greater preparations made by sea and land. The whole summer, until September, was employed in grinding flour, in making biscuits. . . .

Many of the rich men of France were forced to pay a third or fourth of their property, in order to build vessels of a sufficient size; and the poorer sort were taxed as much as they were worth to pay the men at arms.

There was not a vessel of any size from the port of Seville to Prussia, that the French could lay hands on, but was seized by fair or foul means, for the king of France. Provisions arrived from all quarters. Very great quantities of wine, salted meats, oats, trusses of hay, onions, verjuice, biscuit, flour, butter, and yolks of eggs in powder and rammed in barrels, and every other necessary, were sent from Flanders. . . .

Lords and knights, at great distances, were written to, to request they would accompany the king of France in this expedition. . . .

Never, since God created the world, were there seen such numbers of large ships, as filled the harbours of Sluys and Blanckenburgh; for, when they were counted, in the month of September, this same year, they were twelve hundred and eighty-seven ships. Their masts, on coming from sea, appeared like a thick forest. . . .

Whoever had been at Damme, Bruges, or Sluys at this time, and had seen how busily all were employed in loading the vessels with hay in trusses, garlic, onions, biscuit in sacks, pease, beans, cheese-bowls, barley, oats, rye, wheat, wax-candles, housings, shoes, boots, helmets, spurs, knives, hatchets, wedges, pick-axes, hooks, wooden pegs, boxes filled with ointments, tow, bandages, coverlids for sleeping on, horseshoe nails, bottles of verjuice and vinegar, iron, stone ware, pewter and wooden pots and dishes, candlesticks, basins, vases, fat pigs, hasters, kitchen furniture, utensils for the buttery, and for the other offices, and every article necessary to man or beast, would have been struck with astonishment. [60]

An item more in the spirit of the generally entertaining character of the *Chronicles* and more suited, therefore, to provide a farewell to Froissart is the story he tells of Bertrand du Guesclin, the French hero who helped save France after the disaster at Poitiers—how he managed to secure his freedom. Bertrand was among the prisoners taken by the Black Prince in the fighting in Spain in the spring of 1367. That he was not only a remarkably successful tactician but a wily fellow as well appears evident from this story.

Now it happened (as I have been informed) that one day, when the prince was in great good humour, he called Sir Bertrand du Guesclin, and asked him how he was. "My lord," replied Sir Bertrand, "I was never better: I cannot otherwise but be well, for I am, though in prison, the most honoured knight in the world." "How so?" rejoined the prince. "They say in France," answered Sir Bertrand, "as well as in other countries, that you are so much afraid of me, and have such a dread of my gaining my liberty, that you dare not set me free; and this is my reason for thinking myself so much valued and honoured." [The prince] answered, "What! Sir Bertrand, do you imagine that we keep you a prisoner for fear of your prowess. By St. George, it is not so; for, my good sir, if you will pay one hundred thousand francs, you shall be free."

Sir Bertrand was anxious for his liberty, and now, having heard upon what terms he could obtain it, taking the prince at his word, replied, "My lord, through God's will, I will never pay a less sum." The prince, when he heard this, began to repent of what he had done. It is said, that some of his council went farther, and told him: "My lord, you have acted very wrong in thus granting him so easily his ransom." They wanted to break through the agreement;

but the prince, who was a good and loyal knight, replied: "Since we have granted it, we shall keep it, and not act any way contrary; for it would be a shame, and we should be blamed by every one for not agreeing to his ransom, when he has offered to pay so largely for it as one hundred thousand francs."

From the time of this conversation, Sir Bertrand was taking great pains to seek the money, and was so active, that by the assistance of the king of France and the duke of Anjou, who loved him well, he paid in less than a month the hundred thousand francs, and went to the aid of the duke of Anjou, with two thousand combatants, in Provence.[61]

CHAPTER 7

Ibn Khaldun

IBN KHALDUN, WHOSE *Muqaddimah* Arnold Toynbee described as "the greatest book of its kind that has ever yet been created by any mind in any time or place,"[1] was born in Tunis in 1332. His ancestry on the paternal side had enjoyed prominence for several centuries. From Yemen to which it traced its origins, the family had moved to Spain in the eighth century, where by the close of the tenth century it had become one of the ruling dynasties in Seville. Ibn Khaldun's progenitors included eminent names in both government and scholarship, not only in Seville but in north Africa, where the family moved shortly before Ferdinand III occupied that city in 1248. From western north Africa the Khalduns made their way to Tunis where Ibn's great grandfather was executed, perhaps because of irregularities in the treasury of which he was the chief minister. Such harsh fate was unusual for members of the Khaldun family. Either by good fortune or political adroitness they managed somehow to be on the winning side in any political revolution. In this respect, none of Ibn Khaldun's ancestors approached his own re-

markable success. One might classify him as an Arab Tal-
leyrand of the late Middle Ages.

Ibn Khaldun's father, who had eschewed politics, provided his son an excellent education based upon the study
of the Koran, *hadith,* the Arabic language and literature,
and the *fikh.* In a very real sense there was never an end to
his education. Throughout his life he continued to acquaint himself with what learning he managed to find
within his reach, including the mysticism of the Sufis and
the philosophy of the Greeks (chiefly through Arabic commentators). Wherever he went it was his wont to hunt out
scholars who had something to tell him, while he in turn
shared his knowledge with those the fame of his learning
had attracted. He achieved greatest distinction for his
ability to propose profound insights into the forces and
factors that influenced the course of civilization, that is,
the "new science" that he unfolded in his *Muqaddimah.*
This remarkable work "itself clearly shows that Ibn
Khaldun had neither the desire nor the equipment to make
original contributions of note to any of the established
disciplines."[2]

Ibn Khaldun's parents died when he was seventeen, apparently victims of the Black Death. Soon after this tragedy he entered public service in Tunis. In 1354 he moved to
Fez in Morocco, where he became secretary to the sultan.
The rapidity and ease with which he accomplished these
moves announced his life pattern for the next fifty years.
Between political upheavals not of his own choosing and
his own ambitions, which kept him enmeshed in politics,
his life continued an amazing sequence of high positions
and honors, dismissals and disgraces, which terminated
only with his death in 1406.

The greater part of two years, 1357–58, he spent in
prison in Bougie, where he might have remained longer
but for the death of the sultan who had jailed him for his
intrigues. The new sultan brought him into his chancellery, but discouragement over his insecurity led him to

seek permission to remove to Granada. Granada was at this time the sole Muslim state that had escaped reconquest by the Christians. Its sultan gave Ibn Khaldun a warm welcome; he had become his friend during a period of exile in Fez, where they had met. In 1364 the sultan sent Ibn Khaldun on a peace mission to Pedro the Cruel, the ruler of Castile. So greatly did Ibn Khaldun's urbanity, erudition, and diplomatic skill impress Pedro that he offered to restore Ibn his family's estates in Seville should he remain. But Ibn Khaldun returned to Granada, although not for long. He shortly after moved to Bougie, to the court of the new Hafsid ruler who made him his chamberlain, or prime minister. Political turmoil continued to dog his footsteps for the next eight or nine years, now in Fez, then in Granada, and next in Tlemcen after he was ordered out of Granada.

A rest from politics came in 1375–1378 when he retired to the fortified village of Qal-at Ibn Salamah in the province of Oran. For almost four years he enjoyed the protection of the neighboring Arab tribesmen. These years must have been the most enjoyable of his life. They furnished him one of those rare intervals when he enjoyed the company of his wife and children and, beyond this, the leisure to devote himself to his writing. The product of these years was the *Muqaddimah*, the introduction to his universal history.

It was partly the desire to secure the documents he required in the preparation of this history that took him back to Tunis in 1378. For four years he studied and wrote—and "intrigued," it seems. For not only did he complete his history (*Kitab al-Ibar*), but in 1382, again fearful for his life or freedom, he secured permission to make a pilgrimage to Mecca, something not even the suspicious sultan could refuse him. It appears he kept Ibn Khaldun's wife and children as hostages, however, either to assure himself of Ibn's good behavior while he was away or of his return to Tunis. From Alexandria where Ibn landed, he moved to Cairo where he made his home for the remaining twenty-two years of his life. His family never joined him. Barbuq, the sultan of Egypt, used his good offices to persuade the ruler of Tunis to permit Ibn's wife and daughters to come to Cairo, but the ship bringing them foundered in a storm. Two sons survived; they were not on the ship, but almost nothing is known of them. Ibn Khaldun is strangely silent about family matters.

For Ibn Khaldun, life in Egypt proved no more settled than in Tunis and north Africa, although it seems his life was never in danger. He could usually count on the favor of the sultan. But under pressure from emirs and other influential people, even that potentate on occasion had to dismiss the savant from positions to which he had appointed him. The highest office he held was that of Malikite Chief Cadi, a position to which he was appointed five times and as often dismissed. A sixth appointment came in February 1406, a few weeks before his death.

Several circumstances may have accounted for his continued troubles. It is possible that the painful experiences of his earlier years had not entirely stifled his propensity for political intrigue. Without doubt his classification as a "foreigner," an identity he aggravated by his insistence upon wearing Maghrib garb, furnished fuel to the growing resentment of Egyptian politicians who objected to the puritanical rigorism with which they accused him of interpreting and applying the law. There is no question that he considered Egypt in a degenerate state despite the brilliance of its culture; nor is there much doubt that he refused to condone practices, perhaps traditional in Egypt, that violated his less sophisticated sense of propriety.

What proved the most remarkable episode in Ibn Khaldun's colorful career came during his residence in Cairo. Late in 1400, Faraj, who had succeeded his father Barbuq on the throne, had him accompany the army to Damascus to oppose the Mongol conqueror Timur the

Lame, who was approaching the city from the north. Scarcely had they reached Damascus than a rumor of an impending coup had Faraj and his emirs hurrying back to Cairo. Ibn Khaldun remained in Damascus for reasons that are not clear, although it appears he tried to stay neutral in the discussions among various leaders as to whether to accept Timur's demands or suffer a siege.[3] Whatever, the case, Timur seems to have asked to meet the renowned scholar. Because a group that did not wish to negotiate with Timur controlled the gates of the city, Ibn Khaldun was let down from the wall by means of a rope to make his way to the Mongol camp.

For the next thirty-five days Ibn Khaldun was free to come and go between the Mongol camp and Damascus. He was favored with a number of interviews with Timur the Lame. Their discussions were made possible with the aid of interpreters and touched on a variety of subjects, including great men of history and Khaldun's own theories about history. Timur evinced particular interest in Egypt and north Africa and directed the scholar to prepare him a survey of the Maghrib. If Khaldun made this study deliberately unattractive to a would-be conqueror as has been suggested, he may claim some credit for diverting Timur's interest from Egypt and turning it toward China. He did, in any event, win Timur's permission for his friends and himself to return to Egypt. On his return he must have succeeded in convincing Faraj that he had not compromised his interests during his interviews with Timur the Lame. He was reappointed Malikite Chief Cadi and held that office, off and on, until his death.

Were it not for Ibn Khaldun's *Muqaddimah*, which was the introduction to his universal history, modern scholars would accord him nothing beyond a simple mention alongside other Arab historians of the late Middle Ages. He did compose several smaller pieces, a treatise on arithmetic, for example, and an outline of logic, but few of these have survived, with no great loss to posterity. One minor work

is deserving of higher appraisal: his autobiography
(Ta'rif), which he prepared toward the close of his life. The
autobiography as a form of literature was not uncommon
in the Muslim world and neither is Ibn's unique. From the
Western point of view it is disappointing. It lacks personal
information about which the reader is curious; it fails to
note Ibn Khaldun's writings except for the survey he prepared for Timur the Lame; it contains digressions on historical and other diversified subjects that have little or no
connection with his life. But it does leave the picture that
Ibn Khaldun wanted posterity to have of him.[4]

Ibn Khaldun prepared the first draft of his *Muqaddimah* during his sojourn in Qal-at Ibn Salamah. Several
sections of the history itself also date from this period,
although he completed the bulk of his history and revised
these sections during his later years in Cairo. The entire
work, entitled *Kitab al-Ibar*, consists of seven volumes, of
which the *Muqaddimah* constitutes the first. Volumes
two through five deal with the pre-Islamic world and Arab
and eastern Muslim history, volumes six and seven treat
of the Muslim west. The extensiveness of the *Muqaddimah*[4] and its peculiar character led to its recognition as an
independent study during Ibn Khaldun's lifetime.

The universal history, however, has proved something
of a disappointment to scholars. Given the exceptional
nature of the *Muqaddimah* and the perceptive insights it
offers in explaining the rise and fall of civilizations, the
reader anticipated a historical narrative appreciably superior to any that had yet appeared. He looked forward to
reading what so brilliant an analyst would propose, for
instance, in explaining the fall of the Assyrian and Chal-
dean empires. But he looked in vain. Only in the case of the
Jews does Ibn Khaldun attempt to apply his sociophilosophical views concerning the history of a people. His history of Egypt centers on developments at the court and
limits itself to political and military events. Ibn Khaldun

even fails to mention a famine that struck Egypt during his period. In the case of conflicting traditions concerning Zoroaster's life, he makes no effort to harmonize them but contents himself, in the manner of the annalists, simply with recording them.

Still in extenuation of these deficiencies, Ibn Khaldun could point to the inadequacy of the historical sources at his disposal. That he considered the Christian apologist Orosius the most valuable source for the history of the non-Arab and pre-Islamic world suggests the pitiful nature of the limitations under which he labored. So while his survey of Egyptian history and that of the eastern Muslim world is not superior to the accounts of other historians, what he has to say of the Maghrib, particularly of the Berbers, is better than anything extant. One might be forced to admit, nevertheless, that it is probably best to attribute the superiority of his history of the Maghrib to his personal acquaintance with that part of the world; he was even an eyewitness to some of the events he records. That he reveals some disinterest in precise dates is what one might expect of a philosopher of history, whose intellectual aloofness would also explain scattered inconsistencies in chronology.

As indicated above, only in the case of the Jews does he attempt to apply his sociophilosophical views concerning the history of a people. One of these theories is that a dynasty does not ordinarily endure beyond three or four generations. To substantiate this position he offers the record of the success the Jews enjoyed under the four patriarchs Abraham, Isaac, Jacob, and Joseph who followed one another, and of the decline that then set in. He also discovers in the biblical account of how the Israelites spent forty years in the Sinai desert before entering Canaan the basis for the period of forty years that he assigns the life of a generation. According to Ibn Khaldun, it was necessary for the Israelites to spend forty years, that is, a generation in the desert so that their group consciousness (*asabiya*) might revive from the deterioration it had suffered during the years of slavery in Egypt.[5]

Whatever the deficiencies of Ibn Khaldun's history, these do not dim in any way the brilliance of the *Muqaddimah*. This work remains on all counts the most advanced study of civilization and philosophy of history before the modern era. Several circumstances explain the preeminence of the work. First, the author demonstrates remarkable perceptivity in a field of intellectual endeavor that had received little consideration. Then Ibn Khaldun's personal acquaintance with a variety of cultures, each revealing a different level of sophistication, furnished him an admirable basis for his study. These cultures ranged all the way from the primitive mores possessed by some of the Berber tribes of the Maghrib, to the brilliant world of Granada, to the decadent though still imposing civilization of Egypt. Ibn Khaldun spent years in many different countries; he was actively involved in political affairs wherever he went; and he was thoroughly acquainted with the intellectual accomplishments of the peoples among whom he lived. A scholar with Ibn Khaldun's interest in human society must have found the relative position of these peoples on the way to or away from cultural maturity most provocative. A final circumstance that might have influenced Ibn Khaldun in his role of sociophilosopher in the study of the etiology of civilization was his own genuine attraction to mysticism.

Ibn Khaldun appears to have drawn upon the works of scholars such as al-Masudi (d.c. 956) for thoughts they may have expressed in their analysis of social phenomena or their interpretation of history. To what extent, however, scholars can only speculate. Of these earlier writers, al-Masudi was surely the most prolific and probably the most erudite, but only a fraction of his works survive. Because nothing of an earlier age approaches the level of Ibn Khaldun's own interpretations of society and history, scholars are generally in accord in giving him full title to the ideas he expressed in the *Muqaddimah.* They agree that one can find an adequate explanation for the precocity of his views in his remarkable talents at judging human nature and in his good fortune of living an active life amid a variety of cultural environments. Had Ibn Khaldun attempted to compose the *Muqaddimah* before his visit to culturally brilliant Granada, for instance, what he would have had to say would have been appreciably less impressive. For this reason the reader of the *Muqaddimah* may regret that the author had but limited acquaintance with the Christian world of Byzantium and Latin Europe. He might otherwise have had some truly arresting observations to offer relative to the influence of Christian monogamy upon the cultural development of Europe as opposed, for example, to the influence that the polygamy preached in the Koran might have exerted upon the Muslim world.

Scholars disagree in their assessment of the degree that the metaphysical sciences influenced the thought of Ibn Khaldun. Muhsin Mahdi insists that no thinker before Ibn Khaldun, nor any contemporary for that matter, related the history of society to political philosophy and attempted to develop a science of society within the framework of traditional philosophy. According to Mahdi, the "new science" of society that Ibn Khaldun presented the world was the fruit of his efforts to apply the principles of Greek philosophy in his study of social phenomena against the background of the theological interpretation of the universe contained in the Koran.[6]

Franz Rosenthal maintains, on the other hand, that Ibn Khaldun mistrusted speculative reasoning despite his considerable knowledge of Greek philosophy and its Arab commentators. He believes Ibn Khaldun based the principles of his new science, not on interpretations that drew their justification from philosophy but from observation; that he proposed to find the answer to the question of why nations and civilizations rose and fell, not in the operation of metaphysical forces but in the influence of economic and social factors. The social principle to which Ibn Khaldun appears to have attributed greatest influence in the rise and fall of civilizations was that of *asabiya* or "group feeling," a principle to which none of the philosophers had referred.[7] In the judgment of Rosenthal, one might indeed be tempted to identify Ibn Khaldun as a medieval forerunner of modern materialism were it not that he credits much influence in the development of civilizations to such psychological forces as religion.

Whatever the case, Ibn Khaldun appears to have exerted little or no influence on his contemporaries in the fields of political philosophy and social science, nor for several centuries to come. Had he lived two centuries earlier when Western scholars were feverishly translating Arabic works, he might have left a significant imprint upon Western thought. As it was, he was largely ignored by his contemporaries and considered too "dated" when the West discovered him in the eighteenth century.

Ibn Khaldun opens the *Muqaddimah* with an invocation to Allah. He writes:

> In the name of God, the Merciful, the Compassionate. Pray, O God, for our lord Muhammad and his Family and the Men around him.
> The Servant of God who needs the mercy of God who is so rich in His kindness, Abd-ar-Rahman b. Muhammad b. Khaldun al-Hadrami — God give him success! says:
> Praised be God! He is powerful and mighty. In His hand, He holds royal authority and kingship. His are the most beautiful names and attributes. His knowledge is such that nothing, be it revealed in secret whispering or (even) left unsaid, remains strange to Him. His power is such that nothing in heaven and upon earth is too much for Him or escapes Him.[8]

There is more to this prayer. While this kind of pious introduction was conventional with Islamic writers, in the case of Ibn Khaldun, from the regularity with which he refers to the inscrutable and almighty will of Allah, one may conclude that it was less tradition than genuine piety that prompted the expression of these sentiments.

Ibn Khaldun then follows with a foreword. This defines the meaning of history, comments on the deficiencies of earlier historians, and provides a sketch of the contents and arrangement of his history. The opening paragraphs of the foreword read:

> History is a discipline widely cultivated among nations and races. It is eagerly sought after. The men in the street, the ordinary people, aspire to know it. Kings and leaders vie for it.
>
> Both the learned and the ignorant are able to understand it. For on the surface history is no more than information about political events, dynasties, and occurrences of the remote past, elegantly presented and spiced with proverbs. It serves to entertain large, crowded gatherings and brings to us an understanding of human affairs. (It shows) how changing conditions affected (human affairs), how certain dynasties came to occupy an even wider space in the world, and how they settled the earth until they heard the call and their time was up.
>
> The inner meaning of history, on the other hand, involves speculation and an attempt to get at the truth, subtle explanation of the causes and origins of existing things, and deep knowledge of the how and why of events. (History), therefore, is firmly rooted in philosophy. It deserves to be accounted a branch of (philosophy).[9]

Ibn Khaldun lists as shortcomings of earlier historians the introduction of gossip and false reports, a lack of critical spirit, a blind trust in the validity of tradition, and an uncritical acceptance of what is written. The writings of many historians, furthermore, were dull "or, (at any rate) did not try not to be dull." (I,9) A criticism suggestive of the new approach he would employ in writing his own history was his charge that some historians "disregarded the changes in conditions and in the customs of nations and races that the passing of time had brought about. . . . They neglected the importance of change over the generations in their treatment of the (historical material), because they had no one who could interpret it for them."[10] All these shortcomings he hoped to correct, although the foreword concludes with an acknowledgment of his own inadequacy, perhaps a conventional disclaimer. "Still, after all has been said, I am conscious of imperfection when (I look at) the scholars of (past and contemporary) times. I confess my inability to penetrate so difficult a subject."[11]

In the lengthy introduction that follows, Ibn Khaldun discusses the value of historiography, the different methods employed by historians, and the errors these scholars committed. "It should be known," he writes,

> that history is a discipline that has a great number of (different) approaches. Its useful aspects are very many. Its goal is distinguished. (History) makes us acquainted with the conditions of past nations as they are reflected in their (national) character. It makes us acquainted with the biographies of the prophets and with the dynasties and policies of rulers. Whoever so desires may thus achieve the useful result of being able to imitate historical examples in religious and worldly matters.[12]

This is all Ibn Khaldun offers by way of a justification for the study of history, which seems strange given the length and analytical character of the *Muqaddimah*. He moves directly to a consideration of certain weaknesses historians display. One of these is their carelessness about citing statistics. "For example," he points out,

> al-Masudi and many other historians report that Moses counted the army of the Israelites in the desert. He had all those able to carry arms, especially those twenty years and older, pass muster. There turned out to be 600,000 or more. In this connection, (al-Masudi) forgets to take into consideration whether Egypt and Syria could possibly have held

such a number of soldiers. Every realm may have as large a militia as it can hold and support, but no more. This fact is attested by well-known customs and familiar conditions. Moreover, an army of this size cannot march or fight as a unit. The whole available territory would be too small for it. If it were in battle formation, it would extend two, three, or more times beyond the field of vision. How, then, could two such parties fight with each other, or one battle formation gain the upper hand when one flank does not know what the other flank is doing![13]

A more specific error for which Ibn Khaldun censured historians was that of perpetuating the damaging story concerning al-Abbasah, the sister of the caliph Haroun ar-Rashid, and his boon companion Ja'far. The usual story, based largely on al-Tabari, had it that because the caliph enjoyed the company of both his sister and of Ja'far, he arranged a formal marriage between the two so that the young man might be free to enter the royal harem. It was understood, however, that this marriage was not to be consummated. But al-Abbasah fell in love with Ja'far, then managed to have intercourse with him when he was drunk. When Haroun learned about the child that was born to them, he "flew into a rage" and later had Ja'far beheaded.

Ibn Khaldun dismissed the story as rank gossip. He found it impossible to believe that a woman of such noble ancestry as al-Abbasah's could have done such a thing.

Al-Abbasah was the daughter of a caliph and the sister of a caliph. She was born to royal power, into the prophetical succession (the caliphate), and descended from the men around Muhammad and his uncles. She was connected by birth with the leadership of Islam, the light of the revelation, and the place where the angels descended to bring the revelation. She was close in time to the desert attitude of true Arabism, to that simple state of Islam still far from the habits of luxury and lush pastures of sin. Where should one look for chastity and modesty, if she did not possess them? Where could cleanliness and purity be found, if they no longer existed in that house? How could she link her pedigree with (that of) Ja'far b. Yahya and stain her Arab nobility with a Persian client?[14]

If the modern reader remains unconvinced, he will at least agree with Ibn Khaldun that this scandal, even had it occurred, was probably not what provoked Haroun into destroying Ja'far, his father, and his brother, the so-called Barmecides. One may not discount the possibility that Ibn Khaldun knew his denunciation of the story about al-Abbasah's moral lapse would please his royal readers as would his condemnation of the slander about Haroun's alleged "winebibbing." The abrupt manner with which Ibn Khaldun dismisses the authenticity of the story about al-Abbasah and Ja'far furnishes a striking example of how mistaken the greatest scholars may be who permit theories to blind them to the vagaries of human nature.

Ibn Khaldun discusses similar stories of moral misconduct on the part of certain early caliphs then offers an explanation that might apply to any age.

> There are many such stories. They are always cropping up in the works of the historians. The incentive for inventing and reporting them is a (general) inclination to forbidden pleasures and for smearing the reputation of others. People justify their own subservience to pleasure by citing men and women of the past (who allegedly did the same things they are doing). Therefore, they often appear very eager for such information and are alert to find it when they go through the pages of (published) works.[15]

The remedy for this evil is better trained and more responsible historians. Today's scholar, Ibn Khaldun writes,

> needs to know the principles of politics, the (true) nature of existent things, and the differences among nations, places, and periods with regard to ways of life, character qualities, customs, sects, schools, and everything else. He further needs a comprehensive knowledge of present conditions in

all these respects. He must compare similarities or differences between the present and the past (or distantly located) conditions. He must know the causes of the similarities in certain cases and of the differences in others. He must be aware of the differing origins and beginnings of (different) dynasties and religious groups, as well as of the reasons and incentives that brought them into being and the circumstances and history of the persons who supported them. His goal must be to have complete knowledge of the reasons for every happening, and to be acquainted with the origin of every event. Then he must check transmitted information with the basic principles he knows.[16]

Ibn Khaldun says the first book of his *Muqaddimah* deals with civilization and its essential characteristics. These include "royal authority, government, gainful occupations, ways of making a living, crafts, and sciences, as well as with the causes and reasons thereof."[17] He declares his purpose to be the writing of true history, that is, a kind of history that will approximate "an independent science." In preparing this new history he will depend principally on information gleaned from penetrating research, not from rhetoric or, for that matter, from the study of politics.[18] He declares his study may be viewed as "an entirely original science," although he is willing to accept the possibility that earlier scholars, some among the ancient Persians and Chaldeans, for instance, might have contributed thoughts on the subject. While on the one hand he declares his book unique in that "it contains unusual knowledge and familiar if hidden wisdom," he confesses his "inability to penetrate so difficult a subject." He hopes scholars "would look at the book with a critical, rather than a complacent eye, and silently correct and overlook the mistakes they come upon."[19]

He is now ready to embark on his discussion of the nature of civilization in its different manifestations, a study that will presumably furnish the bases and principles for his universal history. He agrees with other writers that man is social by nature and as such requires the assistance of his fellows in order to live in a manner consistent with his nature. He writes:

> The power of the individual human being is not sufficient for him to obtain (the food) he needs, and does not provide him with as much food as he requires to live. Even if we assume an absolute minimum of food – that is, food enough for one day, (a little) wheat, for instance – that amount of food could be obtained only after much preparation such as grinding, kneading, and baking. Each of these three operations requires utensils and tools that can be provided only with the help of several crafts, such as the crafts of the blacksmith, the carpenter, and the potter. Assuming that a man could eat unprepared grain, an even greater number of operations would be necessary in order to obtain the grain: sowing and reaping, and threshing to separate it from the husks of the ear. Each of these operations requires a number of tools and many more crafts than those just mentioned. It is beyond the power of one man alone to do all that, or (even) part of it, by himself.[20]

Ibn Khaldun notes other circumstances when the assistance of the group is essential to the well-being of the individual. He needs help when he must defend himself against wild animals, for instance, or against aggression within the group. In this last instance it is the ruler who provides the assistance. "It has thus become clear that royal authority is a natural quality of man which is absolutely necessary to mankind."[21] And Ibn Khaldun insists that the emergence of the ruler does not necessarily presuppose the wish of God that this should happen, nor that the ruler has his authority from God, as some philosophers had maintained.

Ibn Khaldun next considers the earth, "a grape floating upon water,"[22] the seas and oceans, and rivers. The Nile, he writes, had its origin at the foot of a large mountain, sixteen degrees beyond the equator: "No higher mountain is known on earth."[23] He supplies the reader a map to enable him to better follow the discussion of the seven zones into which the earth is divided. The geographical information he presents resembles that generally accepted in his day. As he himself indicates, much of it had "been given by men such as Ptolemy in the *Geography* and, after him, by the author of the *Book of Roger* (by al-Idrisi)."[24]

He devotes most attention to the third, fourth, and fifth zones, all of which make up the temperate zones. It is the people who lived in these temperate climes who were the most civilized. He explains:

> The human inhabitants of these zones are more temperate (well proportioned) in their bodies, color, character quali-
> ties, and (general) conditions. They are found to be ex-
> tremely moderate in their dwellings, clothing, foodstuffs
> and crafts. They use houses that are well constructed of
> stone and embellished by craftsmanship. They rival each
> other in production of the very best tools and implements.
> Among them, one finds the natural minerals, such as gold,
> silver, iron, copper, lead, and tin. In their business dealings
> they use the two precious metals (gold and silver). They
> avoid intemperance quite generally in all their conditions.
> Such are the inhabitants of the Maghrib, of Syria, the two
> Iraqs, Western India (as-Sind), and China, as well as of
> Spain; also the European Christians nearby.[25]

Ibn Khaldun judged the health of desert people to be superior to the health of those who dwelt in the hills, a superiority he attributed to their more frugal diet. People who were content with a frugal food supply were also more religious as a rule and lived longer lives. These superior virtues or qualities were the products of their environ-ment. But God might directly endow certain human be-ings with unusual powers of perception as he had done in the case of the Prophets. Ibn Khaldun clearly accepted the authenticity of these powers, as he did the ability of some men to interpret dreams, the "glimpse (of the supernatu-ral)," which the soul obtained "while it is asleep." He believed that there were men who could predict the future by gazing into mirrors or bowls of water, furthermore, that "statements concerning supernatural things are also placed upon the tongues of the insane."[26]

The reader whose high estimate of Ibn Khaldun's profundity may have been shaken by these last revelations will find much in the second chapter of Book I to reassure himself concerning that scholar's eminent reputation. Here Ibn Khaldun sets forth what was surely the most learned analysis to that time of the civilization of the Bedouins and of nomadic peoples in general. His opening paragraphs sketch the pattern of life as it progresses from that of the most primitive tribe to that of the most advanced civilization. He writes:

> Some people adopt agriculture, the cultivation of vegetables and grains, (as their way of making a living). Others adopt animal husbandry, the use of sheep, cattle, goats, bees, and silkworms, for breeding and for their products. Those who live by agriculture or animal husbandry cannot avoid the call of the desert, because it alone offers the wide fields, acres, pastures for animals, and other things that the settled areas do not offer. It is therefore necessary for them to restrict themselves to the desert. Their social organization and co-operation for the needs of life and civilization, such as food, shelter, and warmth, do not take them beyond the bare subsistence level, because of their inability (to provide) for anything beyond those (things). Subsequent improvement of their conditions and acquisition of more wealth and comfort than they need, cause them to rest and take it easy. Then, they cooperate for things beyond the (bare) necessities. They use more food and clothes, and take pride in them. They build large houses, and lay out towns and cities for protection. This is followed by an increase in comfort and ease, which leads to formation of the most developed luxury customs. They take the greatest pride in the preparation of food and a fine cuisine, in the use of varied splendid clothes of silk and brocade and other (fine materials), in the construction of ever higher

buildings and towers, in elaborate furnishings for the buildings, and the most intensive cultivation of crafts in actuality. They build castles and mansions, provide them with running water, build their towers higher and higher, and compete in furnishing them (most elaborately). They differ in the quality of the clothes, the beds, the vessels, and the utensils they employ for their purposes. Here, now, (we have) sedentary people. "Sedentary people" means the inhabitants of cities and countries, some of whom adopt the crafts as their way of making a living, while others adopt commerce. They earn more and live more comfortably than Bedouins, because they live on a level beyond the level of (bare) necessity, and their way of making a living corresponds to their wealth.[27]

In the judgment of Ibn Khaldun most sedentary peoples had once been Bedouins and had lived at a nomadic level of civilization. Because Bedouins were obliged to concern themselves with the necessities of life, not with luxuries and pleasure,

their evil ways and blameworthy qualities are much less numerous. They are closer to the first natural state and more remote from the evil habits that have been impressed upon the souls of (sedentary people) through numerous and ugly, blameworthy customs.[28]

The introduction of laws and the reliance upon them for protection mark a major step in the decline of civilization. Until that point the virtues natural to man are sufficient to protect him. When laws make their appearance they destroy man's fortitude and power of resistance. To those who would ask Ibn Khaldun whether the same dictum applied to the laws laid down in the Koran, he would hasten to explain that the restraint imposed by these religious laws came from the people themselves, "not a result of technical instruction or scientific education. . . . Their fortitude remained unabated, and it was not corroded by education or authority. . . . (The influence of) religion,

then, decreased among men, and they came to use restraining laws."[29] In other words, laws derived from government or education tend to destroy fortitude because
their restraining influence comes from outside. The influence exercised by religious laws, on the other hand, does
not bring about a weakening of fortitude because its restraining force is something inherent.

It is here that Ibn Khaldun introduces the principle of
group feeling, or *asabiya*, a concept for which he is especially famous and to which he gave his own meaning.
What enabled Bedouin tribes to defend themselves
against their enemies, that is, beyond the exhortations
and orders of their sheiks, was this group feeling. He explains:

> Their defense and protection are successful only if they are
> a closely-knit group of common descent. This strengthens
> their stamina and makes them feared, since everybody's
> affection for his family and his group is more important
> (than anything else). Compassion and affection for one's
> blood relations and relatives exist in human nature as
> something God put into the hearts of men. It makes for
> mutual support and aid, and increases the fear felt by the
> enemy.[30]

Asabiya extends also to clients and allies because it
"leads to close contact exactly, or approximately in the
same way, as does common descent."[31] All these people,
those descended from a common ancestor, together with
their allies and clients, are willing, by reason of their group
feeling, to recognize the leadership of one of their members. They have become a people.

But a people once united by *asabiya* may lose it as they
come in contact with other peoples or when they turn to a
sedentary life. With some peoples it is the delusion of
group feeling that holds them together. This was true of
the Israelites, Ibn Khaldun writes.

> The Israelites are the most firmly misled in this delusion.
> They originally had one of the greatest "houses" in the

world, first, because of the great number of prophets and messengers born among their ancestors, extending from Abraham to Moses, the founder of their religious group and law, and next, because of their group feeling and the royal authority that God had promised and granted them by means of that group feeling. Then, they were divested of all that, and they suffered humiliation and indigence. They were destined to live as exiles on earth. For thousands of years, they knew only enslavement and unbelief. Still, the delusion of (nobility) has not left them. They can be found saying: "He is an Aaronite"; "He is a descendant of Joshua"; "He is one of Caleb's progeny"; "He is from the tribe of Judah."[32]

This group feeling is a sensitive virtue. It refuses to accept the leadership (nobility) of a particular family beyond the fourth generation. The most striking instance of this phenomenon is also provided by the Israelites. They accepted the rule of one family — Abraham, Isaac, Jacob, and Joseph — for four generations, then split up. From this "historical fact" Ibn Khaldun goes on to unfold his "four-generation theory."

The builder of the glory (of the family) knows what it cost him to do the work, and he keeps the qualities that created his glory and made it last. The son who comes after him had personal contact with his father and thus learned those things from him. However, he is inferior in this respect to (his father), in as much as a person who learns things through study is inferior to a person who knows them from practical application. The third generation must be content with imitation and, in particular, with reliance upon tradition. This member is inferior to him of the second generation, in as much as a person who relies (blindly) upon tradition is inferior to a person who exercises independent judgment.

The fourth generation, then, is inferior to the preceding ones in every respect. This member has lost the qualities that preserved the edifice of their glory. He (actually) despises (those qualities). He imagines that the edifice was not built through application and effort. He thinks that it is something due his people from the very beginning by virtue of the mere fact of their (noble) descent, and not something that resulted from group (effort) and (individual) qualities. For he sees the great respect in which he is held by the people, but he does not know how that respect originated and what the reason for it was. He imagines that it is due to his descent and nothing else. He keeps away from those in whose group feeling he shares, thinking that he is better than they. He trusts that (they will obey him because) he was brought up to take their obedience for granted, and he does not know the qualities that made obedience necessary. Such qualities are humility (in dealing) with (such men) and respect for their feelings. Therefore, he considers them despicable, and they, in turn, revolt against him and despise him. They transfer (political) leadership from him and his direct lineage to some other related branch (of his tribe), in obedience to their group feeling, as we have stated. . . . This is the case with rulers who have royal authority.[33]

Group feeling itself declines, as is the case with everything in the universe. "Minerals, plants, all the animals including man, and the other created things come into being and decay, as one can see with one's own eyes. The same applies to the conditions that affect created things."[34] Although the goal of group feeling is to acquire superiority over other peoples, once this position has been attained, the advent of decline is inexorable. What chiefly produce this decline are the wealth and luxury the nation had accepted while it was establishing its superiority. As the toughness of desert life wanes, group feeling and courage weaken. Then comes defeat, followed by subjection to the rule of another nation, and finally extinction.

The Arabs, as a people, supplied Ibn Khaldun with the bulk of the cultural materials upon which he bases his interpretations. And it is his understanding of the Arabs and his analysis of their traits that constitute the most perceptive parts of his work. He held them to be savage by nature, given to plunder and destruction. They were enemies of civilization. He writes:

> The reason for this is that (the Arabs) are a savage nation, fully accustomed to savagery and the things that cause it. Savagery has become their character and nature. They enjoy it, because it means freedom from authority and no subservience to leadership. Such a natural disposition is the negation and antithesis of civilization. All the customary activities of the Arabs lead to travel and movement. This is the antithesis and negation of stationariness, which produces civilization. For instance, the Arabs need stones to set them up as supports for their cooking pots. So, they take them from buildings which they tear down to get the stones, and use them for that purpose. Wood, too, is needed by them for props for their tents and for use as tent poles for their dwellings. So, they tear down roofs to get the wood for that purpose. The very nature of their existence is the negation of building, which is the basis of civilization.[35]

The Arabs possessed still other traits that made them enemies of civilization. They neglected to encourage the development of crafts and skills; they lacked concern for laws that would restrain those inclined to do evil; all Arabs had the ambition to be leaders. It was fortunate, therefore, that there appeared a force that in time managed to tame the savage Arab and enable him to develop a flourishing civilization. That force was religion. Religion

> causes rudeness and pride to disappear and exercises a restraining influence on their mutual envy and jealousy. . . . Besides, no people are as quick (as the Arabs) to accept (religious) truth and right guidance, because their natures have been preserved free from distorted habits and uncontaminated by base character qualities. The only (difficulty) lies in the quality of savagery, which, however, is easily taken care of and which is ready to admit good (qualities), as it has remained in its first natural state and

remote from the ugly customs and bad habits that leave
their impress upon the soul.[36]

Ibn Khaldun now considers royal authority, as opposed
to tribal leadership, and its relationship with group feeling. Even though an empire composed of a number of
tribes might be so extensive as to obscure such factors as
asabiya, this group consciousness remained a force among
the families that competed for leadership. Once a particular family had established its superiority, the circumstances that attended its success in achieving that leadership were forgotten. Then it became traditional for all
members of the tribe to accept its direction. When this
point had been attained the dynasty could safely disre-
gard any further concern over group feeling because religion now supplied the dynamic energy that held the people
together.

Ibn Khaldun believed that the accomplishments of a
dynasty, notably the physical monuments it left to posterity, were proportionate to its original power. The enormous extent of the Islamic empire during the reign of
Al-Mamun, for example, the incredible amount of wealth
that the government had at its command, the large number of men whose labor it could requisition, explained the
impressive achievements of that caliph. Lest the reader
reject reports of accomplishments for which he found no
observable parallels in his own time, Ibn Khaldun tells
how the vizier of the sultan of Merinid answered his own
query concerning the credibility of a certain Ibn Battutah.

Be careful not to reject such information about the conditions of dynasties, because you have not seen such things
yourself. You would then be like the son of the wazir who
grew up in prison. The wazir had been imprisoned by his
ruler and remained in prison several years. His son grew up
in prison. When he reached the age of reason, he asked his
father about the meat which he had been eating. (His father) told him that it was mutton, and he asked him what

that was. When his father described a sheep to him in all details, (the son said), "Father, you mean it looks like a rat?" His father was angry with him and said, "What has a sheep to do with a rat?" The same happened later about beef and camel meat. The only animals he had seen in prison were rats, and so he believed that all animals were of the same species as rats.[37]

After surveying the history of the Muslim caliphates, Ibn Khaldun introduces a sketch of the history of the Christian church. He declares Christ brought his religion to the Jews, abolished certain laws of the Torah, also "performed marvelous wonders, such as healing the insane and reviving the dead."[38] He mentions how Christ sent his messengers (apostles) to all parts of the world, then tells that his prestige and influence so aroused the envy of Herod that he persuaded the emperor Augustus to permit Christ's execution.

Ibn Khaldun describes the policy that the Roman state adopted toward Christianity as ambivalent, now hostile, then indifferent, until the emergence of Constantine who established it as the state religion. He writes of the dissensions over doctrine that disrupted the Christian community, of the first general council at Nicaea, and the evolution of the papacy. While his knowledge of the history of the Christian church is reasonably accurate, his interpretation of the relationship between the pope and the Holy Roman emperor reveals a startling lack of acquaintance with those officials. What he wrote of them might have been accepted as true on certain occasions in the earlier Middle Ages, but that was surely not the case in his own day. He writes:

It is the custom of the Pope with respect to the European Christians to urge them to submit to one ruler and have recourse to him in their disagreements and agreements, in order to avoid the dissolution of the whole thing. His purpose is to have the group feeling that is the strongest among them (concentrated upon one ruler), so that (this ruler) has power over all of them. The ruler is called "Emperor," (*Emperador*) with the middle letter (pronounced somehow) between dh and z. (The pope) personally places the crown upon the head of the (emperor), in order to let him have the blessing implied (in that ceremony). The emperor, therefore, is called "the crowned one." Perhaps that is the meaning of the word "emperor."[39]

Ibn Khaldun next turns his attention to the officials who serve in the government, their responsibilities and titles, and the relative importance of those who deal with the sword as opposed to those who use the pen. Whatever the number and competency of these officials, the real burden of governing successfully remains on the shoulders of the ruler. He

> must exercise political leadership and get people to submit to him to the degree he desires and be satisfied, both with his intentions regarding them and with the fact that he alone has all the glory and they have none. This requires an extraordinary measure of psychology. A noble sage has said: "Moving mountains from their place is easier for me than to influence people psychologically."[40]

In his discussion of war, Ibn Khaldun distinguishes between a just and an unjust conflict. It appears he judged those wars to be just that "the religious law calls 'the holy war,' "[41] and also a war that is fought to force obedience upon "seceders." Next he considers methods of warfare as employed by different peoples. His analysis of the factors that determine ultimate victory in any war might profitably be pondered by all those who would seek to make their fortunes by that means.

> There is no certainty of victory in war, even when the equipment and the numerical (strength) that cause victory (under normal circumstances), exist. Victory and superiority in war come from luck and chance. This is explained by

the fact that the causes of superiority are, as a rule, a combination of several factors. There are external factors, such as the number of soldiers, the perfection and good quality of weapons, the number of brave men, (skillful) arrangement of the line formation, the proper tactics, and similar things. Then, there are hidden factors. (These hidden factors) may be the result of human ruse and trickery, such as spreading alarming news and rumors to cause defections (in the ranks of the enemy); occupying high points, so that one is able to attack from above, which surprises those below and causes them to abandon each other; hiding in thickets or depressions and concealing oneself from the enemy in rocky terrain, so that the armies (of one's own side) suddenly appear when (the enemy) is in a precarious situation and he must then flee to safety (instead of defending himself), and similar things. These hidden factors may also be celestial matters, which man has no power to produce for himself. They affect people psychologically, and thus generate fear in (them). They cause confusion in the centers of (armies), and there are routs. Routs very often are the result of hidden causes, because both parties make much use of (the opportunities offered by) them in their desire for victory. One of them must by necessity be successful in their use. Wherefore, Muhammad said: "War is trickery." An Arab proverb says: "Many a trick is worth more than a tribe."[42]

The reader who may reject as unscientific Ibn Khaldun's reference to "celestial" factors in the outcome of battles will react more sympathetically to what that scholar has to offer on the subject of public finance. In their early history dynasties are content to impose modest taxes, according to Ibn Khaldun, because the revenue realized will meet the simple needs set forth by religious law. During this period of low taxes, people possess the incentive to be active, to expand, and to undertake greater enterprises. The result is that the cultural level of such dynasties rises. But with the years comes the adoption of luxurious practices on the part of the maturing dynasty, practices that require the imposition of heavier taxes, which in turn produce a slowing down of economic and cultural growth.

> When the dynasty continues in power and their rulers follow each other in succession, they become sophisticated. The Bedouin attitude and simplicity lose their significance, and the Bedouin qualities of moderation and restraint disappear. Royal authority with its tyranny, and sedentary culture that stimulates sophistication, make their appearance. The people of the dynasty then acquire qualities of character related to cleverness. Their customs and needs become more varied because of the prosperity and luxury in which they are immersed. As a result, the individual imposts and assessments upon the subjects, agricultural laborers, farmers and all the other taxpayers, increase. Every individual impost and assessment is greatly increased, in order to obtain a higher tax revenue. Customs duties are placed upon articles of commerce and (levied) at the city gates, as we shall mention later on. Then, gradual increases in the amount of the assessments succeed each other regularly, in correspondence with the gradual increase in the luxury customs and many needs of the dynasty and the spending required in connection with them. Eventually, the taxes will weigh heavily upon the subjects and overburden them. Heavy taxes become an obligation and tradition, because the increases took place gradually, and no one knows specifically who increased them or levied them. They lie upon the subjects like an obligation and tradition.[43]

The reader will suspect what the ultimate result of spiraling taxes will be. When assessments go beyond the limits of equity, a dynasty's subjects lose their interest in industrial enterprises. The inevitable consequence is that less revenue becomes available, which in turn leads to still higher imposts to make up the deficiency. The result is the destruction of civilization.

> If (the reader) understands this, he will realize that the strongest incentive for cultural activity is to lower as

much as possible the amounts of individual imposts levied upon persons capable of undertaking cultural enterprises. In this manner, such persons will be psychologically disposed to undertake them, because they can be confident of making a profit from them.[44]

Heavy exactions laid upon people, on the other hand, weaken and gradually extinguish the incentive to increase the amount of property. Once people conclude that the increase they make in the volume of their income will simply be siphoned off by the government, they lose their incentive to expand their cultural undertakings.

In Chapter IV of Book II Ibn Khaldun takes up the subject of cities with their imposing buildings and monuments as products of a sedentary civilization. These can only appear after royal authority has emerged and a dynasty has been established.

The explanation for this is that building and city planning are features of sedentary culture brought about by luxury and tranquility, as we have mentioned before. Such (features of sedentary culture) come after Bedouin life and the features that go with it.

Furthermore, towns and cities with their monuments, vast constructions, and large buildings, are set up for the masses and not for the few. Therefore, united efforts and much cooperation are needed for them. They are not among the things that are necessary matters of general concern to human beings, in the sense that all human beings desire them or feel compelled to have them. As a matter of fact, (human beings) must be forced and driven to (build cities). The stick of royal authority is what compels them, or they may be stimulated by the promise of reward and compensation. (Such reward) amounts to so large a sum that only royal authority and a dynasty can pay for it. Thus, dynasties and royal authority are absolutely necessary for the building of cities and the planning of towns.[45]

In Chapter V of the *Muqaddimah* Ibn Khaldun turns to

a discussion of various occupations, of the ranking of workers according to their skills, then of the crafts themselves. Of commerce he writes:

> Commerce is a natural way of making profits. However, most of its practices and methods are tricky and designed to obtain the (profit) margin between purchase prices and sales prices. This surplus makes it possible to earn a profit. Therefore, the law permits cunning in commerce, since (commerce) contains an element of gambling. It does not, however, mean taking away the property of others without giving anything in return. Therefore, it is legal.[46]

Ibn Khaldun declared the Arabs to be the least skilled of all peoples in the crafts. He explains:

> The reason for this is that the Arabs are more firmly rooted in desert life and more remote from sedentary civilization, the crafts, and the other things which sedentary civilization calls for (than anybody else). (On the other hand,) the non-Arabs in the East and the Christian nations along the shores of the Mediterranean are very well versed in (the crafts), because they are more deeply rooted in sedentary civilization and more remote from the desert and desert civilization (than others).[47]

Ibn Khaldun next takes up various crafts for consideration, but not all of them, for this would be impossible. They "are so numerous as to defy complete enumeration."[48] Of all the crafts, he found agriculture to be the most ancient. Carpentry, he believed, had been introduced by Noah; at least that is what tradition maintained. "With its help, he constructed the ship of salvation (the Ark)."[49] He presents a lengthy description of the "craft of midwifery." In his discussion of the "craft of medicine," he notes the general belief and one he shared that "the origin of all illnesses is in food, as Muhammad said in the comprehensive tradition on medicine." He goes on to say that "the stomach is the home of disease. Dieting is the main medi-

cine. The origin of every disease is indigestion."⁵⁰ He classified the craft of calligraphy as "a noble craft, since it is
one of the special qualities of man by which he distinguishes himself from the animals."⁵¹ The craft of making
books was limited to cities that had a rich cultural background, while music was the craft "concerned with the
setting of poems to music."⁵²

Ibn Khaldun next turns to a discussion of the sciences,
using the word *science* in the sense of knowledge that man
can acquire through observation, study, and experimenta-
tion. Included with the sciences are the study of the angels
and the prophets; also jurisprudence, speculative theology, Sufism, dream interpretation, numbers, astronomy,
physics, sorcery, alchemy ("We know of no one in the world
who has attained the goal (of alchemy) or got any desirable
result out of it"⁵³), and astrology. Ibn Khaldun condemns
astrology on both religious and natural grounds and because an astrologer might encourage the enemies of a dynasty to revolt should the signs appear propitious for such
an undertaking. He further discusses the education of children and the methods of instruction employed in Muslim
cities. Although he judged scholars to be essential to civilization, he declares they made poor politicians.

> The reason for this is that (scholars) are used to mental
> speculation and to a searching study of ideas which they
> abstract from the *sensibilia* and conceive in their minds as
> general universals, so that they may be applicable to some
> matter in general but not to any particular matter, individ-
> ual, race, nation, or group of people. (Scholars) then make
> such universal ideas conform (in their minds) to facts of the
> outside world. . . .
>
> Thus, in all their intellectual activity, scholars are accus-
> tomed to dealing with matters of the mind and with
> thoughts. They do not know anything else. Politicians, on
> the other hand, must pay attention to the facts of the
> outside world and the conditions attaching to and depend-

ing on (politics). (These facts and conditions) are obscure. . . . The conditions existing in civilization cannot (always) be compared with each other. They may be alike in one respect, but they may differ in other. . . .

(Now) scholars are accustomed to generalizations and analogical conclusions. When they look at politics, they press (their observations) into the mold of their views and their way of making deductions. Thus, they commit many errors, or (at least) they cannot be trusted (not to commit errors). . . .

The average person of a healthy disposition and a mediocre intelligence has not got the mind (for speculation) and does not think of it. Therefore, he restricts himself to considering every matter as it is, and to judging every kind of situation and every type of individual by its particular (circumstances). His judgment is not infected with analogy and generalization. Most of his speculation stops at matters perceivable by the senses and he does not go beyond them in his mind. . . .

Such a man, therefore, can be trusted when he reflects upon his political activities. He has the right outlook in dealing with his fellowmen.[54]

From here Ibn Khaldun proceeds to a lengthy discussion of grammar and literature, and with this he concludes the *Muqaddimah*. One would have to say that only in the broadest meaning of history as the record of culture can the modern scholar justify such considerations in an introduction to history.

Reference has earlier been made, in connection with the origins of Muslim historiography, to the manner scholars used chains of authorities to establish the authenticity of what they were seeking to confirm. The first scholars to do this were interested in verifying the genuineness of statements attributed to Muhammad, with historians employing the same method somewhat later to prove the historicity of events from the past. In his *Muqaddimah* Ibn Khaldun offers an excellent illustration of the use of chains of authorities concerning the validity of traditions

about the Mahdi, the man many Muslims believed would
appear at the end of time to bring about the triumph of
justice and of Islam.[55]

We are now going to mention here the various traditions
concerning (this matter). (We are also going to mention)
the attacks upon these traditions by those who disapprove
(of the matter), and the evidence upon which they base
their disapproval. This, then, will be followed by a report
on the statements and opinions of the Sufis. Thus, the true
situation will become clear, if God wills.

We say: A number of religious leaders have published
traditions concerning the Mahdi, among them at-
Tirmidhi, Abu Dawud, al-Bazzar, Ibn Majah, al-Hakim,
at-Tabarani, and Abu Ya'la al-Mawsili. They mention a
number of the men around Muhammad as transmitters of
these traditions: 'Ali, Ibn 'Abbas, Ibn 'Umar, Talhah, Ibn
Mas'ud, Abu Hurayrah, Anas Abu Sa'id al-Khudri, Umm
Habibah, Umm Salimah, Thawban, Qurrah b. Iyas, 'Ali
al-Hilali, and 'Abdallah b. al-Harith b. Jaz, among others.
(They also mention) their chains of transmitters, which
have often been found objectionable by those who disapprove (of the matter). We shall mention this now, because
hadith scholars acknowledge negative criticism to have
precedence over positive criticism. If we find that some
person in the chain of transmitters is accused of negligence, poor memory, weakness, or poor judgment, it af-
fects and weakens the soundness of the tradition. . . .

As-Suhayli reports with reference to Abu Bakr b. Abi
Khaythamah that the latter did a thorough job of collecting the traditions of the Mahdi. (As-Suhayli) said: "The
tradition with the strongest chain of transmitters is the
one mentioned by Abu Bakr al-Iskaf in the *Fawa'id al-
Akhbar.* It goes back to Malik b. Anas, who had it on the
authority of Muhammad b. al-Munkadir, who had it on the
authority of Jabir, who said that the Messenger of God
said: 'He who does not believe in the Mahdi is an unbe-
liever, and he who does not believe in the Anti-Christ is a
liar.' He said something similar with regard to the rising of
the sun in the west, I think." One could not find a more

extremist statement. The soundness of his chain of transmitters between (Abu Bakr) and Malik b. Anas (also) is
problematic. Abu Bakr al-Iskaf is considered by (*hadith*
scholars) as suspect and as a forger of traditions.

With their chain of transmitters going back to Ibn
Mas'ud, at-Tirmidhi and Abu Dawud have published the
following tradition through 'Asim b. Abi n-Najud, one of
the seven authoritative Qur'an readers, on the authority of
Zirr b. Hubaysh, on the authority of 'Abdallah b. Mas'ud,
on the authority of the Prophet: "If no more than one day
remained of the world — said Za'idah — God would cause
that day to last until there be sent a man from me — or:
from my family — whose name will tally with my name, and
the name of whose father will tally with the name of my
father."

This is the recension of Abu Dawud. Abu Dawud did not
add any remarks critical of it, and he said in his well-known
Epistle that everything to which he did not append critical
remarks in his book was all right. . . .

Al-Hakim said that the tradition was transmitted by
ath-Thawri, Shu'bah, Za'idah, and other Muslim religious
leaders, on the authority of 'Asim. He said: "Everything
transmitted by 'Asim, on the authority of Zirr, on the authority of 'Abdallah, is sound, according to the rules I have
laid down for using information derived from 'Asim as evidence, for he is an authoritative Muslim religious leader."
However, Ahmad b. Hanbal said about 'Asim that he was
a pious man, a reader of the Qur'an, and a good and reliable
person, but that al-A'mash had a better memory than he.
Shu'bah used to prefer al-A'mash to him for establishing
(the soundness of) traditions. Al-'Ijli said: "There was some
difference of opinion about his (reliability) with regard to
Zirr and Abu Wa'il." In this way, he alluded to the weakness of the material he transmitted on authority. Muhammad b. Sa'd said: "He was reliable; however, he made many
errors in his traditions." Ya'qub b. Sufyan said: "There is
some confusion in his traditions." 'Abd-ar-Rahman b. Abi
Hatim said: "I said to my father: 'Abu Zur'ah says that
'Asim is reliable.' My father replied: 'He does not fall into
that category.' " Ibn 'Ulayyah discussed 'Asim (adversely)

and said: "Everyone named 'Asim has a bad memory." Abu
Hatim said: "So far as I am concerned, he falls into the
category of truthful transmitters whose traditions are all
right. But he was not a (great) *hadith* expert." An-Nasai
expressed a different opinion about him. Ibn Khirash said:
"His traditions contain things that are unknown." Abu
Ja'far al-'Uqayli said: "There was nothing the matter with
him except a bad memory." Ad-Daraqutni said: "There was
something the matter with his memory." Yahya al-Qattan
said: "I have never found a man named 'Asim who did not
have a bad memory."

Ta'rif

Without question the most exciting episode in the tur-
bulent career of Ibn Khaldun was his meeting with Timur
the Lame, the Mongol chieftain whose name struck fear
into the hearts of the rulers of Europe and Asia and who in
time went on to establish one of the world's greatest empires. The fact that Ibn Khaldun did meet this dread warrior was generally accepted, but it was only recently that
the historian's autobiography (*Ta'rif*) came to light to confirm that fact and to furnish us a detailed and colorful
account of this extraordinary encounter. Here follows an
excerpt from the *Ta'rif* in Ibn Khaldun's own words.[56]

When the news reached Egypt that Emir Timur had conquered Asia Minor, had destroyed Siwas, and had returned to Syria, Sultan Faraj gathered his armies, opened
the bureau of stipends, and announced to the troops the
march to Syria.

At that time I was out of office, but Yashbak, the Sultan's dawadar, summoned me and urged me to accompany
him in the royal party. When I tried to refuse his offer he
assumed a firm attitude toward me, though with gentleness of speech and considerable generosity.

So I departed with them on the next morning. . . . We
reached Gaza; here we rested for several days awaiting
news. Then we set out for Damascus in order to forestall

the Tartars, encamped at Shaqhab, and then set out at night, arriving at Damascus in the morning. . . .

The Sultan erected his tents and [other] structures in the plain of Qubbat Yalbugha. Emir Timur, despairing of taking the city by assault, remained for more than a month on a hillock above Qubbat Yalbugha, watching us while we observed him. The two armies engaged three or four times, during this period, with varying success.

Then the Sultan and his chief emirs learned that some of the other emirs were engaged in a seditious plot and were planning to flee to Egypt to bring about a revolt there. So they agreed to return to Cairo. . . .

The inhabitants of Damascus the next morning were perplexed because news of what had happened was vague. The judges and jurists then came to see me. . . , and it was agreed to ask Emir Timur for security for their homes and families. . . . The cadi with the sheikh of the Sufis . . . went out [to Timur]. He consented to grant immunity and sent them back to summon the notables and the other cadis. . . .

The cadi . . . informed me that Timur had asked about me and whether I had left with the armies of Egypt or whether I was still in the city. He [the cadi] had replied that I was still staying in the college where I had been before. We accordingly spent that night making preparations to go to him.

Then a dispute arose among some of the men in the Great Mosque, because some of them disapproved of the reliance which had been placed on what had been said [concerning the surrender]. A report of this reached me late in the night and I feared some rash attempt on my life. I therefore arose at dawn and went to the group of judges who were at the city gate. I requested permission of them to go out, or to descend the wall. . . . They at first refused me permission, then in the morning they lowered me down the wall.

Near the gate I found some of his [i.e. Timur's] retinue. . . . [They] offered me a mount and sent with me one of the Sultan's retinue, who conducted me to him. . . . When my name was announced, the title "Maghribi Malikite Cadi" was added to it; he summoned me, and as I entered the audience tent to [approach] him he was reclining on his elbow while platters of food were passing before him which he was sending one after the other to groups of Mongols sitting in circles in front of his tent.

.Upon entering, I spoke first, saying, "Peace be upon you," and I made a gesture of humility. Thereupon he raised his head and stretched out his hand to me, which I kissed. He made a sign to me to sit down; I did so just where I was, and he summoned from his retinue one of the erudite Hanafite jurists . . . to serve as interpreter between us.

He asked me from where in the Maghrib I had come, and why I had come. I replied, "I left my country in order to perform the pilgrimage. . . ."

Next he asked me, "Where is your birthplace?" I replied, "In the inner Maghrib, [where I was] secretary to the greatest king there."

He said, "What is the meaning of 'inner' in describing the Maghrib?" [My description of Maghrib proved unsatisfactory.] He said, "I am not satisfied. I desire that you write for me [a description of] the whole country of the Maghrib — its distant as well as its near-by parts, its mountains and its rivers, its villages and its cities — in such a manner that I might seem actually to see it."

I said, "That will be accomplished under your auspices."

Then he gave a signal to his servants to bring from his tent some of the kind of food which they call "rishta" and which they were most expert in preparing. Some dishes of it were brought it, and he made a sign that they should be set before me. I arose, took them, and drank, and liked it, and this impressed him favorably.

[Ibn Khaldun then describes his discussions with Timur, his return to his lodging in Damascus, and Timur's decision to attack the city.]

Then [Timur] pressed the siege of the Citadel in earnest; he erected against it catapults, naphtha guns, ballistas, and breachers, and within a few days sixty catapults and other similar engines were set up. The siege pressed ever harder upon those within the Citadel, and its structure was destroyed on all sides. . . .

From the inhabitants of the town he confiscated under torture hundredweights of money which he seized after having taken all the property, mounts, and tents which the ruler of Egypt had left behind. Then he gave permission for the plunder of the houses of the people of the city, and they were despoiled of all their furniture and goods. The furnishings and utensils of no value which remained were set on fire, and the fire spread to the walls of the houses, which were supported on timbers. It continued to burn until it reached the Great Mosque; the flames mounted to its roof, melting the lead in it, and the ceiling and walls collapsed. This was an absolutely dastardly and abominable deed, but the changes in affairs are in the hands of Allah—he does with his creatures as he wishes, and decides in his kingdom as he wills. . . .

When I had met him and been let down the wall to him, as already related, one of my friends who from previous acquaintance with them knew their customs advised me to present him some gift. . . . I therefore chose from the book market an exceedingly beautiful Qur'an copy . . . a beautiful prayer rug, a copy of the famous poem al-Burda by al-Busiri . . . and four boxes of the excellent Cairo sweetmeats. I took these gifts and entered to him while he [Timur] was in the Qasr al-Ablaq, sitting in its reception hall.

When he saw me arriving he stood up and made a sign to me to sit at his right, where I took a seat, some of the leaders of the Jaghatai being on both sides of him. After having sat there for a little while, I moved over in front of him and pointed to the presents which I have mentioned and which were in my servants' hands. I set them down, and he turned toward me. Then I opened the Qur'an, and when he saw it he hurriedly arose and put it on his head. Then I presented the Burda to him; he asked me about it and about its author, and I told him all I knew about it. I next gave him the prayer rug, which he took and kissed. Then I put in front of him the boxes of sweets and took a bit of them, according to the custom of courtesy, and he distributed the sweetmeats in the box among those present at his council. He accepted all this and indicated that he was pleased with it. . . .

When the time for Timur's journey approached and he decided to leave Damascus, I entered to him one day. After we had completed the customary greetings, he turned to me and said, "You have a mule here?"

I answered, "Yes." He said, "Is it a good one?" I answered, "Yes." He said, "Will you sell it? I would buy it from you." I replied, "May Allah aid you – one like me does not sell to one like you; but I would offer it to you in homage, and also others like it if I had them." He said, "I meant only that I would requite you for it with generosity." [Timur was true to his word and also provided for Khaldun's safe departure for Egypt.]

The Reign of the Two Sultans Abou Sa'id and Abou Tsabit, Sons of 'Abd Er-Rah'man and Grandsons of Abou Yah'ia Yagkmorasan[57]

So provocative is Ibn Khaldun's writing in the *Muqaddimah* that the reader usually forgets the historian intended that section simply as an introduction to his universal history. And because the *Muqaddimah* is so much more valuable than the universal history itself, here is one book where the introduction, often skipped or passed over quickly in most books, receives the most attention, while the heart of the book generally goes unnoticed. Still, one section of the universal history does merit reading, that which concerns the Magrib, roughly north Africa west of Egypt. What Ibn Khaldun has to say about the Berber tribes there is far superior in both detail and extent to anything else that is extant. From the excerpt of the universal history that follows, one might conclude that the kind of never-ending tribal warfare described has characterized life in that part of Africa for centuries, up to the present century.

These two princes resembled two moons that shone in the heavens of the empire of the 'Abd El-Wadite (otherwise plunged into darkness), two stars shining with nobility and grandeur, two formidable champions to whom the people looked for security. The one was a model of loyalty and piety; the other, whenever there was fighting, resembled a lion intent upon his prey. The first was a veritable fountain of justice, the second an ocean of generosity and kindness, a source of good fortune to the realm which had been deprived of it. These two alone resolved the difficulties of a situation which had appeared beyond solution. They devoted themselves to restoring that which had been destroyed (during the rule of the Merinids), to repair the walls of the capital which had been partly destroyed, and to reestablish the renown which had been lost to the empire.

They gathered together the scattered members of the family of the 'Abd El-Wadite from the unhealthy grazing lands to which they had been exiled. They showed their clansmen the road to glory. They rivaled each other in their efforts to bring prosperity to this great empire and to reestablish proper procedures in the business of politics and government. They applied themselves, the one to carry on war, the other to the practice of piety, this one managing internal affairs, the other pursuing the Arabs to their mountain retreats. Both were models of virtue and each maintained cordial relations with the other which closed the door to misunderstanding. . . . These sovereigns were successful in their undertakings, gained the upper hand over their formerly victorious enemies, repaired the damages, inaugurated a wise administration, and spread far and wide the shining glories of the empire.

Alas! Time brings to destruction the most noble efforts. A day arrives when the steel refuses to give a spark, when the best sword is blunted. Does not the time come that brings an end to the most unyielding bodies? Does not good fortune find itself replaced with misery? The empire which will never perish is from God alone, the Creator (of all things).

The two new sovereigns of the empire of the 'Abd El-Wadite took possession of Tlemcen on Wednesday the 22nd of djoumada II 749 (September 1348), as we noted above. The morning of the day following, the tribe of the Beni 'Abd el-Wad solemnly proclaimed the blessed sultan Abou Sa'id king – may he enjoy the fullness of the mercy of Allah! Political exigencies forced him to arrest 'Otsman ben Yah'ia ben Djarrar, who died in prison during Ramad'an of this same year (Nov.–Dec. 1348).

The sovereigns Abou Sa'id and Abou Tsabit chose for vizier Yah'ia ben Dawoud ben 'Ali ben Madjn and for secretary 'Abd el-Wah'id ben Moh'ammed ez-Zawwaq, who was afterwards dismissed because of unscrupulous acts of which he was found guilty. They appointed in his place 'Ali ben Moh'ammed ben So'oud after his return from Tunis, as we will report later on, if it pleases God.

To discharge the duties of the cadi there were appointed the jurist Abou-l-'Abbas Ah'med ben Ah'med ben 'ali el-Qaisi, known by the name of El-Mochawwich, and later Abou-'l-'Abbas Ah'med ben el-Il'asan ben Sa'id.

That done, each of the two princes assumed the insignia of royalty, received popular investiture, and promulgated ordinances for appointments and the raising of taxes. But the throne itself was occupied by Abou Sa'id whose name was cited in the Sermon and also engraved on the money, while the sultan Abou Tsabit was entrusted with the military administration of those matters affecting the provinces and war. This last arrangement was evidence of the respect and affection of his brother which he had earned. This disposition of affairs was accepted by their elder brother Maoula, the pious and great Abou Ya'qoub, who retired to Nedroma in order to devote himself to his prayers. . . .

On the coast (in the region of the Koumiya, between Tlemcen and Rachgoun), Ibrahim ben 'Abd el-Malik el-Koumi raised the standard of revolt, intending to recover the throne of 'Abd el-Moumin ben 'Ali to his own profit. The sultan Abou Tsabit – may Allah grant him pardon! – the head of his powerful tribe, marched against the rebel, ten radjah (October 1348), cut through and conquered the entire region along the shore (the present region of the Trara), sowing death and taking prisoners. He seized Nedroma, Honain, and came with his troops to besiege Oran (which was commanded by) 'Abbou ben Sa'id ben Adjana. Abou Tsabit maintained the siege of the city for several days; but the Beni Rachid defected and promised Ibn Adjana assistance in the struggle against the Beni 'Abd el-Wad. The governor of Oran then made a sortie and the Beni Rachid gave ground. Moh'ammed ben Yousof ben 'Inan ben Faris ben Zaiyan ben Tsabit ben Moh'ammed was slain, the camp of the ('Abd el-Wadite) was given over to pillage, but the sultan Abou Tsabit was able to flee to his capital, thanks to the speed of his horse.

He made preparations for a second expedition against Oran, but in this he was prevented by the news he received of the arrival of 'En-Nacir, son of the sultan Abou-'l-Il'asan, of Tunis, at the head (of the Arab tribes) of Sowaid, Ed-Dyalim, El-'At't'af and H'ocain. (The king of Tlemcen) sent to warn the sultan Abou 'Inan and (abandoning his projects against Oran) prepared to march against the army of his old and more formidable enemies which was approaching.

At the beginning of the month of moh'arram 750 (March–April 1349) all the Beni 'Abd el-Wad who had been taken to Maghrib in the service of the Merinids, arrived at Tlemcen in the name of the sultan Abou 'Inan in order to support the efforts of the king of this city against En-Nacir. Among them (Abou Tsabit) found his nephew Abou Zaiyan, son of the sultan Abou Sa'id – may Allah grant him pardon! This prince had taken refuge at Fas (Fez) with the consent of his father, at the time of the departure of the latter for Ifriqua with the sultan Abou-'l-H'asan.

The sultan Abou Tsabit – may Allah grant him pardon! – left then to meet En-Nacir and the enemy army during the second ten days of the month of moh'arram. He dispatched an ambassador to Maghrawa to notify them that they (should) come to join him, according to the terms of the treaty between them; but they refused to respond to his appeal.

Abou Tsabit continued his march (toward the east by the plain of Chelif) and met the enemy bands on the banks of the wadi Ourk, in the country of El-'At't'af at the end of the month of rabl' I (June 1349). He dealt them a sound

defeat, and the jurist Abou-'Il'asan 'Ali ben So'oud, who
was made prisoner at this time, was brought to him and
pardoned. The sultan of the 'Abd el-Wadite returned then
to his capital where he made his entry at the end of the
month rabl' II of this same year (July 1349). He bore a
grudge deep in his heart against the Maghrawa, who had
refused their help against a common enemy, thereby vio-
lating the pact (which united them). . . .

As his displeasure concerning Maghrawa increased and
his enmity for them grew, Abou Tsabit left to attack them
on Sunday the 23rd chawwal 750 (the beginning of January 1350). Their encounter came on the banks of the wadi
Rihou, Friday the 26th of dsou-'l-qa'da. The battle was
furious and the struggle lasted until the moment when
Maghrawa suffered defeat and their battalions were completely destroyed. The vanquished retreated to the sum-
mit of their mountain and the bottom of the valleys. The
city of Mazouna acknowledged the sovereignty of the sultan, the late Abou Sa'id.

The events which we have read had just taken place
when the sultan, the late Abou Tsabit, received news at the
beginning of the year 751 (1350–51) of the landing in Algiers of the sultan Abou-'l-H'asan and of the support given
to his sovereign by the sheik Abou Ya'quob Wanzamar ben
'Arif and by the Toudjin commanded by 'Adi ben Yousof
who recruited troops among the El-'At't'af, Ed-Dyalim and
H'ocain. The king of Tlemcen — may Allah grant him
pardon — then made peace with the Maghrawa and prepared to fight these new enemy bands. After having
crossed the plateau of Mindas, he halted at El-Modairisa in
the Sersou, at the beginning of the month of rabl' I (May
1350). He forced the sheik Wanzamar ben 'Arif and the
troops which he commanded to flee before him. The sultan
Abou Tsabit was still there when he was joined by the
Yah'ia ben Rah'ou (ben Tachfin ben Mo't'i) at the head of a
troop of Merinid soldiers which the sultan Abou 'Inan sent
to help him. He then left for the east, going before his
adversaries, and stopped before Medea which he occupied.
The H'ocain having retired into the mountains of Tit't'eri,
the king of Tlemcen left 'Imran ben Mousa El-Djanouni at

Medea and hurried to crush them. He stormed the mountain which they had fortified and took hostages. He then established his authority over the country of H'amza, subjected the region to his rule, reduced the rebels, razed their fortresses, and took the road to the west in order to return to his capital, that of the 'Abd el-Wadite. He reached the place known by the name of El-Achbour in the country of the H'ocain. There he met 'Isa ben Solaiman ben Mancour ben 'Abd el-Wah'id ben Ya'quob ben 'Abd el-H'aqq who had been sent by the sultan Abou 'Inan to take command of the soldiers (Merinids) and to assure himself of the person of Yah'ia ben Rah'ou whom he suspected of having conspired with the sultan Abou-'l-Hasan. From there Abou Tsabit hastened to return to his capital where he made his entry the sixth day of radjah of this same year (751) 10 September 1350.

Shortly after he received news that En-Nacir, son of the sultan Abou-'l-H'asan, had slain 'Imran ben Mousa El-Djanouni and had seized Medea, Milyana, and Timzourat, and that the sultan Abou-'H'san was marching toward the west at the head of innumerable warriors recruited from among the Solaim, Ryah, Sowaid, Ed-Dyalim, El-'At't'af, H'ocain, and Toudjin, without counting the Merinids who accompanied him together with their allies. He further learned that 'Ali ben Rachid el-Maghrawi had fled with his tribe at their approach and was retreating into the country of 'Abd el-Wadite.

At this news, the sultan Abou Tsabit, burning with a bravery which never faltered, left Tlemcen. He was preoccupied with the disastrous results of battle but in no way was seeking to escape. (He was) full of courage and as immovable as a mountain, full of an ardor which he communicated more and more to his formidable troops, filled with a patriotism whose example penetrated his soldiers more and more as they advanced. He took possession of Taghit-ou-Nfif, where 'Ali ben Rachid el-Maghrawa rejoined him with his tribe. The two chiefs, after having exchanged greetings while on horseback, discussed at length the manner they might attack the enemy. The sultan Abou Tsabit assumed responsibility for the sultan Abou-'l-

H'asan, while the son of the latter and his supporters would be attacked by 'Ali ben Rachid. On Wednesday the tenth of cha'ban (October 14, 1350), the encounter took place at a place called Ti'zizin in the vicinity of Chelif. The struggle was furious on all sides, dreadful to the point of causing the hair of a child to turn white or to cause it to jump with fright. El-Maghrawi and his tribe were routed and the sultan Abou Tsabit assured the greatest victory of contemporary times.

Abou-'l-H'asan and his army were routed at the beginning of the night. A number of his troops were put to death, among them (we will list) his son En-Nacir, Moh'ammed ben ('Ali ben) El-'Azfi, commander of the fleet; Barakat ben H'occoun ben El-Bawwaq, the minister of the interior; 'Ali ben El-Qabaili, his private secretary and writer of the l'alama. The victors seized the riches of Abou-'l-H'asan, and his goods, wives, and daughters fell into his hands. The world is indeed changing; wars are full of chance; but the eternal power is given to God alone!

(Abou-'l-H'asan) owed his life to the speed of his horse. He fled with Wanzamar ben 'Arif from near the country of the Sowaid, the tribe of the latter. From there the defeated sultan took them toward the west, across the desert (the high steppes) toward Sidjilmassa, thus approaching his former realm of Maghrib. The sultan Abou Tsabit — may Allah grant him pardon — returned to his capital covered with laurels, (greater than all the others), bringing back rich and incomparable booty. He entered Tlemcen at the beginning of chawwal of this same year (December 1350).

Notes

Introduction

1. *Procopius,* H. B. Dewing, Trans., 7 vols. (Cambridge, Mass.: Harvard University Press, 1914–1940), vol. II, p. 21. Hereafter, volumes I–IV will be cited as *Wars,* volume VI as *Secret History,* and volume VII as *Buildings.*
2. Alfred Bel, ed. and trans., *Histoire Des Beni 'Abd El-Wad Rois De Tlemcen Jusqu' au Regne D'Abou H'Ammou Mousa II* par Abou Zakarya Yah'ia Ibn Khaldoun. (Algiers: P. Fontana, 1903), p. 211.
3. *Sir John Froissart's Chronicles of England, France, and the Adjoining Countries,* 5 vols., Thomas Johnes, trans. (London: The Haford Press, 1803–10), vol. I, p. 517.
4. See p. 95.
5. *Chronique De Abou-Djafar-Mohammed-Ben-Djarirben Yezid Tabari,* Hermann Zotenberg, trans. (Paris: Imprimerie Imperiale, 1958), vol. I, p. 9.
6. Bel, *Histoire Des Beni 'Abd El-Wad Rois De Tlemcen,* p. 213.
7. Ibid., p. 209.
8. *Procopius,* vol. IV, p. 221.
9. See p. 233.

10. See p. 10.
11. See p. 48.
12. See p. 139.
13. See p. 212.
14. But see pp. 263–64, for his handling of the affair between al-Abbasah and Ja'far.
15. See p. 204.
16. See p. 47.
17. See p. 10.
18. See p. 133.
19. See pp. 213 and 218.
20. Matthew Paris, *Matthew Paris's English History*, J. A. Giles, trans. (London: H. G. Bohn, 1854), vol. III, p. 115.
21. *Procopius*, vol. V, p. 203.
22. See p. 15.
23. See p. 64.
24. See p. 100.
25. See p. 135.
26. Paris, *Matthew Paris's English History*, vol. I, p. 487.
27. See p. 249.
28. See p. 274.
29. See p. 115.

Chapter 1/Procopius

1. *Secret History*, pp. 97, 99.
2. *Wars*, vol. IV, pp. 71–72.
3. *Buildings*, p. 3.
4. A recent biographer believes Procopius was busy with the *Buildings*, a panegyric of Justinian, and the *Secret History* at the same time. See J. A. S. Evans, *Procopius* (New York: Twayne Publishers, 1972), p. 78.
5. *Buildings*, pp. 25, 27, 29.
6. *Wars*, vol. I, pp. 3, 5.
7. *Wars*, vol. II, p. 95.
8. *Wars*, vol. I, p. 3.
9. *Wars*, vol. I, p. 5.
10. *Buildings*, p. 3.
11. *Secret History*, p. 3.
12. *Secret History*, pp. 5, 7.

13. The architects.
14. *Buildings,* pp. 29, 31.
15. *Wars,* vol. II, p. 43.
16. *Wars,* vol. IV, p. 191. On at least two earlier occasions Roman standards had fallen into the hands of the enemy – at Carrhae in 53 B.C., when Crassus was slain, and in 9 A.D., when the Germans annihilated three legions in the Teutoburg forest.
17. *Wars,* vol. II, pp. 3, 5.
18. *Secret History,* p. 5.
19. H. B. Dewing, *Secret History,* p. ix.
20. *Secret History,* p. 105.
21. *Secret History,* p. 149, 151.
22. *Secret History,* pp. 97, 99, 101.
23. So writes G. A. Williamson, *Procopius, The Secret History* (Baltimore: Penguin Books, 1966), p. 29.
24. *Wars,* vol. III, pp. 41, 43.
25. *Secret History,* pp. 189, 191.
26. See *Wars,* vol. I, p. 291.
27. *Secret History,* pp. 75, 77.
28. *Wars,* vol. IV, p. 419.
29. *Secret History,* p. 199.
30. From the Greek word for goat.
31. *Wars,* vol. IV, pp. 11, 13, 15.
32. *Wars,* vol. III, pp. 83, 85.
33. *Wars,* vol. III, pp. 317, 319.
34. *Wars,* vol. I, p. 3.
35. *Secret History,* pp. 21, 23.
36. *Wars,* vol. II, pp. 95, 97.
37. *Wars,* vol. III, pp. 89, 91.
38. *Wars,* vol. I, p. 223.
39. *Wars,* vol. III, pp. 253, 255, 257.
40. *Wars,* vol. III, pp. 201, 203, 205, 207.
41. *Wars,* vol. I, pp. 109, 111, 113.
42. *Wars,* vol. II, p. 21.
43. A captain in Narses' army.
44. *Wars,* vol. V, p. 397.
45. *Wars,* vol. V, pp. 385, 387.
46. *Wars,* vol. I, p. 453.
47. *Wars,* vol. I, p. 341.

48. Still Procopius admitted that he could not always understand why God did, or permitted, what took place. In writing of Chosroes' destruction of Antioch, he declared, "I become dizzy as I write of such a great calamity." *Wars,* vol. I, p. 343.
49. *Wars,* vol. II, p. 115.
50. *Wars,* vol. I, p. 287.
51. *Wars,* vol. IV, p. 405.
52. Terracina is located on the seacoast between Rome and Naples.
53. *Wars,* vol. III, p. 109.
54. *Wars,* vol. V, p. 61.
55. *Buildings,* p. 69.
56. *Wars,* vol. I, pp. 51, 53.
57. The view that since Peter, the first of the apostles, was the first bishop of Rome, his successors there inherited his position of primacy.
58. *Wars,* vol. III, p. 25.
59. *Wars,* vol. III, p. 221.

Chapter 2/The Venerable Bede

1. S. J. Crawford, *Anglo-Saxon Influence on Western Christendom, 600–800* (New York: Barnes and Noble, 1966), p. 103.
2. The rule observed at Wearmouth-Jarrow was not strictly that of St. Benedict, although Benedict Biscop, the founder, had relied heavily on it in composing the rule he instituted. See *Bede's Ecclesiastical History of the English People,* Bertram Colgrave and R.A.B. Mynors (Oxford: Clarendon Press, 1969), p. xxiii. All passages quoted from Bede's *History* are from this edition. They will be cited simply as *Bede's History.*
3. *Bede's History,* p. 567 (v.24). The v.24 indicates the twenty-fourth chapter of the fifth book.
4. See *Bede's History,* p. 585, a quote from a letter of Cuthbert, a pupil of Bede, who later became the abbot of Jarrow.
5. Virgil was the Latin author most frequently studied in medieval schools. Many also believed that the poet's allusion in

    Eclogue IV to the birth of a boy who would usher in the golden age was a prophetic announcement of Christ's own appearance.

6. He was "authoritatively recognized as saint" only in 1899. See *Butler's Lives of the Saints,* ed. Herbert Thurston and Donald Attwater (New York: Kenedy, 1956), vol. II, p. 404.

7. Charles W. Jones, *Bedae Pseudepigrapha: Scientific Writings Falsely Attributed to Bede* (Ithaca: Cornell University Press, 1939), p. 1.

8. Bede's "system of dating by the year of grace . . . is his main contribution to historical writing." *Bede's History,* p. xix.

9. Four years, six months after he had begun to reign, Caesar, because of his arrogance, fell victim to an attack by sixty or more Roman senators and equestrians who had conspired against him. *Monumenta Germaniae Historica, Auctores Antiquissimi,* ed. Theodor Mommsen (Berlin: Hildebrand, 1961), vol. XIII, p. 280.

10. Crawford, *Anglo-Saxon Influence,* p. 103.

11. *Bede's History,* p. 3. Preface.

12. Ibid.

13. Ibid., pp. 3, 5, 7. Preface.

14. Ibid., p. 7. Preface.

15. Ibid.

16. Ibid., pp. 133, 135 (ii.1).

17. Jarrow was located just a few miles from the eastern end of Hadrian's wall.

18. That is, Brittany. Actually Britons fled to the mainland in such numbers during the fifth and sixth centuries that they gave the land their name (Brittany) and culture.

19. *Bede's History,* pp. 15, 17 (i.1).

20. Ibid., pp. 19, 21 (i.1).

21. Caesar made two expeditions: the first in 55 B.C., the second in 54.

22. *Bede's History,* pp. 21, 23 (i.2).

23. Ibid., pp. 29, 31, 33 (i.7).

24. Ibid., p. 39 (i.10).

25. Ibid., p. 45 (i.12).

26. Ibid., pp. 55, 57 (i.17).

27. Ibid., pp. 63, 65 (i.20).

28. Ibid., p. 69 (i.22).

29. Ibid., p. 107 (i.30).
30. Ibid., pp. 77, 79 (i.26).
31. Ibid., pp. 127, 129 (ii.l).
32. Ibid., p. 165 (ii.9).
33. Ibid., p. 183 (ii.13).
34. Ibid., p. 183 (ii.13).
35. Ibid., p. 185 (ii.13).
36. Ibid., pp. 185, 187 (ii.13).
37. Ibid., p. 215 (iii.1).
38. See *Venerabilis Baedae Historiam Ecclesiasticam Gentis Anglorum....* Recognivit ... Instruxit Carolus Plummer (Oxford: Clarendon Press, 1961), pp. lxiv-lxv.
39. *Bede's History,* pp. 243, 245 (iii.9).
40. Aidan had come from Ireland upon King Oswald's request for missionaries.
41. *Bede's History,* pp. 257, 259, 261 (iii.14).
42. Ibid., pp. 265, 267 (iii.17).
43. Ibid., pp. 299, 301 (iii.25).
44. Ibid., p. 301 (iii.25).
45. Ibid., pp. 307, 309 (iii.25).
46. Ibid., p. 309 (iii.26).
47. Ibid., pp. 333, 335 (iv.2).
48. Ibid., p. 389 (iv,18).
49. Ibid., p. 415 (iv,24).
50. Ibid., p. 417 (iv.24).
51. Ibid., p. 419 (iv.24).
52. Ibid., p. 513 (v.17).
53. Ibid., p. 515 (v.18).
54. Ibid., p. 557 (v.23).
55. This is a reference to the defeat the Saracens suffered at Tours in 732, which Bede may have added when the *History* was in its final preparation.
56. *Bede's History,* p. 571 (v.24).

Chapter 3/Al-Tabari

1. Muhsin Mahdi, *Ibn Khaldun's Philosophy of History* (Chicago: University of Chicago Press, 1964), p. 135.
2. Sacred tradition, based upon Muhammad's words and actions.

3. *Selections from the Annals of Tabari*, ed. M. J. De Geoje (Leiden: E. J. Brill, 1902), p. ix.

4. Religious law, jurisprudence in general.

5. "We may well doubt whether it would have been in his power to compose a history ten times the bulk of that which has been preserved, and probably this story should be dismissed as fabulous." D. S. Margoliouth, *Lectures on Arabic Historians* (Calcutta: University of Calcutta, 1930), p. 110.

6. Ibid., p. 41.

7. "The invention, as cheapening the process of production, is to be compared with that of printing." Ibid., p. 4.

8. The descriptions of such victories were known as *maghazi*.

9. See the beginning of Tabari's history (p. 95). He writes as a theologian.

10. An example of the use of chains of authorities in doctrinal matters appears in chapter 8 (pp. 283–285).

11. A. J. Butler, *The Treaty of Misr in Tabari* (Oxford: Clarendon Press, 1913), pp. 8–11.

12. "Tabari is more a collector of traditions than a historian." Margoliouth, *Lectures*, p. 16.

13. Mahdi, *Khaldun's Philosophy*, p. 136.

14. See *The Reign of Al-Mu'tasim*, trans. Elma Marin (New Haven: American Oriental Society, 1951), p. xvi.

15. From Ibn Khaldun's *Ta'rif*. See Walter J. Fischel, *Ibn Khaldun and Tamerlane* (Berkeley: University of California Press, 1952), p. 37.

16. It has been suggested that al-Tabari left out of his account certain matters unfavorable to the Abbasids. See Franz Rosenthal, *A History of Muslim Historiography* (Leiden: E. J. Brill, 1968), p. 135.

17. *Chronique De Abou-Djafar-Mohammed-Ben-Djarirben Yezid Tabari*, trans. Hermann Zotenberg (Paris: Imprimerie Impériale, 1958), vol. I, pp. 9–11. Translation by author.

18. Ibid., pp. 455–69.

19. *Geschichte Der Perser Und Araber Zur Zeit Der Sasaniden Aus Der Arabischen Chronik Des Tabari*, trans. Th. Nöldeke (Leyden: E. J. Brill, 1879), pp. 151–72, 238–53, 386–99. English translation by the author.

20. E. W. Brooks, *English Historical Review* (London, 1900), vol. XV, pp. 736–47.

21. Harun al-Rashid.
22. The ruling caliph, the father of Aaron (Harun al-Rashid).
23. As quoted in *The History of the Decline and Fall of the Roman Empire* by Edward Gibbon (Philadelphia: John D. Morris & Co., 1845), vol. V, pp. 446–47.
24. Ibid., p. 447.
25. The point of the poet's verses that follow was that it was the illness of the caliph that prevented the wazirs from speaking to him for some time after the news about Nikephoros had arrived.

Chapter 4/Otto of Freising

1. *The Deeds of Frederick Barbarossa by Otto of Freising*, trans. C. C. Mierow (New York: Columbia University Press, 1953), p. 5. Hereafter, this work will be cited as *Deeds*.
2. Ibid., p. 79.
3. Ibid., pp. 246–47.
4. The edition used in this study is that translated by C. C. Mierow, entitled *The Two Cities: A Chronicle of Universal History to the Year 1146 A.D. by Otto, Bishop of Freising* (New York: Columbia University Press, 1928). Hereafter, this volume will be cited as *Two Cities*.
5. *Deeds*, p. 28.
6. *Two Cities*, p. 205.
7. Ibid., p. 172.
8. Ibid., pp. 93–94.
9. Ibid., p. 96.
10. Ibid., p. 191.
11. *Deeds*, p. 24.
12. *Two Cities*, pp. 87–88.
13. Ibid., pp. 88–89.
14. Ibid., p. 89.
15. Ibid., p. 93.
16. Ibid., pp. 95–96.
17. Ibid., p. 187.
18. Ibid., p. 160.
19. *Deeds*, p. 159.
20. *Two Cities*, p. 417.
21. Ibid., p. 384.

22. *Deeds*, p. 101.
23. *Two Cities*, pp. 279–80.
24. Otto's account is not accurate.
25. Otto often refers to the Alps as the Pyrenees.
26. One may detect some tipping of Otto's hand in favor of the church in his reference to the "antipope" Clement as "Dement."
27. *Deeds*, pp. 28–30.
28. *Two Cities*, pp. 90–91.
29. *Deeds*, p. 51, and note 89.
30. *Two Cities*, p. 96.
31. Ibid., pp. 443–44.
32. Ibid., pp. 411–12.
33. Ibid., p. 378.
34. *Deeds*, pp. 124–25.
35. *Two Cities*, p. 382.
36. Ibid., p. 283.
37. Ibid., pp. 240–41.
38. *Deeds*, pp. 120–22.
39. *Two Cities*, p. 435.
40. Ibid., pp. 428–29.
41. Ibid., pp. 227–28.
42. Ibid., pp. 167–68.
43. Ibid., p. 91.
44. Ibid., p. 93.
45. Ibid., pp. 323–24.
46. Ibid., pp. 215–16.
47. Ibid., p. 462.
48. Ibid., pp. 478–79.
49. Ibid., p. 514.
50. Ibid., p. 141.
51. Ibid., p. 196.
52. Ibid., pp. 271–72.
53. *Deeds*, pp. 80–81.
54. *Two Cities*, p. 429.
55. Ibid., p. 349.
56. Ibid., pp. 156–57.
57. Ibid., p. 146.
58. *Deeds*, pp. 142–43.
59. Ibid., p. 144.

60. *Two Cities*, pp. 272-73.
61. Ibid., p. 274.
62. Ibid., p. 274.
63. Ibid., p. 95.
64. Regulus, a Roman consul who had been captured by the Carthaginians, had been permitted to return to Rome on the understanding that he would seek to convince the Senate to make peace. When Regulus reached Rome he used his eloquence to convince the Senate rather to continue the war, then, since he had given the Carthaginians his word, he returned to Carthage and was executed. Historians question the melodramatic aspects of the story.
65. *Two Cities*, pp. 193-94.
66. *Deeds*, pp. 69-70.
67. *Two Cities*, p. 277.
68. *Deeds*, pp. 118-23.
69. Ibid., p. 79.
70. Ibid., p. 142.
71. Ibid., p. 83.

Chapter 5/Matthew Paris

1. See Richard Vaughan, *Matthew Paris* (Cambridge: University Press, 1958), p. 5.
2. See Vaughan, *Matthew Paris*, p. 7 and plate I; see also *Matthaei Parisiensis, Monachi Albani Chronica Majora*, ed. Henry Richards Luard (London: Longman and Co., 1880), vol. V, p. 748 and note.
3. *Chronicles and Memorials of Great Britain and Ireland during the Middle Ages* (London: Public Record Office, 1858-1896).
4. *Chronica Majora*, vol. III, p. 199.
5. Ibid., vol. III, p. 194.
6. *Matthaei Parisiensis, Monachi Sancti Albani, Historia Anglorum*, ed. Frederick Madden (London: Longmans, Green, Reader, and Dyer, 1869), vol. III, pp. 51-52, and note 3. See also Vaughan, *Matthew Paris*, pp. 121-22.
7. Ibid.
8. *Matthew Paris's English History*, trans. J. A. Giles (London: H. G. Bohn, 1854), vol. III, p. 220.

9. *Chronica Majora;* vol. IV, pp. 644–45.
10. *Matthew Paris's English History,* vol. II, p. 415.
11. *Chronica Majora,* vol. II, p. 466.
12. *Matthew Paris's English History,* vol. II, p. 502.
13. Ibid., vol. III, p. 231.
14. Ibid., vol II, p. 242.
15. Ibid., pp. 467–68.
16. Ibid., vol. I, p. 344.
17. Ibid., vol. III, p. 251.
18. Ibid., vol. I, p. 312.
19. Ibid., pp. 268–71.
20. Ibid., vol. III, pp. 166–67.
21. Ibid., vol. I, p. 38.
22. Ibid., vol. I, pp. 38–39.
23. Ibid., p. 332.
24. Ibid., pp. 277–78.
25. Ibid., vol. II, pp. 196–97.
26. Ibid., p. 433.
27. Ibid., p. 247.
28. Ibid., vol. I, pp. 67–68.
29. Ibid., vol. I, pp. 155–56.
30. Ibid., vol. III, pp. 115–16.
31. Matthew questions the accuracy of the emperor's figure. He observes that "a credible Italian asserted, that Milan, with its dependencies, raised an army of six thousand armed men with iron-clad horses." Ibid., vol. I, p. 95.
32. *Matthew Paris's English History,* vol. I, pp. 93–95.
33. Ibid., pp. 137–38.
34. Ibid., vol. II, p. 22.
35. Ibid., p. 54.
36. Ibid., vol. I, p. 47.
37. Ibid., pp. 335–36.
38. Boniface, a Savoygard and uncle of the queen, owed his "election" to Henry's influence.
39. *Matthew Paris's English History,* vol. I, p. 459.
40. Ibid., vol. III, p. 305.
41. The Fourth Lateran Council (1215) had forbidden the establishment of new orders.
42. *Matthew Paris's English History,* vol. II, p. 35.
43. Dominicans and Franciscans.

44. *Matthew Paris's English History*, vol. I, pp. 475–76.
45. Ibid., vol. III, p. 140.
46. Ibid., pp. 163–64.
47. Ibid., p. 76.
48. See ibid., vol. I, pp. 314–15; also ibid., pp. 15–20.
49. Ibid., vol. II, p. 278.
50. Ibid., pp. 401–2.
51. Ibid., vol. I, p. 388.
52. Ibid., p. 193.
53. Ibid., p. 451.
54. Ibid., vol. II, p. 251.
55. Ibid., vol. III, pp. 312–13; see also pp. 265 and 283.
56. Ibid., p. 115.
57. Ibid.
58. Ibid., vol. II, p. 42.
59. Ibid., p. 405.
60. Ibid., pp. 405–10.
61. Ibid., vol. III, p. 1.
62. Ibid., vol. I, p. 481.
63. Ibid., vol. III, p. 257.
64. Ibid., vol. I, p. 461.
65. Ibid., vol. III, p. 183.
66. Ibid., vol. II, p. 410.
67. It appears he drew most, if not all, these quotations from an anthology.
68. *Matthew Paris's English History*, vol. III, p. 244.
69. Ibid., vol. III, p. 100.

Chapter 6/John Froissart

1. The edition of Froissart's chronicles used in this study is *Sir John Froissart's Chronicles of England, France, and the Adjoining Countries,* trans. Thomas Johnes, 5 vols., (London: The Haford Press, 1803-1810). Hereafter cited as *Chronicles.*
2. In a strict sense Froissart was not a Frenchman. He was a native of Hainault which today lies on the French side of the Belgian border. "He betrays the local dialect in his writing and, no doubt, spoke French with a Walloon accent." Charles Dunn, "Introduction" in *The Chronicles of England,*

France and Spain by Sir John Froissart (New York: Dutton, 1961), p. v.

3. *Chronicles,* vol. I, p. 2.
4. Ibid., vol. IV, p. 13.
5. Ibid., p. 300.
6. Ibid., p. 426.
7. Ibid., p. 409.
8. Ibid., p. 368.
9. Ibid., vol. III, p. 72.
10. Ibid., vol. I, p. 1.
11. Ibid., vol. III, p. 414.
12. Ibid., p. 475.
13. Ibid., p. 475.
14. Ibid., p. 642.
15. Ibid., p. 414. For a study in support of Froissart's reliability, see Leonard Manyon, "An Examination of the Historical Reliability of Froissart's Account of the Campaign and Battle of Crecy," *Papers of the Michigan Academy of Science, Arts and Letters,* VII (1927), pp. 207-24.
16. *Chronicles,* vol. II, p. 649.
17. Ibid., vol. IV, p. 13.
18. Ibid., vol. III, p. 503.
19. Ibid., p. 209.
20. Ibid., p. 10.
21. Ibid., vol. IV, p. 4.
22. Ibid., vol. I, p. 31.
23. Ibid., vol. III, p. 593.
24. Ibid., vol. I, p. 392.
25. Ibid., p. 613.
26. Ibid., vol. II, p. 361.
27. Ibid., p. 308.
28. Ibid., vol. III, pp. 364-65.
29. Ibid., vol. IV, p. 202.
30. Ibid., vol. III, p. 452.
31. Ibid., vol. IV, pp. 12-13.
32. Ibid., p. 390.
33. Ibid., p. 73.
34. Ibid., p. 69.
35. Ibid., vol. II, p. 400.
36. Ibid., vol. III, p. 383.

37. Froissart did actually do some searching of archives. He says he saw copies of the decisions and agreements made at Calais in 1359 "in the chanceries of the two kings." Ibid., vol. I, p. 572.

38. *The Chronicles of Froissart,* trans. John Bourchier, Lord Berners (London: D. Nutt, 1903), p.v.

39. *Chronicles,* vol. II, pp. 459–60.

40. Ibid., p. 61.

41. Ibid., pp. 66–67.

42. Ibid., vol. I, 205–10.

43. Ibid., pp. 199–201.

44. Ibid., pp. 226–27.

45. Ibid., vol. III, p. 643.

46. Ibid., vol. II, p. 663.

47. Ibid., vol. I, pp. 48–51.

48. Ibid., pp. 443–44.

49. Ibid., pp. 448–49.

50. Ibid., pp. 791–92.

51. Ibid., vol. II, pp. 247–49.

52. Ibid., pp. 382–85.

53. Ibid., vol. IV, pp. 229–34.

54. Ibid., vol. I, pp. 549–50.

55. Ibid., pp. 31–32.

56. Ibid., pp. 323–25.

57. Ibid., p. 440.

58. Ibid., pp. 269–74.

59. Ibid., pp. 647–51.

60. Ibid., vol. III, pp. 286–87.

61. Ibid., vol. I, pp. 753–54.

Chapter 7/Ibn Khaldun

1. Arnold Toynbee, *The Study of History* (Oxford: Oxford University Press, 1934), vol. III, p. 322.

2. *Ibn Khaldun: The Muqaddimah; An Introduction to History,* trans. Franz Rosenthal (New York: Pantheon Books, 1958), vol. I, p. xliii. Hereafter cited as *Ibn Khaldun.*

3. See Walter J. Fischel, *Ibn Khaldun and Tamerlane* (Berkeley: University of California Press, 1952), p. 69, n. 48. Timur the Lame is also known as Tamerlane.

4. The *Muqaddimah* suffers from redundancy. "It may even be said that the *Muqaddimah* could easily be reduced to about half its size and would then be a more readable work." *Ibn Khaldun*, vol. I, p. lxix.
5. For a discussion of Ibn Khaldun's treatment of Jewish history, see Walter J. Fischel, *Ibn Khaldun in Egypt* (Berkeley: University of California Press, 1967), pp. 152–55.
6. See Muhsin Mahdi, *Ibn Khaldun's Philosophy of History* (Chicago: University of Chicago Press, 1957), chaps. 2 and 3. See also m. m. Sharif, ed., *A History of Muslim Philosophy* (Wiesbaden: Harrassowitz, 1966), vol. II, *Political Thought*, chap. 49.
7. Ibn Khaldun gave this term a meaning different from that common to Muslim literature. It originally meant something like "making common cause with one's agnates." In time it acquired the meaning of "bias," or an unquestioning support of one's group regardless of the justice of its position. Ibn Khaldun uses the term in a more constructive way. He gives it the meaning of the feeling that a human being has for his relatives, then for those sprung from a common ancestor, and finally, for those associated with this group by long contact. See *Ibn Khaldun*, vol. I, p. lxxviii.
8. *Ibn Khaldun*, vol. I, p. 3.
9. Ibid., p. 6.
10. Ibid., p. 9.
11. Ibid., p. 14.
12. Ibid., p. 15.
13. Ibid., pp. 16–17.
14. Ibid., p. 29.
15. Ibid., p. 40.
16. Ibid., pp. 55–56.
17. Ibid., p. 11.
18. He finds Aristotle's work on this subject deficient on a number of counts.
19. *Ibn Khaldun*, vol. I, p. 14.
20. Ibid., p. 89.
21. Ibid., p. 92.
22. Ibid., p. 95.
23. Ibid., p. 101.
24. Ibid., p. 97.

25. Ibid. pp. 167–68.
26. Ibid., p. 214.
27. Ibid., pp. 249–50.
28. Ibid., p. 254.
29. Ibid., p. 260.
30. Ibid., p. 263.
31. Ibid., p. 264.
32. Ibid., p. 275.
33. Ibid., pp. 279–80.
34. Ibid., p. 278.
35. Ibid. pp. 302–3.
36. Ibid., pp. 305–6.
37. Ibid., p. 371.
38. Ibid., p. 476.
39. Ibid., p. 481.
40. Ibid., vol. II, p. 3.
41. Ibid., p. 74.
42. Ibid., pp. 85–86.
43. Ibid., p. 90.
44. Ibid., p. 91.
45. Ibid., p. 235.
46. Ibid., p. 317.
47. Ibid., p. 353.
48. Ibid., p. 356.
49. Ibid., p. 365.
50. Ibid., p. 373.
51. Ibid., p. 377.
52. Ibid., p. 395.
53. Ibid., vol. III, p. 271.
54. Ibid., pp. 308–10.
55. Ibid., vol. II, pp. 157–62.
56. *Ibn Khaldun and Tamerlane: Their Historic Meeting in Damascus, 1401 A.D. (803 A.H.):* A study based on Arabic manuscripts of Ibn Khaldun's *Autobiography* with a translation into English and a commentary by Walter J. Fischel (Berkeley: University of California Press, 1952), pp. 29–43.
57. *Histoire Des Beni 'Abd El-Wad Rois De Tlemcen Jusqu'au Regne D'Abou H'Ammou Mousa II* par Abou Zakarya Yah'ia Ibn Khaldoun. Ed. and tr. Alfred Bel (Algiers: P.

Fontana Publishers, 1903), pp. 199–208. English translation by the author.

Bibliography

Anderson, Gillian, and William Anderson, eds. *The Chronicles of Jean Froissart*. Carbondale: Southern Illinois University Press, 1963.

An Arab Philosophy of History: Selections from the Prolegomena of Ibn Khaldun of Tunis. Translated by Charles Issawi. London: John Murray, 1950.

Archambault, Paul. *Seven French Chroniclers*. Syracuse: Syracuse University Press, 1974.

Barnes, Harry Elmer. *A History of Historical Writing*, 2d. rev. ed. New York: Dover, 1962.

Blair, Peter. *The World of Bede*. New York: St. Martin's Press, 1971.

Bonner, Gerald. *Famulus Christi: Essays in Commemoration of the Thirteenth Centenary of the Birth of the Venerable Bede*. London: S.P.C.K., 1976.

Browne, G. F. *The Venerable Bede, His Life and Writings*. New York: Macmillan, 1930.

Butler, A. J. *The Treaty of Misr in Tabari*. Oxford: Clarendon Press, 1913.

Colgrave, Bertram, and R. A. B. Mynors, eds. *Bede's Ecclesiastical History of the English People*. Oxford: Clarendon Press, 1969.

315

Coulton, G. G. *The Chronicler of European Chivalry.* London: The Studio, Ltd., 1930.

Crawford, S. J. *Anglo-Saxon Influence on Western Christendom, 600-800.* New York: Barnes and Noble, 1966.

The Chronicles of Froissart. 6 vols. Translated by John Bourchier, Lord Berners, with an introduction by W. P. Ker. London: D. Nutt, 1901-1903.

Dunn, Charles W. "Introduction." In *The Chronicles of England, France, and Spain.* H. P. Dunster's condensation of the Thomas Johnes translation. New York: Dutton, 1961.

Evans, J. A. S. *Procopius.* New York: Twayne Publishers, 1972.

Fischel, Walter J. *Ibn Khaldun and Tamerlane.* Berkeley: University of California Press, 1952.

Fischel, Walter J. *Ibn Khaldun in Egypt: A Study in Islamic Historiography.* Berkeley: University of California Press, 1967.

Gillett, H. M. *Saint Bede the Venerable.* London: Burns, Oates, and Washbourne, Ltd., 1935.

Grandsen, Antonia. *Historical Writing in England, c. 550 to c. 1307.* Ithaca: Cornell University Press, 1974.

von Gruenbaum, G. E. *Medieval Islam, 275-87.* Chicago: University of Chicago Press, 1946.

Ibn Kahldun, The Muqaddimah: An Introduction to History. Translated by Franz Rosenthal. New York: Pantheon Books, 1958.

Jolliffe, John, ed. and trans. *Froissart's Chronicles.* London: Harvill Press, 1967.

Ker, W. P. *Essays on Medieval Literature.* London: Macmillan, 1905.

Knowles, David. "Introduction." In *Bede's Ecclesiastical History of the English Nation,* rev. ed. New York: Dutton, 1970.

Lewis, B., and P. M. Holt, eds. *Historians of the Middle East.* Oxford: Oxford University Press, 1962.

Mahdi, Muhsin. *Ibn Khaldun's Philosophy of History.* Chicago: University of Chicago Press, 1964.

Margoliouth, D. S. *Lectures on Arabic Historians.* Calcutta: University of Calcutta, 1930.

Otto of Freising. *The Deeds of Frederick Barbarossa.* Translated by C. C. Mierow. Records of Civilization. New York: Columbia University Press, 1953.

Otto of Freising. *The Two Cities: A Chronicle of Universal History to the Year 1146 A.D.* Translated by C. C. Mierow. Records of Civilization. New York: Columbia University Press, 1928.

Paris, Matthew. *Matthew Paris's English History.* Translated by J. A. Giles. London: H. G. Bohn, 1854.

Paetow, L. J. *A Guide to the Study of Medieval History,* rev. ed. Millwood, N.Y.: Krauss Reprint Co., 1973.

Procopius. 7 vols. Translated by H. B. Dewing. Cambridge, Mass.: Harvard University Press, 1914–1940.

Procopius: Secret History. Translated by Richard Atwater, foreword by Arthur Boak. Ann Arbor: University of Michigan Press, 1961.

Rabi, Muhammad Mahmoud. *The Political Theory of Ibn Khaldun.* Leiden: E. J. Brill, 1967.

The Reign of Al-Mu'tasim. Translated by Elma Marin. New Haven: American Oriental Society, 1951.

Rosenthal, E. I. J. *Political Thought in Medieval Islam.* Cambridge: University Press, 1958.

Rosenthal, Franz. *A History of Muslim Historiography,* rev. ed. Leiden: E. J. Brill, 1968.

Sauvaget, J., and C. Cahen. *Introduction to the History of the Muslim East: A Bibliographic Guide.* Berkeley: University of California Press, 1965.

Schmidt, N. *Ibn Khaldun, Historian, Sociologist, and Philosopher.* New York: Columbia University Press, 1930.

Sherley-Price, Lee, ed. and trans. *Bede: A History of the English Church and People.* Harmondsworth, Middlesex: Penguin Books, 1955.

Sir John Froissart's Chronicles of England, France, and the Adjoining Countries, 5 vols. Translated by Thomas Johnes. London: The Haford Press, 1803–1810.

Smalley, Beryl. *Historians in the Middle Ages.* New York: Charles Scribner's Sons, 1974.

Thompson, A. Hamilton, ed. *Bede, His Life, Times, and Writings: Essays in Commemoration of the Twelfth Centenary of His Death.* Oxford: Clarendon Press, 1935.

Thompson, J. W., and B. J. Holm. *A History of Historical Writing,* 2 vols. New York: Macmillan, 1967.

Thurston, Herbert, and Donald Attwater, eds. *Butler's Lives of the Saints.* New York: Kenedy, 1956.

Vaughan, Richard. *Matthew Paris.* Cambridge: University Press, 1958.

Vryonis, Speros, ed. *Readings in Medieval Historiography.* Boston: Houghton Mifflin Co., 1968.

Williamson, G. A. "Introduction." In *Procopius, The Secret History.* Baltimore: Penguin Books, 1966.

Index